METHODS OF MARKING FISH AND SHELLFISH

Support for the publication of this book
was provided by

Sport Fish Restoration Act Funds

administered by the

**U.S. Fish and Wildlife Service
Division of Federal Aid**

METHODS OF MARKING FISH AND SHELLFISH

Larry A. Nielsen

Department of Fisheries and Wildlife Sciences
Virginia Polytechnic Institute and State University
Blacksburg, Virginia

American Fisheries Society
Special Publication 23

American Fisheries Society
Bethesda, Maryland 1992

The American Fisheries Society Special Publication series is a registered serial.
A suggested citation format follows.

Nielsen, L. A. 1992. Methods of marking fish and shellfish.
American Fisheries Society Special Publication 23.

98 97 96 95 94 93 92   6 5 4 3 2 1

Library of Congress Catalog Card Number: 92-74200

ISBN 0-913235-80-6

ISSN 0097-0638

Printed in the United States of America

This publication is printed on acid-free, recycled paper

Published by and available from the American Fisheries Society
5410 Grosvenor Lane, Suite 110, Bethesda, Maryland 20814, USA

Dedication

To
My family,
Near and far,
Whose marks I
Carry proudly
And permanently
As son,
Brother,
Husband,
Father,
And friend.

Contents

Preface

This book is the final product of a three-step educational project sponsored by the U.S. Fish and Wildlife Service and the American Fisheries Society. The first step was the 1988 International Symposium and Educational Workshop on Fish-Marking Techniques, held in Seattle, Washington. The symposium gathered together more than 400 professionals with fish marking experience or interests. The second step was the publication of *Fish-Marking Techniques,* the 879-page proceedings of the symposium. The proceedings contains substantial information about a variety of techniques, based mostly on project-specific case studies.

The third step, and the one toward which the first two steps pointed, is this book, intended as a synthesis of fish marking techniques. The synthesis was needed to compile existing information into a common format that would treat all major marking techniques to the same level of detail. Most chapters in this book share a common outline, and I have generalized to the extent possible, using the symposium results and other literature. It is clear that writing this book would not have been possible without the symposium as an original source of both data and experiences. I gratefully acknowledge the symposium authors' contributions to this text; approximately half the citations come from the symposium.

It is equally clear that the symposium proceedings itself would never suffice as a comprehensive technical manual or textbook. External marks, for example, including fin clips, brands, and dyes, were covered sparingly in the symposium. Books like this, which compile, assess, and synthesize the primary literature, are critically needed in fisheries. The extent to which we create such texts will determine the extent to which our science and management succeed in coming years.

The preparation of the book—and the book itself—demonstrated to me the unevenness of information about marks, their applicability, and their effects. Virtually all marks have been used on some taxa (such as salmon), providing an enormous comparative information base. And some marks (such as coded wire tags) have been tried on many taxa. But for most marks and most taxa, reliable information is quite sparse. Very few studies have examined the performance of a mark on a variety of taxa or the performance of a variety of marks on a single taxon. One of my strong beliefs is that such methodological studies are ideal projects for graduate student research, adding critically needed information that can be performed in a short time on a small budget. I encourage university faculty, graduate students, funding agencies, and private marking businesses to work together to fill the gaps in our knowledge of this essential set of techniques.

The need for comprehensive information on marks was the stimulus for this project, and many readers will undoubtedly be disappointed by the book's failure to produce many and profound generalizations. Other readers will be able to cite instances that conflict with the generalizations that are included. I have deliberately tried to balance my personal tendency to generalize and the limited scope of the available literature, which is consistently site specific, and project specific.

Readers will also note that the book deals primarily with fish and secondarily with molluscs and crustaceans, which we have chosen to call shellfish. The coverage also reflects the availability of information; relatively few publications treat molluscs or crustaceans comprehensively or in detail.

Many reviewers have contributed substantially to the book, which evolved considerably through four drafts. These reviewers include, in alphabetical order, Pete Bergman, Sylvia Behrens Yamada, Henry Booke, Ed Brothers, Dan Coble, Eric Hallerman, Wayne Hubert, Al Knight, Sandy McFarlane, Jess Muncy, Dave Philipp (and colleagues), Earl Prentice, Bob Sousa, and Dick Wydoski. I gratefully acknowledge their help, as they have kept me from making many serious mistakes. Their reviews, however, do not assure that the book is either good or accurate, and all remaining errors—of omission or commission—are mine.

Several reviewers of the entire text have sought more generalization. Several expert reviewers of individual chapters have sought higher endorsement for their favorite techniques, assuring me that the technique was more widely applicable, less technically difficult, more reliable, or less costly than I had depicted. Other reviewers objected to extrapolations, desiring much more specificity and qualification of statements in the text. All reviewers provided excellent ways to improve the text, and I have incorporated those wherever possible. But I have not incorporated many other suggestions which I thought were unsubstantiated or which conflicted with the general purpose of the book.

Writing this book has taught me the enormous value of a supportive editorial environment. The American Fisheries Society has a real treasure in its editorial office. Bob and Sally Kendall were consistently expert and gentle in their guidance; as friends and editors, they are top-notch. Amy Moore, Meredith Donovan, and Beth McAleer of the editorial staff were equally helpful and timely. Kathy Barker typed several versions of the text, and Sharon Nielsen, my wife, prepared the index (and tolerated me through the entire process).

A supportive university environment is equally important to a book project. Our Department of Fisheries and Wildlife Sciences at Virginia Tech values our professional contributions and especially supports those oriented to our instructional mission. Although the vast majority of my work on this book occurred at home, many colleagues—faculty, staff, and students—helped along the way, and I thank them.

It is a great privilege to have the opportunity to prepare this book on behalf of the American Fisheries Society, my colleagues, and our students. I hope it helps.

LARRY NIELSEN

September 1992
Blacksburg, Virginia

Common and Scientific Names of Species Mentioned in the Text

American eel .... *Anguilla rostrata*
American lobster .... *Homarus americanus*
American shad .... *Alosa sapidissima*
Arctic char .... *Salvelinus alpinus*
Atlantic cod .... *Gadus morhua*
Atlantic herring .... *Clupea harengus*
Atlantic rock crab .... *Cancer irroratus*
Atlantic salmon .... *Salmo salar*
ayu .... *Plecoglossus altivelis*
billfishes .... FAMILY Istiophoridae
blue crab .... *Callinectes sapidus*
bluefin tuna .... *Thunnus thynnus*
bluegill .... *Lepomis macrochirus*
brook trout .... *Salvelinus fontinalis*
brown bullhead .... *Ameiurus nebulosus*
brown trout .... *Salmo trutta*
channel catfish .... *Ictalurus punctatus*
chinook salmon .... *Oncorhynchus tshawytscha*
chum salmon .... *Oncorhynchus keta*
coho salmon .... *Oncorhynchus kisutch*
common carp .... *Cyprinus carpio*
dabsonfly .... *Protohermes grandis*
greater amberjack .... *Seriola dumerili*
haddock .... *Melanogrammus aeglefinus*
herrings .... FAMILY Clupeidae
jacks .... FAMILY Carangidae
king mackerel .... *Scomberomorus cavalla*
lake trout .... *Salvelinus namaycush*
largemouth bass .... *Micropterus salmoides*
leopard shark .... *Triakis semifasciata*
mackerels .... FAMILY Scombridae
northern pike .... *Esox lucius*
ocean quahog .... *Arctica islandica*
Pacific herring .... *Clupea pallasi*
pinfish .... *Lagodon rhomboides*

pink salmon .... *Oncorhynchus gorbuscha*
rainbow trout .... *Oncorhynchus mykiss*
red drum .... *Sciaenops ocellatus*
red king crab .... *Paralithodes camtschaticus*
sablefish .... *Anoplopoma fimbria*
sailfish .... *Istiophorus platypterus*
salmonids .... FAMILY Salmonidae
sauger .... *Stizostedion canadense*
scombrids .... FAMILY Scombridae
shortnose sturgeon .... *Acipenser brevirostrum*
shovelnose sturgeon .... *Scaphirhynchus platorynchus*
skipjack tuna .... *Katsuwonus pelamis*
smallmouth bass .... *Micropterus dolomieu*
snow crab .... *Chionoecetes opilio*
sockeye salmon .... *Oncorhynchus nerka*
spinner dolphin .... *Stenella longirostris*
spot .... *Leiostomus xanthurus*
spot shrimp .... *Pandalus platyceros*
striped bass .... *Morone saxatilis*
sturgeons .... FAMILY Acipenseridae
swordfish .... *Xiphias gladius*
walleye .... *Stizostedion vitreum*
white bass .... *Morone chrysops*
white marlin .... *Tetrapturus albidus*
white sturgeon .... *Acipenser transmontanus*
white sucker .... *Catostomus commersoni*
yellow perch .... *Perca flavescens*

Chapter 1

Styles and Uses of Marking

1.1 INTRODUCTION

Marking is an essential technique for fisheries researchers and managers. Actually, it is an essential technique for all human activity. Consider your wallet, which may contain your driver's license, credit cards, library card, staff identification, health and auto insurance verifications, membership cards, and a gallery of photographs. Each of us carries an anthology of marks that distinguishes us among the five billion humans on this planet.

We carry these marks because we wish to be identifiable and because we want to identify other people—for the same reasons fisheries workers mark aquatic animals. We wear Chicago Cubs hats to identify ourselves as elite members of the general stock of baseball fans, just as we identify the stock origin of fish in a mixed fishery. We verify young persons' ages from their driver's licenses, just as we verify fish ages from marks. Immigration officials stamp passports of arriving and departing travelers, so their migrations can be monitored, analogous to fish movement studies. Librarians keep track of our book borrowing habits, just like a fish behaviorist watches the foraging habits of a marked reef fish.

Aquatic observers have been marking animals for hundreds of years, in dozens of ways. Izaak Walton wrote in 1653 that stream watchers tied ribbons to the tails of Atlantic salmon (McFarlane et al. 1990). Since then, marks have evolved into a smorgasbord of buttons, clamps, clips, punches, threads, beads, streamers, dyes, stains, transmitters, chemicals, molecular profiles, and statistical tricks. The end is nowhere in sight.

Some of this diversity is demanded by the diversity of animals to be marked. Numerous varieties of fish have been marked, in numerous kinds of habitats. So have all sorts of invertebrates, from lobsters to clams to insect larvae. Even rocks and tree trunks have been marked, so researchers could follow their passive movements downstream.

1.2 USES OF MARKING

All this creative energy flows into marking methods for good reason. Marking is an essential way to collect data for research and for evaluation of management programs. In general, marking programs provide three broad categories of information.

First, *marking labels individual animals for specific handling*. If each animal is particularly valuable, as are the members of an endangered species, each can be individually marked, watched, and cared for. The spawning adults in an aquaculture operation may be individually marked so that the breeding history of each animal can be rigorously controlled and so that each animal's reproductive condition can be monitored with minimal handling as it approaches maturity. Many other captive situations, such as public aquaria and research experiments, also require individual identification so each animal can be weighed, measured, medicated, and otherwise handled.

Second, *marking allows animals to be identified as they move and mingle with other animals*. Marking has uncovered the large-scale migrations of fishes throughout the world, enhancing our understanding of the life cycles of many mysterious species. Fisheries managers need to know the origins of fish that spawn in separate locations but move back together during the fishing season. Marking allows analysis of the stock composition, providing the basis for the subsequent regulation and allocation of harvest to protect the stocks. Most large-scale marking techniques and studies today are designed for stock composition analysis. Marking can also tell us where stocked animals go—and sometimes how rapidly—so that the value of stocking can be evaluated. Multiple observations of marked animals also can reveal the local habitats used by them and their behavior under various conditions.

Third, *marking provides a means for collecting population statistics*. The most familiar use of marking is undoubtedly the mark–recapture estimation of abundance. Marking allows the direct assessment of an animal's growth, because the same animal's size can be compared on several recapture dates. The repeated measurement of marked animals is also useful as verification of growth estimates based on population or cohort means. Recovery of marked fish after known intervals offers a check on age determinations. Mortality is estimated from marked animals, by measuring the rate of harvest based on tag returns.

1.3 STYLES OF MARKING

Many people have defined the characteristics of an ideal mark (Box 1.1), but no single marking system approaches that ideal. Hence, the pursuit of new and better marking techniques has obsessed fisheries workers through time. No one has attempted a complete listing of marking styles or materials, but the fact that more than 900 scientific articles have described marking techniques indicates that the search is far from over (McFarlane et al. 1990).

Classifying this array of techniques into tidy groups is difficult. Marks have been organized by taxonomy of the marked animals (Stonehouse 1978), marking materials (Wydoski and Emery 1983), style of attachment (Jones 1979), and historical development (McFarlane et al. 1990). This book is organized primarily by the style of identification, that is, by the way the animals are marked. Under this taxonomy, seven major marking styles exist.

External tags (Chapter 3) are physical devices attached to animals so that the devices are visible outside the animal's body. The tags pass into and sometimes through the body, requiring a shaft that permanently penetrates the animal's skin. Without question, external tagging is the most diverse marking style. Because of the presence of the physical tag, however, external tagging also has more disadvantages than most other techniques.

External marks (Chapter 4) are alterations to the animal's appearance that

Box 1.1   The Perfect Mark

The pursuit of the perfect mark has produced many lists of characteristics and criteria. Rounsefell and Kask (1945), writing at a time when most tags were buttons, straps, or body cavity plates, listed these criteria for selection of the proper tag:

(1) length of time the tag remains on the fish (the longer the better);
(2) ease of application (the easier and more uniform, the better);
(3) likelihood of being seen when the fish is recaptured.

Kelly (1967) described characteristics of an ideal dye (injected as a mark). His test is applicable, however, to most types of marks:

(1) long-lasting (preferably for the fish's lifetime);
(2) permanent on every fish;
(3) nontoxic and nonirritating;
(4) no effect on growth;
(5) requires little or no extra formulation (that is, little special preparation);
(6) allows rapid marking;
(7) inexpensive;
(8) nonencumbering;
(9) easily visible to an untrained observer;
(10) provides several different mark combinations;
(11) requires little specialized equipment.

Stott (1971) described the more general characteristics of an ideal mark:

(1) permanent on any fish;
(2) unmistakably recognizable (preferably individually) to anyone;
(3) no effect on growth, mortality, or behavior;
(4) no effect on predation rate or vulnerability to fishing gear.

Everhart and Youngs (1981), expanding on earlier work with Rounsefell, brought the characteristics of an ideal mark to an even dozen:

(1) remains unaltered during the fish's lifetime;
(2) no effect on behavior or vulnerability to predators;
(3) does not tangle with weeds or nets;
(4) inexpensive and easily obtained;
(5) fits any size fish with little alteration;
(6) easy to apply without anesthetic and with little or no stress on fish;
(7) identifies fish at least to group;
(8) creates no health hazard;
(9) does not harm food or aesthetic value of fish;
(10) easy to detect in the field by untrained individuals;
(11) causes no confusion in reporting;
(12) remains unaffected by preservation.

enable the animal to be identified externally. Fin clips (partial amputations) are the most familiar style, but brands, tattoos, pigments, and dyes are also common. External marks are the easiest to apply and probably the most widely used marks for short-term and geographically restricted projects.

Internal tags (Chapter 5) are physical devices that are implanted entirely within an animal's body. Although a variety of internal tags has been applied in the past, most internal tagging today uses coded wire tags, nearly microscopic bits of wire that are notched with a binary code. Recovering internal tags usually requires sacrificing the animal, but new styles of internal tags and new techniques of implantation are being developed that allow the tags to be read externally or excised without harm to the animal.

Natural marks (Chapter 6) represent a variety of ways to identify animals based on patterns in their shape or markings. These include measures or observations of scale and otolith patterns, morphological dimensions, and parasite loads. The common characteristic of natural marks is that they do not require attaching a tag to an animal or directly marking it. Thus, natural marks may have a smaller effect on animals than traditional marking or tagging methods.

Biotelemetric tags (Chapter 7) are devices that transmit signals detected by a receiver at a remote listening station. Although the tags could be classified as external or internal tags according to the method of attachment, they are distinguished by the style of data recovery. The animals themselves need not be recaptured and handled because the tags send information continuously to a remote observer or computer-linked sensor. Biotelemetric tags become more popular each year, as the sizes and prices of the tags decrease and their quality and longevity increase.

Genetic identifiers (Chapter 8) are entirely different from the other marking styles. Genetic identification uses the precise genetic profile of an animal based on biochemical tests. The most common technique is electrophoresis, by which slightly different forms of enzymes or DNA fragments are identified and quantified for each animal. Because the presence and abundance of enzyme forms are genetically controlled and DNA is the material of genes, the tests can reveal which animals belong to which reproductive group. Although genetic marks can be considered natural marks because the animals create the marks themselves, the genetic basis for the analyses and the statistical nature of data make genetic marking a distinctly different—and sophisticated—technique.

The last style is *chemical marking* (Chapter 9). Chemical marking depends on the detection of harmless chemicals that have been accumulated naturally by an animal or introduced into it during captivity. The most commonly used chemical is tetracycline, an antibiotic that attaches to hard tissues and fluoresces under ultraviolet light. Chemical marking has been the subject of much experimentation through time, but has yet to be used widely in routine marking operations.

1.4   STEPS IN A MARKING PROJECT

A marking project is complicated. Like all fisheries projects, it will be most successful when conceived from beginning to end as a unified program (Figure 1.1; Box 1.2). In general, a marking project has seven operational steps, described briefly here and explored in greater detail in Chapter 2.

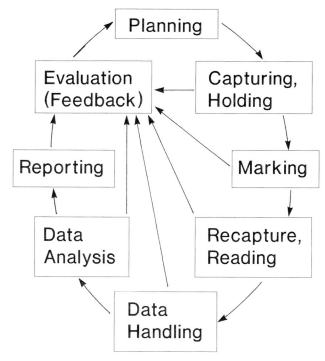

Figure 1.1 Seven operational steps of a marking project. All the steps should include evaluation (feedback) to the planning process so the next project can be planned better.

The first step in a marking project is *planning*. Every project must have a clear definition of the purpose and the intended results. Because no mark is perfect, knowing the precise objectives of a study will allow the best choice among the available marking techniques. After the objectives are set, the entire process must be explicitly organized. Organizational complexities grow with the magnitude of the program; large-scale marking projects usually involve the staffs of many agencies as well as the general public, working through all the steps of the project. Prescribing precisely who will do what, when, where, and how is critical for smooth execution.

The second step is *capturing and holding the animals to be marked*. This step is crucial because the validities of many assumptions are determined at this point. The collection process must assure that the marked animals represent the entire population from which they are drawn. Because the animals will be released after marking, with the assumption that the process has not affected their subsequent behavior or survival, they must be handled with greatest care.

The *marking process* itself is the third step. The animals also must be treated with the utmost care during the marking process. Marking requires highly standardized procedures to assure that animals are treated uniformly, marks are applied expertly, and data are recorded accurately. The marking process must be rigorously monitored so quality remains high as the tediousness of repetitive marking sets in. For certain marking techniques, like genetic identification, the marking process does not occur per se. In its place is a sampling process to provide a data base that will be used later as the standard to which captured animals are compared.

After the animals have been released and living at large for some time, they are *recaptured and the marks are read*—the fourth step in the process. Recapture is labor-intensive because many unmarked animals will be captured for every marked animal recovered. Many marking projects underestimate the time and money required for an adequate recapture process. Most analysts suggest that the recapture effort should be at least equal in magnitude to the marking effort.

After the animals are recaptured, the information must be extracted from the marked animals. External tags and marks should be the easiest to read or decode, but even these can be difficult to interpret if the marks are old. Many other marking techniques require elaborate steps to recover the mark information. Miniaturized tags may be embedded in the animal's tissue, requiring dissection and then microscopic examination. Biotelemetric information may be electronic codes, requiring extensive programming and computer processing. The data may consist of colored dots on an electrophoresis gel, requiring expert interpretation. Reading the results, therefore, may be as difficult as the marking and recovery processes themselves.

Once they have been collected, *the data must be carefully and consistently handled* as the fifth step in a marking project. Because marking studies often

---

Box 1.2   A Large-Scale Tagging Program

The Southeast Fisheries Center of the U.S. National Marine Fisheries Service operates the Cooperative Game Fish Tagging Program for agencies working in the Atlantic Ocean, Gulf of Mexico, and Caribbean Sea. The program is a good example of the complexities of a major marking effort and the planning necessary for success. The following description is adapted from Scott et al. (1990).

Planning

Since the program was created in 1954, its goal has been to advance biological knowledge about the population characteristics of major game fishes. The program began with the objective of determining movement patterns, stock structure, life span, growth rate, and survival rate of bluefin tuna. As the program has evolved, it has added similar objectives for billfishes, jacks, mackerels, red drum, and other species.

Capture and Holding

Because fisheries agencies cannot afford to capture these large fishes directly in sufficient numbers for an effective study, this program uses recreational and commercial fishers as well as scientists to capture the fish for marking. Currently, about 2,500 volunteers participate, along with many organized fishing clubs. Volunteers live in the USA, Canada, Mexico, South America, Africa, Europe, and the Caribbean. Project officials send each volunteer a tagging kit including instructions, record-keeping forms, and tagging equipment. The Southeast Fisheries Center provides individually

Continued.

Box 1.2   Continued.

numbered tags to each cooperator and requires that all tagging be reported
back to them. Because the fish are large, fishers are instructed to reduce
stress on the fish by keeping the fish in the water next to the boat for tagging.

Marking

Bluefin tuna are tagged with dart-style tags (see Chapter 3), which are
inserted from the end of a tagging pole—much like a harpoon would be used.
Similar techniques are used with other species. Several improvements in tag
design and tagging method have been made, increasing the quality of tagging
and, hence, the retention of tags. Since 1954, volunteers have tagged more
than 120,000 fish of 78 species in these proportions:

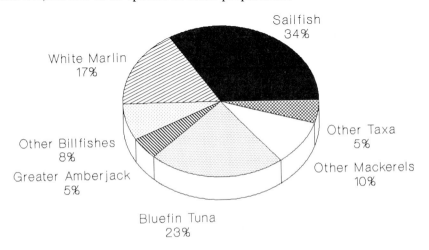

Recapture and Reading

Commercial and recreational fishers also recapture tagged fish. Each tag
carries the word "reward" and the address of the Southeast Fisheries
Center. Various rewards are offered as incentives to fishers for returning the
tags. Information about the fish is sent back to the fisher, as an additional
incentive for participating. For this program, tag reading is routine because
the information is written as a number on the external shaft of the tag.

Data Handling

Information about thousands of tagged and recaptured fish is received
each year by the Southeast Fisheries Center. In recent years, the amounts
and kinds of data and requests for their use have increased exponentially.
The Center, therefore, is developing a computerized system to store,
manipulate, and retrieve information. Data are entered into a comprehensive
data base that serves as an information resource for all scientists working
with the tagging program. When fully operational, the system will maintain
the data base on a mainframe accessible through microcomputers throughout the world. The intention is also to provide access to other tagging data
collected independently by other state, federal, and international agencies.

Continued.

Box 1.2 Continued.

Data Analysis

Data analysis is an individual procedure for each study and cannot be described in detail here. One example of the caution needed in analyzing data, however, has been revealed through this program. Because fishers tag their catches in the water, they must estimate the length and weight of the fish rather than accurately measuring them. Like fishers everywhere, the volunteer taggers often overestimate the size of their catch. Subsequent analysis has shown that the estimated weights of as many as one-third of the marked fish are greater than actual, measured weights when the fish are later recaptured:

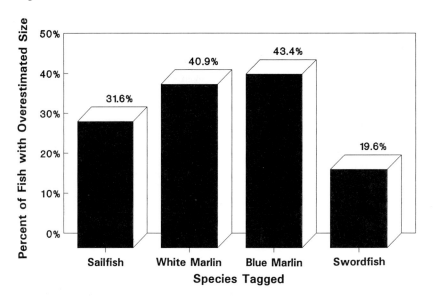

Reporting

The program has produced an annual report since 1974. The report summarizes the program activities for the year, including the numbers of cooperators, fish tagged, and fish recovered. It also highlights the particularly successful cooperators. As needed, the report discusses ways to improve the fish capture, handling, and tagging procedures—such as making better estimates of the size of the tagged fish!

involve several groups who are marking and recapturing animals, specific and explicit protocols must guide data handling. Like the early steps in a marking project, the data handling procedures may seem routine. Considering the effort spent to acquire each datum, however, the proper care and handling of data are as important as the proper care and handling of the marked animals.

The sixth step is *data analysis*. This step is anything but routine, as many identification techniques, like genetic, natural and chemical marking, are now entirely statistical. Scientists continue to develop new methods for calculating estimates and comparing them statistically. Statistical research with marking data continually shows the biases in earlier computational methods, suggesting that all marking analyses should be scrutinized rigorously. And, because the results of marking projects are likely to be used for management decisions, the analysis must be explicitly described, repeatable, and defendable.

The seventh operational step in a marking project is *reporting the results.* Because so many people need the results, the reporting process must be managed as carefully as all other steps. For continuing projects, a regular, standardized reporting program is probably necessary, including newsletters, information bulletins, technical reports, and news releases. For one-time projects, reporting is just as important, even if less dramatic.

An eighth step is essential for the overall improvement of marking projects—*evaluation, or feedback.* Evaluation provides the information for better planning of the next project and for development and research activities. As with all fisheries activities, evaluation must be a planned activity within the marking project. The seven other steps should contain mechanisms for recording data and observations useful for evaluation and subsequent planning.

1.5   CHOOSING A MARKING TECHNIQUE

The appropriate marking technique for a study will be a difficult choice. No available technique meets all the criteria for an ideal mark (Table 1.1). The utility of each mark depends on the objectives of the study, the characteristics of the animals to be marked, and the style of data collection. These considerations must be explicitly examined for each marking study, so that the best mark is always chosen. Choosing a mark because it has been successful elsewhere or because the study team has experience with it may yield suboptimal results for the study.

Table 1.2 lists various criteria that influence marking choice. The table also lists which marking styles generally are applicable for each criterion. This table can serve as a guide for the initial exploration of possible marks for a study, along with the more detailed information available for each technique in subsequent chapters. Final selection of a marking technique, however, should involve careful study of the literature and consultation with experienced professionals.

The first set of criteria affecting mark selection relates to the study *objectives; that is, to the kind of data being collected.* Two basic considerations affect mark selection. First is the need for identifying individuals or groups of animals. If each individual needs to be identifiable, then the marking system must provide a large number of unique codes. For these studies, an external, internal, or biotelemetric tag is generally needed. For many studies, however, only groups of animals need to be identified, allowing the use of marks that have fewer coding options but are less stressful for the animals.

Another aspect of data type relates to the frequency of identification. If animals need only be recaptured and identified once, the mark can be internal, even if its detection requires sacrifice of the animal. If animals need to be identified repeatedly, the identification system must be external or externally decipherable (biotelemetric tag, passive integrated transponder, visible implant tag). A related consideration is whether the recaptured animals must be kept alive. Endangered species, brood stock, and trophy animals must be protected. Therefore, marking, handling, and data collection must be as nonintrusive as possible.

The second set of criteria relates to the *characteristics of the animals being studied*. Several characteristics are important. First, of course, is the taxonomy of the species. Most marks have been developed for bony fishes, but many are adaptable for other fishes and for invertebrates. Furthermore, most modern marking techniques were invented for salmonids, which are routinely marked in large numbers in the Pacific Northwest. Careful consideration is needed in extrapolating marking results from salmonids to other fishes. For example, although branding works well on fine-scaled salmonids and ictalurids, it is much less useful for large-scaled taxa like centrarchids and percids. Also, fast-swimming fishes need marks that do not increase substantially the drag on the body. Researchers are increasingly interested in marking commercial invertebrates, raising unique marking problems associated with exoskeletons and molting. In general, invertebrate marking should be approached experimentally before any large management projects are undertaken.

Another crucial animal characteristic is shape. The various marking techniques often require—or at least work best on—very specific body shapes. Tattoos, for example, work best where a large, flat, relatively light-colored body surface is

Table 1.1 Comparison of marking techniques to characteristics of an ideal mark, adapted from the criteria of Everhart and Youngs (1981) to be more general. Relative to the ideal characteristic, H = high, M = median, and L = low conformity.

Characteristic of ideal mark	External tags	External marks	Internal tags	Natural marks	Bio-telemetry	Genetic identifiers	Chemical marks
Remains useful during entire life span	M	L	H	M	L	H	L
No effect on behavior, predation	L	M	H	H	L	H	H
Does not tangle in nets, weeds	L	H	H	H	L	H	H
Inexpensive	H	H	M	M	L	M	L
Independent of animal size	L	H	H	M	L	H	M
Easy to perform without stress or anesthetic	L	M	M	H	L	L	H
Able to identify groups	H	H	H	H	H	H	H
Able to identify individuals	H	L	M	L	H	L	L
Creates no health hazard	H	H	H	H	H	H	L
Does not harm food or aesthetic value of animal	L	L	M	H	L	H	L
Easy to perform by untrained persons	H	M	L	L	L	L	L
Causes no confusion in detection or analysis	H	L	H	L	H	M	M
Unaffected by storage	H	L	H	M	H	H	L

Table 1.2 General applicability of various marking systems to important selection criteria.

Criterion	External tags	External marks	Internal tags[a]	Natural marks	Bio-telemetry	Genetic identifiers	Chemical marks
Identification can be							
Groups	X	X	X	X		X	X
Individuals	X		X		X		
Recapture can be							
Once	X	X	X	X		X	X
Repeated	X	X			X		
Dead	X	X	X	X		X	X
Alive	X	X			X	X	
Animal can be							
Fish	X	X	X	X	X	X	X
Invertebrate	X	X	X		X	X	
Large	X	X	X	X	X	X	
Small		X	X	X		X	X
Study can be							
Short	X	X	X	X	X		
Long	X		X	X		X	X
Recapture can be							
Professional	X	X	X	X	X	X	X
Volunteer	X	X	X				

[a]Some newly developed techniques, such as use of visible implant tags and of new injection sites for coded wire tags, allow internal tags to be read or extracted without death of the animal. Most internal tagging, however, involves ultimate loss of the animal.

available (e.g., on sturgeons). External tags anchored inside the body work best on wide-bodied animals with ample muscle tissue for embedding the anchor. Flatfishes, obviously, cannot be marked with tags that protrude beneath their bodies. Fishes that live within reefs or in other structurally complex environments should not be tagged with protruding tags.

The size of the marked animals also affects marking style. Most external tags are large and cannot be used on small animals. If small animals are to be marked, external marks, internal tags, natural marks, genetic marks, and chemical marks are appropriate. The opposite problem—how to mark large animals—often occurs in studies of marine pelagic species. Because these species cannot be brought on board the vessel for marking, the technique used must allow marking alongside the boat, often under difficult conditions. Whether the animal is large or small at marking, its growth during the marking study also must be considered. The mark chosen must remain present and readable as the animal grows and must not impair natural growth or behavior.

The third set of criteria relates to the *style of data collection* that will be used to recover information from the marked animals. Two considerations are important here. The first is the length of the study. If the study is short-term, then marks with a limited life span are useful. These include most external marks (fin clips, brands, dyes), external tags, biotelemetric tags, and chemical marks. Many studies are long-term, however, requiring several years before recaptures are possible. In these studies, the marks must be stable for long periods and over a variety of different life stages of the marked animals. Most newer marking systems, including internal tags and genetic identification techniques, are designed to be useful over long periods.

The second consideration concerns who will actually recapture the animal. If professionals perform the recaptures, then the marks can be subtle, training can be extensive, and elaborate handling and data recording requirements can be established. If volunteers collect the recaptured animals, then the process must be simple and the marks must be immediately visible, with the necessary reporting instructions attached. This requires brightly colored tags large enough to contain a telephone number or address, an extensive publicity campaign, and incentives for participation; alternatively, volunteers can be instructed to leave animals with obvious external marks at highly publicized drop-off locations.

1.6 HOW TO USE THIS BOOK

This book summarizes the nature of marking projects (Chapter 2) and surveys the various marking methods commonly used today (Chapters 3–9). It briefly describes the main techniques along with their uses, assumptions, advantages, and disadvantages. It describes the basic process for using each method, and it provides current references to other manuals and studies that detail each technique. In general, the book is designed to help professionals decide which technique to use.

One short book cannot describe the details for performing each of the major techniques and their various adaptations. The references in each chapter should be reviewed for details of methodology and for specific effects related to the animals under study. Experts on the particular technique should be contacted. These experts include authors of the cited writings and representatives of companies that supply the marking equipment. Finally, local users of the technique should be consulted to determine any particular problems or adaptations associated with local application of the technique.

The information referenced here comes primarily from the published literature, especially from American Fisheries Society Symposium 7 (Parker et al. 1990). Therefore, it represents studies and opinions that are several years old. Consultation with current users of techniques and with manufacturers is likely to provide new information that should be considered in a marking project. Because old techniques are constantly being improved and because new techniques are constantly being developed, disadvantages are rapidly disappearing and utility is increasing. In general, an open mind is a very useful marking tool.

1.7 REFERENCES

Everhart, W. H., and W. D. Youngs. 1981. Principles of fishery science, 2nd edition. Cornell University Press, Ithaca, New York.

Jones, R. 1979. Materials and methods used in marking experiments in fishery research. FAO (Food and Agriculture Organization of the United Nations) Fisheries Technical Paper 190.

Kelly, W. H. 1967. Marking freshwater and a marine fish by injected dyes. Transactions of the American Fisheries Society 96:163–175.

McFarlane, G. A., R. S. Wydoski, and E. D. Prince. 1990. Historical review of the development of external tags and marks. American Fisheries Society Symposium 7:9–29.

Parker, N. C., A. E. Giorgi, R. C. Heidinger, D. B. Jester, Jr., E. D. Prince, and G. A.

Winans. 1990. Fish-marking techniques. American Fisheries Society Symposium 7, Bethesda, Maryland.

Rounsefell, G. A., and J. L. Kask. 1945. How to mark fish. Transactions of the American Fisheries Society 73:320–365.

Scott, E. L., E. D. Prince, and C. D. Goodyear. 1990. History of the Cooperative Game Fish Tagging Program in the Atlantic Ocean, Gulf of Mexico, and Caribbean Sea, 1954–1987. American Fisheries Society Symposium 7:841–853.

Stonehouse, B., editor. 1978. Animal marking. University Park Press, Baltimore, Maryland.

Stott, B. 1971. Marking and tagging. Pages 82–97 in W. E. Ricker, editor. Methods for the assessment of fish production in fresh waters, 2nd edition. Blackwell Scientific Publications, Oxford, UK.

Wydoski, R., and L. Emery. 1983. Tagging and marking. Pages 215–237 in L. A. Nielsen and D. L. Johnson, editors. Fisheries techniques. American Fisheries Society, Bethesda, Maryland.

Chapter 2

Designing a Marking Program

2.1 PROGRAM CONCEPT

Marking programs are like icebergs. The mark and the marking activities are the small, visible parts of the project. The mass of the program, like the mass of an iceberg, is invisible. A successful marking program requires extensive pre- and postmarking planning, organization and execution. As the magnitude of a marking program increases, so does the importance of careful planning.

Consider salmonid marking on the northern Pacific coast of North America (Johnson 1990). Each year more than 40 million salmon are tagged with coded wire tags. The tagging occurs in at least 300 hatcheries in the USA and in many Canadian hatcheries. More than 1,200 new tagging codes are used annually. The tagged fish migrate to sea, where they mix with fish tagged in Japan and Russia. Eventually they are harvested by thousands of commercial fishers, who report the capture location of tagged fish in hundreds of statistical areas. Then various agencies collect the data and try to make sense of them—no mean task.

Planning is equally important for small-scale marking programs. Although small programs do not share the logistic nightmares of large programs, they also do not have the luxury of an extensive marking and recovery network that can compensate for an occasional error. In a small marking program, planning is vital because each datum is of such relatively high value. And, for a project with only one marking or recovery period, a delay may jeopardize the entire project.

The manager of a successful marking study, therefore, will think in terms of a program from objective setting to final report. She will pay close attention to all the stages of planning and execution. This chapter describes the seven stages of a marking program, with advice about how to make the best decisions at each stage. Although most of the examples cover large-scale programs, the concepts are equally appropriate for small-scale and one-time projects.

2.2 PROGRAM PLANNING

Every successful project begins with a stated goal and stated objectives. A goal describes the overall purpose of the project. For example, the project might intend to "estimate the abundance of largemouth bass in Smith Mountain Lake," or "determine the stock composition of sockeye salmon harvest in Bristol Bay." The types of information that marking techniques can provide were listed in Chapter 1; goals for marking programs generally should be phrased in those terms.

Objectives define precisely what will be accomplished. Objectives must be specific, measurable, and achievable; they must tell what will be done, when, and with what resources. For example, the goal of estimating largemouth bass abundance might be translated into an objective to "estimate abundance of all largemouth bass age 3 and older for five consecutive years, with a variance no greater than 25% of the point estimate, costing annually no more than $5,000 and 30 worker-days." There is little doubt now about what the project will achieve, and explicit bases exist for evaluating the project's success.

The next planning step is to consider alternative strategies for achieving the objective. At this stage, a long list of alternatives should be created, without judging of their relative merits. For most mark–recapture studies, several approaches are available. For the largemouth bass example, all appropriate fish could be marked each year with a temporary fin clip and recaptured a few weeks later. Alternatively, each new year-class of appropriate fish could be marked each year with external tags and recaptured the following year, allowing replicate estimates of abundance for older year-classes in succeeding years. Or, the fish could be tagged in the spring and recaptured throughout the fishing season by anglers; or they could be tagged in the fall and recaptured in the spring by electrofishing. It is critical to follow this explicit listing process, so that each possibility can be examined objectively (Heimbuch et al. 1990).

The next step is to evaluate the characteristics of each alternative and choose the best one. Characteristics include the sample sizes necessary to achieve the desired statistical precision, the costs of capturing, marking, and recapturing the animals, the type of analysis possible, and the time needed to perform the study by that alternative. When these characteristics are assessed objectively and written explicitly, the choice of general approach and specific techniques should be easier. Of course, almost every program will require some compromise

---

Box 2.1   Setting Program Objectives

The restoration of striped bass on the Hudson River is a long-term management program. One element of that program is stocking striped bass fingerlings that presumably will add to the spawning population in later years. Project managers chose to evaluate that presumption through a marking and recapture project. They marked fingerling striped bass in the hatchery with coded wire tags. The remaining problem was when and how to collect recaptures. They analyzed the problem via goals, objectives, and methodological alternatives, as described here (adapted from Heimbuch et al. 1990).

Study Goal

The study's goal was to assess the contribution of hatchery-raised fingerlings to the Hudson River stock of striped bass.

Study Objective

The specific objective was to measure the proportion of hatchery-raised fish in the Hudson River striped bass population with a confidence level of ±25% and a probability of type I error of 5%, using no more than two boat crews and 60 days of field time.

Continued.

Box 2.1 Continued.

Alternative Methods

Heimbuch and his colleagues considered many different life stages, times, and locations for collecting recapture samples, based on their knowledge of fish distribution and river conditions:

(1) age-0 fish in the fall after hatchery release;
(2) age-1 fish in the winter at the mouth of the river;
(3) age-1 fish in the spring below the spawning grounds;
(4) age-2 and older fish in winter at the mouth of the river;
(5) mature females in the spring below the spawning grounds;
(6) fish of mixed ages in the coastal fishery.

Analysis of Alternatives

Heimbuch's group examined each of these alternatives in turn, based on the likelihood of achieving the study objectives, concurrence with necessary statistical assumptions, and field requirements. Alternative 1 was rejected because not all parts of the river inhabited by age-0 fish could be sampled and because hatchery-raised and natural fish might not have the same distribution by that time. Alternatives 2–6 were assessed on the basis of needed field time to collect the necessary recaptures (6,100 for alternatives 2–5) or the necessary fish to mark externally (244,000 yearlings for alternative 6). Presuming a boat crew could make eight trawl hauls per day, the group's assessment was:

Alternative	Catch/haul	Hauls needed	Boat-days needed
(2) Age 1 (winter)	12.0	510	64
(3) Age 1 (spring)	0.4	13,555	1,694
(4) Ages 2 and older	≤3.0	≥2,034	≥255
(5) Mature females	0.3	20,000	5,000
(6) Mixed ages (fishery)	18.9	12,910	1,614

Alternatives 3–6 were all rejected because the field requirements were enormous. Alternative 2 was acceptable because assumptions were likely to be met and because the needed number of recaptures (6,100 fish) could be made by one boat and crew in about 64 days. Therefore, alternative 2 was chosen as the method for conducting this project.

between statistical validity and cost. This planning process, however, will allow the compromises to be made openly and with full agreement by all participants. Box 2.1 demonstrates this approach for a marking program for Hudson River striped bass.

The final step is to fully and explicitly plot the entire operation (Vreeland 1990). This plot should be a flow diagram or other description that defines the order of steps in the process, the needed equipment, supplies, and work force, and the time needed to complete each step. It should include contingency plans for equipment breakdown, staff illness, inclement weather, and other potential problems. Because the collection, marking, and recapture of live animals is likely to involve intensive efforts over short periods, proper preparation is crucial (Johnson and Nielsen 1983).

Careful attention to statistical design constraints is also needed. A statistician will say first that a good design makes for easy and valid analysis. Although each study is unique, several features are common to all good designs. First, every study must be designed to meet its stated goals and objectives. This seems obvious, but researchers often repeat another design because it is available and understandable. For Pacific salmonids, this approach has led to repetitious studies that are well designed to provide data for hatchery assessment, but are poorly designed to answer pressing management questions (Johnson 1990).

Second, the design should include specific protocols for avoiding bias. At every step requiring a decision, a specific, justifiable approach should be written. For example, if fish are to be collected from boats landing at a marina, then a protocol should describe which boats will be sampled, on what days, at what times, etc. Any logical reason for a special design should be written explicitly and used rigorously. If no logical reason for a special design exists, then some form of random or systematic sampling is essential (Johnson and Nielsen 1983). Random and systematic sampling are strict protocols to prevent subconscious, undefined bias.

Finally, the design should allow variance calculations for the resulting point estimates. Three methods are available for estimating variance. First, a theoretical variance can be calculated based on the presumed statistical distribution of the data (Newman 1990). These are the familiar variance equations in statistical textbooks. Because catch data are not normally distributed, however, appropriate formulas often must be individually derived by statisticians. Second, computer techniques called bootstrapping and Monte Carlo simulation can create replicate samples from one data set. The replicates can then be used to calculate a simulated value for the true variance (Geiger 1990). Third, and best, the data themselves can be collected so that true variances can be calculated. This process involves using different codes on groups of marked animals, producing replicates of the desired statistic (Newman 1990). Salmonid marking programs on the Pacific coast, for example, have used distinctly different codes on coded wire tags, built into the automated tagging system. Alternatively, the values of the last digit on the tags can be considered different codes for different replicates. Thus, any tagging program using numbered tags has up to 10 replicates automatically built into its routine tagging operation (Rexstad et al. 1990). Similar strategies can be used for group-level markings by using slight variations (e.g., different orientation of branding marks) as replicates.

2.3 CAPTURING AND HOLDING ANIMALS

Most marking programs require the capture of living animals that will be marked and released for recapture at a later time. Obviously, a successful study depends on collecting a statistically reliable sample, holding and handling the animals with minimal stress, and releasing them in appropriate habitats.

The fundamental requirement is that the sample marked be large enough to provide the statistical precision desired. Because statistical precision is defined primarily by the number of animals recaptured, the entire statistical process must

Table 2.1 Commonly cited statistics books and guides, based on citations in *Fish-Marking Techniques* (Parker et al. 1990).

Author(s) and year	Principal contents
Burnham et al. (1987)	Design and analysis of mark–recapture studies
Cochran (1977)	Complete description of sampling designs, emphasizing mathematical analysis
Conover (1980)	Introduction to nonparametric statistics, emphasizing application and assumptions
Lachenbruch (1975)	Discriminant analysis
Ricker (1975)	Guide for calculating and analyzing fisheries data
SAS Institute (1985)	Guide to the use of SAS computerized statistical programs
Seber (1982)	Design and analysis of abundance estimation studies
Snedecor and Cochran (1980)	General statistics, briefly covering experimental and sampling designs and nonparametric techniques
Sokal and Rohlf (1981)	General parametric statistics, emphasizing biological applications
Steel and Torrie (1980)	General statistics, including experimental and sampling design and nonparametric techniques
Zar (1984)	General statistics, both parametric and nonparametric, emphasizing biological applications

be evaluated before the study begins. The objectives for the study should define the statistical precision, including at least the confidence interval and the type I error. The derivation and description of appropriate formulae for calculating precision are beyond the scope of this book, but the principles involved are available in most sampling design texts (Table 2.1).

After the desired recapture sample has been determined, the number of marked animals can be calculated. This number depends on several circumstances concerning mark retention, survival rate of marked animals, efficiency of the recapture method, and amount of recapture effort expended (Figure 2.1), as follows:

$$M = \frac{R}{pS(q_r f_r) A};$$

M = number to be marked;
R = number of recaptures required;
p = mark retention rate;
S = survival rate from marking to recapture;
q_r = catch rate per unit recapture effort;
f_r = units of recapture effort;
A = sampling fraction (awareness factor) (see Section 2.5).

Note that q_r is a fractional rate, representing the proportion of the population captured by every unit of effort. This is calculated in practice as the actual catch rate divided by the estimated population abundance. Thus, a trawl that captured an average of 20 fish per haul in a lake with 40,000 fish would have $q_r = 0.0005$.

Figure 2.1 also illustrates that decisions about capture technique for the

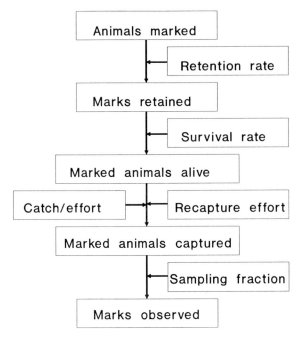

Figure 2.1 Relationship of the number of animals marked to the number that will be recovered, and the factors affecting the relationship. For project planning, one starts with the number of marks that must be recovered to achieve results of a desired precision. This number is multiplied by the reciprocal fractions described in the side boxes to arrive at the number of animals that must be marked originally.

marking sample must consider catch rates, total effort available, and population density.

A critical element in the sampling process is assuring that the marked animals accurately represent the entire population of interest. The best approach, of course, is to mark every animal, a feasible solution only for a few hatchery-based, high-priority programs (Wooley et al. 1990). In most cases, however, some sampling process is needed. When animals are dispersed in a water body, the collection process should cover all the habitat areas occupied by the population (Green et al. 1990). Furthermore, the sampling effort should be distributed so that the various strata (e.g., bays, stream stretches) are sampled in proportion to relative animal abundance, rather than in proportion to area.

Representative sampling is equally important for hatchery-based marking. Subtle biases may occur if animals from only a few culture tanks are marked or if the marked animals all come from early or late spawnings. Animals selected for marking should be checked for disease, so that latent high mortality rates are not unknowingly tied to the marked animals (Wooley et al. 1990). Most important, however, is developing a randomized or systematic procedure for selecting individual fish for marking. An acceptable method is to concentrate the fish into a small part of the culture tank (e.g., the last few feet of a raceway), and then randomly dip out netfuls of fish for marking (Vreeland 1990). Each culture tank must be sampled in this way, so that equal proportions of marked fish come from each tank (Box 2.2).

Animals are invariably stressed during capture, so capture techniques and procedures should be as gentle as possible. Because aquatic species react differently to various collecting techniques, alternative techniques should be evaluated for each situation. For example, marking deep-water pelagic fishes is very difficult because the fish may die when brought to the surface or suffer increased predation when returned to the water. In New Zealand, therefore, scientists are experimenting with breakaway circular hooks that are fished from deep longlines (Murray 1990). The hooks function as jaw tags, printed with numbers and other information. The fish mark themselves, in their preferred habitat, with a minimum of stress.

In general, all handling and holding should be as brief as possible. Collecting equipment should be monitored and emptied much more frequently for marking projects than for more routine collections; gill nets, for example, which are normally left in the water for 12–24 hours during monitoring activities, should be checked at least every 2 hours for markable fish. Trawls and seines should be fished for only a short time—a few minutes for some species and water conditions—before being emptied.

Once captured, the animals must be held in optimum conditions. A marked animal that later dies is a waste of the animal and the marking effort. Moreover, citizens feel rightly appalled if they see fisheries professionals treating fish poorly. The American Society of Ichthyology and Herpetology, the American Fisheries Society, and the American Institute of Fishery Research Biologists have jointly developed general protocols for handling live aquatic animals (ASIH et al. 1988). These protocols (see Appendix, page 195) should guide animal care decisions in all studies.

Four conditions are fundamental to a successful holding process. First, water quality should be kept at ambient or better conditions during all phases of the holding–marking–recovery process. Holding water should be drawn from the animal's natural environment whenever possible, dissolved oxygen levels should be maintained near saturation, and water temperature should be maintained at ambient or cooler levels. Except during specific treatments such as with anesthetics or antibiotics, holding water should be replaced continuously to avoid buildup of toxic chemicals.

Second, handling should be minimized. Animals should be netted, picked up, and moved as few times as possible, and they should be kept submerged as much as possible. This is especially important if water temperatures are high. With careful attention to the design of holding and marking facilities and with some experience, most marking operations can be streamlined and performed with the animal in the water. Ideally, even submerged fish and their water should be shaded from sun (especially in summer) and protected from wind (especially in winter).

Third, anesthesia should be used when possible for complex or intrusive procedures. Anesthesia reduces stress on the animals and improves the likelihood that the mark will be placed on the animal quickly and effectively. Many anesthetics have been used on aquatic organisms, but only two are currently acceptable for use on animals that will be released into the wild or eaten (Summerfelt and Smith 1990). The first is tricaine, licensed under the trade name Finquel™ and familiar to most fisheries professionals as MS-222™, another trade name. Summerfelt and Smith (1990) reported that effective tricaine concentrations vary with species: 15–25 mg/L for salmonids, 25–50 mg/L for channel catfish, and 120–140 mg/L for striped bass, for example. Regulations require that fish treated with tricaine be held for 21 days before release. The second acceptable anesthetic is carbon dioxide, applied directly as gaseous CO_2 or converted from dissolved sodium bicarbonate. Several other anesthetics are available for experiments that

Box 2.2 Sampling Hatchery Fish

Representative sampling for marking hatchery fish should be randomized so all fish have an equal probability of being sampled. Consider a small hatchery with five raceways, each of which can be divided with screens into four equal sections. Approximately 100,000 trout are in the raceways, but they are unevenly distributed because of different hatching and survival rates, as shown here:

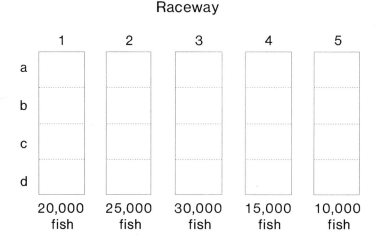

A marking project is planned to mark 10% of the total, or 10,000 fish. Because about 500 fish can be handled at a time by the marking crew, 20 sampling units are required.

A random design is required for representative sampling. Because sampling should be proportional to fish density, each raceway should have a probability of selection equal to relative abundance, as follows:

Raceway	Number of fish	Probability	Random numbers
1	20,000	0.20	00–19
2	25,000	0.25	20–44
3	30,000	0.30	45–74
4	15,000	0.15	75–89
5	10,000	0.10	90–99
1–5	100,000	1.00	

Two-digit random numbers can then be selected without replacement from a random-number table, according to the last column shown above. After that, a die can be tossed, with numbers 1–4 representing raceway sections a–d, respectively. Samples should be collected in the numbered order that they arise.

Continued.

Box 2.2 Continued.

Here is a sample design, based on an actual random draw:

Sample unit	Random number	Die face	Raceway and section	Sample unit	Random number	Die face	Raceway and number
1	78	3	4c	11	36	3	2c
2	33	1	2a	12	60	3	3c
3	68	2	3b	13	38	4	2d
4	76	1	4a	14	39	3	2c
5	18	2	1b	15	00	1	1a
6	82	2	4b	16	31	1	2a
7	65	3	3c	17	90	1	5a
8	21	1	2a	18	32	4	2d
9	94	4	5d	19	07	4	1d
10	03	2	1b	20	74	1	3a

do not release the animals, but these are unlikely to be useful for most marking situations. Details are provided in Summerfelt and Smith (1990). Restrictions on anesthetic use have made anesthesia much less practical in recent years. Nonetheless, anesthesia should be used whenever possible.

Fourth, marked animals should be treated with an antibiotic if the marking procedure and general handling have placed them at risk of infection. Tetracycline is the most popular antimicrobial chemical used on aquatic animals and is registered for use on food animals. It can be used as a bath treatment, as an injection, or as a food additive (Summerfelt and Smith 1990); it is also a chemical mark itself (Chapter 9). Great caution is necessary in the selection and use of chemicals because governmental regulations are becoming increasingly strict and rigorously enforced. A check of current chemical approvals should be undertaken before any prophylaxis is applied to animals that will be released or eaten.

If the animals are released back into natural environments, release should be as near the point of capture as possible so that study assumptions remain valid and physiological and behavioral stresses are reduced. If fish are marked on a boat, the marking operation should be conducted continuously or at frequent intervals, so that the boat has not travelled far from the capture location. If animals are captured remotely and brought to a central location for marking, groups should be held separately according to capture location and returned to that location for release.

2.4 MARKING ANIMALS

The process of marking animals is the subject of most of this book. Chapters 3–9 give the advantages, disadvantages, assumptions, and techniques for the marking methods most common today and most likely to be popular in the future. Regardless of the specific technique used, however, the marking process is identical.

First, the appropriate marking technique must be chosen, with reference to the criteria described in Chapter 1. As described there, explicit evaluation of the objectives and the constraints is essential for making the best choice.

Once a marking technique is chosen, the second step is defining a strict procedure for the marking process. This is equivalent to defining a quality assurance–quality control program in an industrial process (Geoghegan et al. 1990; Figure 2.2). Even the smallest details must be defined and fully described because small differences in the way people apply the mark or record the data may affect results for years. For example, the largest single error in marking programs is error in recording the tag or mark code. Errors are particularly common when a new tagging code is introduced. Geoghegan et al. (1990), therefore, recommended that one person should record the tag number first, before handing the tag to the tagger; the tagger should then read the tag number aloud to the recorder, who checks it against the entry. Standard forms for recording information about the mark, the marked animals, and the marking environment are needed. In general, as much information as possible should be recorded (Vreeland 1990). Acceptable error levels should be set in advance (generally no more than 1%) and monitored regularly.

The physical marking process and the location of the mark on the animal should be completely standardized (Wooley et al. 1990). Marking location affects retention, delayed mortality, and mark recognition rates for recaptured animals. This standardization is even more critical when morphometric techniques, such as scale size, shape, and patterning are used. Scales taken from different parts of a fish's body differ in size and shape; sampling them without precise attention to where scales are collected can invalidate the entire project. Mark locations can be defined in terms of specific scales (e.g., third row above lateral line, 8th scale back from head) or standard morphometric features (e.g., dactylus of third walking leg).

This level of attention to standardization and exact procedures means that extensive training is essential for the marking personnel (van der Elst 1990). In many cases, the level of standardization may eliminate volunteers as the work force. In other cases, the preparation of fully explained and illustrated guides (including videotapes) may provide sufficient training for volunteers. Each volunteer will require a marking kit with all the tools, tags, data forms, instruction manuals, and telephone numbers of project personnel needed to complete the process.

Formalized training, however, is just as necessary for professional personnel as for volunteers. Because professionals may have marked animals previously, they may resist training. Nevertheless, each new marking operation requires training to demonstrate precisely the basic techniques, the modifications being used, and the reasons for them. Practice with the technique should be part of every training regimen.

During the process, marking personnel must judge which animals are unlikely to survive and, hence, should not be marked or released. These include animals highly stressed during capture and holding and those not recovering normally after the marking operations (Ryan 1990; Vreeland 1990). Such animals should be released immediately to enhance the probability that they will survive. As in other steps in the operation, explicit criteria should be developed for judging when an animal is unfit for tagging. Table 2.2 gives an example of stages in the behavior of anesthetized fish that can be used to judge condition of all captive animals.

The final step in the tagging operation is often skipped—a study to determine acute mortality and tag retention rates. A sample of marked animals always

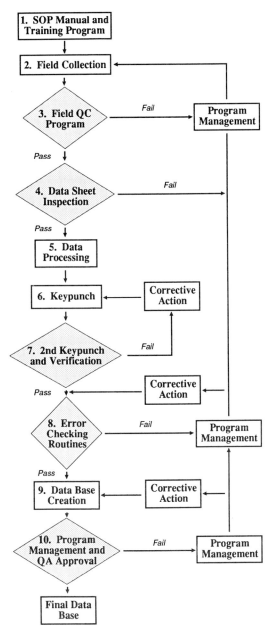

Figure 2.2 The quality assurance control program established for the Hudson River striped bass tagging program. SOP = standard operating procedures, QC = quality control, QA = quality assurance. Reprinted from Geoghegan et al. (1990).

should be retained for at least 24 hours to determine if the marks have been applied correctly and to estimate the rate of immediate tag loss (Vreeland 1990). Even if substantial data exist for use of a specific technique on a specific species, a short-term retention study should be conducted to determine if the marking personnel and marking equipment are working at the expected quality levels.

Table 2.2. Stages of anesthesia, which can be used to judge the condition of fish held in captivity before and after tagging (adapted from Summerfelt and Smith 1990).

Stage of anesthesia	Reaction of fish to light and touch	Rate of opercular movement	Fish equilibrium
0	Normal	Normal	Normal
1	Slightly depressed	Slightly depressed	Normal
2	Only reacts to strong pressure	Slightly depressed	Normal
3	Only reacts to strong touch or vibration	Slightly increased	Erratic swimming, partial loss of muscle tone
4	Loss of spinal reflexes	Slow, but regular	Total loss of equilibrium and muscle tone
5	No response	Slow and irregular	Total loss

Depending on the total number of animals marked, a sample of 300 animals is probably sufficient for statistical purposes (Vreeland 1990).

For novel techniques or applications, a longer study also should be conducted to determine tag retention rates and mortality (Ryan 1990). Various long-term studies have shown that most tag loss occurs within 1 week of marking. Thus, a 7-day program to monitor animals retained in cages within the release environment will probably be sufficient to estimate total tag loss. Data from these two studies can be used to calculate an estimated number of marked animals at large in the environment.

2.5 RECAPTURING ANIMALS AND READING THEIR MARKS

As much as professionals debate about the best mark for any particular situation, they all unite on one point: recapturing marked animals is at least as important as marking them. This is the step that produces results. Unfortunately, this step is difficult and often distantly removed from the marking process. In studies of marked striped bass in Chesapeake Bay, for example, the recapture process required 9 years before enough marked animals were recovered to complete the project (Wooley et al. 1990). Other studies may depend on marking in the headwaters of a spawning stream and recapture thousands of kilometers away by fishers and scientists from other nations.

Perhaps the most important point about recovering and reading marks is the most basic—have a plan. As soon as the marked animals can be presumed to have met the study's dispersal requirements, recaptures can begin. As long as the last marked animal is swimming, recaptures can continue. Between those two times, the project manager must be prepared to receive, record, and maintain recapture data in an organized fashion and to sustain the preestablished coordination links between the personnel and agencies contributing to the project.

Recapture may involve professionals, volunteers, or both (Miyake 1990). If professional crews recapture the animals, the process is decidedly easier to control. A standard and detailed protocol for collecting the marked animals is needed. The fundamental need is to perform a statistically valid sampling process, as was needed for the original capture process (see Section 2.3). For studies in relatively small water bodies (ponds and lakes, short streams), the entire area can be covered and all captured animals examined for marks. In many cases, however, not every captured animal can be examined. The proportion of the catch examined is termed the "sampling fraction." Pacific coast researchers, for example, have set a minimum goal of sampling 20% of the commercial salmonid catch for marks (Johnson 1990).

The more usual manner of collecting marked animals is by fishers, either commercial or recreational, who voluntarily participate in the program. This situation is typical for large water bodies, highly mobile animals, and long-term studies. Volunteers cannot be expected to report all marks, and experience shows that the rate of volunteer mark reporting ranges widely (Palermo 1990). The proportion of recovered marks that are actually reported is called the "awareness factor," and it is analogous to the sampling fraction for commercial catches. Anticipating—and controlling—the awareness factor is a critical element in determining the precision and accuracy of the results.

Successful volunteer recapture programs increase the awareness factor by informing the public about the program and then by providing incentives for fishers to return the data. Anglers must first know about the marking program. Every source should be used to publicize the program. Mass media announcements can spread the news broadly to large segments of the population. Specific important audiences, however, including commercial fishers, charter boat operators, guides, bait and tackle store owners, marina operators, and fishing organizations, should be identified and contacted directly. The publicity program also must be continuous. Stores and restaurants, for example, may post a notice of the marking program for a few weeks, but they will remove the notice if not encouraged to keep it up.

Essential parts of this publicity are instructions to make mark reporting easy. Clearly marked drop-off points at marinas and other high-traffic locations are essential. Also a ready supply of preprinted and return-postage-paid data envelopes must be available if tags are meant to be returned by mail with additional information. People who are likely to collect many tags (for example, charter boat captains or active members of local fishing clubs) should be supplied with personal kits for recording data and returning tags and data at regular intervals to the project manager.

The usual incentive for encouraging mark reporting is a cash reward (Figure 2.3). Most programs use a two-stage reward system consisting of a small reward for every mark reported and an end-of-season lottery providing a larger reward to one or more randomly chosen participants. Although small, the reward for reporting each mark must be large enough to encourage an angler or commercial fisher to take the time to handle the marked animal separately and report the information. Most rewards reported in the late 1980s were $5–10 (Eder 1990; Haas 1990). End-of-season lotteries have paid as high as $1,000. Fishery-related businesses may be willing to sponsor the rewards and lotteries, as well as the entire marking program, in exchange for publicity (van der Elst 1990). Reward systems like these can increase angler returns by more than 50% (Haas 1990). Nonmonetary rewards can also be effective, such as hats advertising the program (Scott et al. 1990) or patches for fishing vests.

An additional incentive for anglers—one that involves them more closely in the entire management program—is to receive information about the animals they

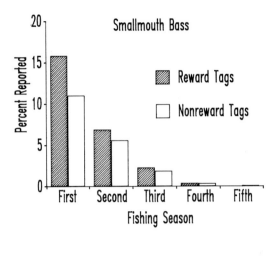

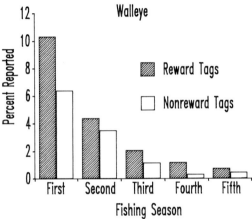

Figure 2.3 Tag return rates by anglers in Michigan. Return rates were consistently and significantly higher for rewarded tag returns. Reprinted from Haas (1990).

captured. A reply card can describe where and when the animal was marked, how much it grew and traveled while free, and how the information is used. This technique is especially valuable if marking programs are expected to continue for many years.

Regardless of the source of recovered marks, they must be recovered so that valid statistical analysis can follow. Several simple measures can assure validity of later calculations and conclusions. First, the sampling fraction or awareness factor should be as large as possible because bias shrinks as the sampling fraction increases (Shaul and Clark 1990). The decision about sampling fraction is part of the larger question about the minimum numbers of marks needed. For many studies, including baseline descriptions of natural genetic and chemical marks, a sample of 100 recaptured, marked animals is considered minimum.

Second, marked fish must be recaptured so that they accurately represent the entire study area. Thus, all landing points must be monitored proportionately to expected landings, and all water areas must be sampled proportionately to expected population abundances. For example, if heads of salmon are being collected at marinas to recover coded wire tags, the capacity of the collection bins at each marina should be proportional to the number of fishing trips ending at each marina.

Third, all data should be checked for accuracy and completeness. Data entered into a computer should be double-keyed and then cross-checked. Data should be matched against known constraints (e.g., the reported tag code should match a code actually used in this area on this species), and impossible or improbable data should be rejected (Green et al. 1990). Because new tag codes can increase reading and recording errors almost tenfold (Perry et al. 1990), special care is needed whenever the routine is changed appreciably.

2.6 DATA HANDLING

Large marking programs produce massive amounts of data. Because marking is often conducted for large, complex, multijurisdictional fisheries, many agencies may mark and recapture animals. These agencies may have different needs and may use different methods for recording and manipulating their data (Lapi et al. 1990). If not handled correctly, the data may never be useful for management. Even for small studies, improper handling can make data useless; because small studies have few data, the loss can be disastrous.

The basic recommendation for large-scale marking programs is that one centralized group should handle the data (Johnson 1990). That group should be overseen by a representative board of the cooperating agencies, and it should act as coordinator for their common interests. This group can maintain the data in a common data base, using standardized coding for species, catch locations, and other data (Davis et al. 1990). It also should assign and monitor marking codes and nomenclature used for all marking programs within its jurisdiction.

This group should maintain quality control for all the marking data it receives. This includes several distinct responsibilities (Lapi et al. 1990). First, the group should provide specific and understandable reporting instructions for persons recapturing animals and reporting the marks. Second, it should validate all incoming data for completeness and reliability, as described in Section 2.5. Third, it should implement a protocol for receiving suggestions for changes in data handling, reviewing those changes, recommending acceptance or rejection to the board, and informing the membership of board-approved changes. Fourth, it should update existing data to the current protocol, so all data can be analyzed as a whole. In the absence of updating, the group should at least keep accurate records and annotate data with the protocol under which each datum is preserved. For small studies, similar functions should be performed by the project leader, always recorded in explicit and complete detail.

The data-handling group for a major ongoing project obviously needs a stable operating base, including funds, facilities, personnel, and authority. The participating organizations must make a long-term and financially stable commitment (Johnson 1990). Generally, the data group should include a full-time staff coordinator, a dedicated computer, and the necessary budget for technical staff support and for communication with the membership.

2.7 DATA ANALYSIS

Data analysis can be as simple as a mark–recapture abundance estimate for largemouth bass in a small pond or as complex as a multivariate discrimination of several sockeye salmon stocks being harvested on a treaty-regulated international fishing ground. The principles of competent analysis in any scientific investigation are also the principles of competent analysis here.

Foremost is the recognition that expert help is almost always needed. Virtually all analytic procedures are more complex than first imagined. Every decision in the study, from choice of mark to method of recapture, affects the data and the resulting conclusions (Schwarz and Arnason 1990). As marking techniques have developed and diversified, the computational techniques also have become more complicated and abstract. Many of the techniques described in later chapters, including morphometric indices, genetic identification, and chemical marking, have little to do with marking per se—they are almost entirely statistical sleuthing exercises.

Fortunately, analytic help is increasingly available. Large marking programs normally have full-time biostatisticians on call for statistical advice, and most fisheries agencies now employ biostatisticians to help design and analyze agency projects. These are the frontline experts who should be consulted before and during marking studies. The computations necessary for most techniques are cumbersome, so many specialized computer programs have been written (e.g., Rexstad et al. 1990). The Computer Users Section of the American Fisheries Society compiles programs in the public domain and reviews newly available programs regularly.[1] Because both statistical and computational understanding advance rapidly, it is prudent to keep in regular contact with colleagues who make their living crunching numbers.

Specific computations and concerns exist for each type of data collected from a marking study. Although all the questions for all the data types cannot be addressed here, a few basic issues can be raised for the major data types.

2.7.1 Stock Contribution Analysis

Stock contribution data are collected to determine the proportional contribution of various stocks to a mixed group, usually at harvest. The basic formula for each stock (after Geiger 1990) is

$$C = \frac{X}{(S \times P)};$$

C = stock contribution to total catch (in numbers of fish);
X = number of marks recovered or reported;
S = sampling fraction or awareness factor;
P = marking fraction (proportion of original stock marked).

The variables under the control of the study are sampling fraction (S) and marking fraction (P). As described earlier, the sampling fraction, or awareness

---

[1]The Section can be reached via the AFS at 5410 Grosvenor Lane, Suite 110, Bethesda, Maryland 20814.

factor, has a major effect on the data. It should be as large as possible. Whereas *S* can be selected for commercial fisheries and for sampling performed by an agency, it must be estimated or measured for recreational fisheries or for reporting that is voluntary. This process adds another source of error to the estimate of stock contribution.

The marking fraction also should be as large as possible. A higher marking fraction increases the probability of recapturing marked animals. In every case, however, the fraction must be known and reported. This requires knowing precisely how many animals are marked and how many in total will be released. If animals have been marked a long time before release (e.g., if they have been held in a hatchery for a month after marking), an additional sampling process may be necessary to estimate the marking fraction at the time of release.

2.7.2   Distribution and Movement Studies

Recapture of marked animals is a primary tool for discovering their migration patterns. The necessary data are simple, recording primarily the presence or absence of marked animals and their relative abundance on a geographical grid. Consequently, rates of tag loss, handling mortality, and the like do not affect the quality of the distributional data, as long as the effects are evenly distributed. The essential design requirement, however, is that all marked animals have equal probability of recapture. That is, the recaptures of animals in different sampling areas must be expressed as recaptures per unit of recovery effort (Sheridan and Melendez 1990). This requirement is frequently overlooked in practice, leading to invalid conclusions. For example, if marked animals are monitored at a series of fishing ports, equally distant from the release location, the absolute number of recaptures will be proportional to both animal density and fishing effort (Box 2.3). Dividing absolute recaptures by fishing effort will make the recovery rate proportional only to animal density, the intended result. Whereas this adjustment is easy if marked animals are recovered by professional crews or even commercial fishers, it is difficult if recoveries are based on recreational or artisanal fishers.

2.7.3   Population Abundance Estimation

The classical use of marking data has been to estimate absolute abundance, via Petersen or similar indices. Abundance estimation is now a well-developed, thoroughly researched subdiscipline, with an expansive literature. Burnham et al. (1987) provided an excellent literature review.

2.7.4   Age and Growth Studies

As with abundance estimation, the analysis of age and growth data are well covered in other works. Marking studies can produce excellent age and growth data because individual animals can be measured and aged repeatedly. The data can be highly misleading when extrapolated to the entire population, however, because the marks themselves can cause differences in growth and longevity. The discussions in later chapters regarding mark influence on growth and behavior should be carefully considered before age and growth statistics are computed.

Box 2.3 Reporting Distributional Data

Imagine that a study is conducted to determine the movement patterns of
lobsters among a series of subtropical islands. The question is whether or not
Center Island lobsters invade other lobster populations in the waters around
neighboring islands. Lobsters are trapped around Center Island, tagged and
released. Lobsters are recaptured by local divers on the islands in the
surrounding archipelago. After 3 years of reporting, the total returns are as
follows:

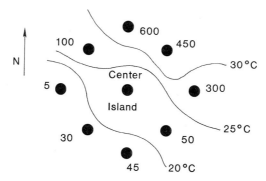

The logical conclusion appears to be that the lobsters move northeast,
towards warmer waters. Analysis of diving activity, however, shows that
diving effort also follows isotherms, as follows:

Temperature	Average diving trips per month	Average hours per trip	Effort index
Over 30°C	100	2.5	250
25–30°C	70	1.0	70
20–25°C	10	0.5	5
Below 20°C	6	0.5	3

When total recaptures are divided by the effort index, the relative
recapture rates are as follows:

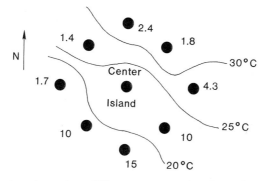

The conclusion is quite different now, showing that lobsters move
generally southward. Lobsters are responding to some factor other than
temperature.

2.8 REPORTING

The final step in a marking program is reporting the results. Although this step will get little attention here, it is obviously the essential end to any project. Each project requires a final report, and long-term projects require a constant flow of progress reports and statistical updates. All intermediate reports should be contained in a named publication series, and each report should carry a date and number for future reference.

Continuing programs must provide three types of information in addition to a comprehensive annual report. Reporting must list the marking codes that are being used, including the newly authorized codes and those still likely to be recovered. The report also must list all recaptures (who, what, where, when, and how) so members can perform the desired analyses on the animals they marked and released. Finally, the reports must describe changes in protocol placed in effect since the previous report. Because most large marking studies require cooperation among agencies and geographically dispersed workers, a comprehensive mailing list is essential.

2.9. REFERENCES

ASIH (American Society of Ichthyologists and Herpetologists), American Fisheries Society, and American Institute of Fishery Research Biologists. 1988. Guidelines for use of fishes in field research. Fisheries (Bethesda) 13(2):16–23.

Burnham, K. P., D. R. Anderson, G. C. White, C. Brownie, and K. H. Pollock. 1987. Design and analysis methods for fish survival experiments based on release–recapture. American Fisheries Society Monograph 5, Bethesda, Maryland.

Cochran, W. G. 1977. Sampling techniques, 3rd edition. Wiley, New York.

Conover, W. J. 1980. Practical nonparametric statistics, 2nd edition. Wiley, New York.

Davis, N. D., K. W. Myers, R. V. Walker, and C. K. Harris. 1990. The Fisheries Research Institute's high-seas salmonid tagging program and methodology for scale pattern analysis. American Fisheries Society Symposium 7:863–879.

Eder, S. 1990. Angler use of black crappie and the effects of a reward-tag program at Jamesport Community Lake, Missouri. American Fisheries Society Symposium 7:647–654.

Geiger, H. J. 1990. Parametric bootstrap confidence intervals for estimating contributions to fisheries from marked salmon populations. American Fisheries Society Symposium 7:667–676.

Geoghegan, P., M. T. Mattson, D. J. Dunning, and Q. E. Ross. 1990. Improved data in a tagging program through quality assurance and quality control. American Fisheries Society Symposium 7:714–719.

Green, A. W., L. W. McEachron, G. C. Matlock, and E. Hegen. 1990. Use of abdominal streamer tags and maximum-likelihood techniques to estimate spotted seatrout survival and growth. American Fisheries Society Symposium 7:623–630.

Haas, R. C. 1990. Effects of monetary rewards and jaw-tag placement on angler reporting rates for walleyes and smallmouth bass. American Fisheries Society Symposium 7:655–659.

Heimbuch, D. G., D. J. Dunning, H. Wilson, and Q. E. Ross. 1990. Sample-size determination for mark–recapture experiments: Hudson River case study. American Fisheries Society Symposium 7:684–690.

Johnson, D. L., and L. A. Nielsen. 1983. Sampling considerations. Pages 1–22 in L. A. Nielsen and D. L. Johnson, editors. Fisheries techniques. American Fisheries Society, Bethesda, Maryland.

Johnson, J. K. 1990. Regional overview of coded wire tagging of anadromous salmon and steelhead in northwest America. American Fisheries Society Symposium 7:782–816.

Lachenbruch, P. A. 1975. Discriminant analysis. Hafner Press, New York.

Lapi, L., M. Hamer, and B. Johnson. 1990. Data organization and coding for a coastwide mark–recovery data system. American Fisheries Society Symposium 7:720–724.

Miyake, P. M. 1990. History of the ICCAT tagging program, 1971–1986. American Fisheries Society Symposium 7:746–764.

Murray, T. 1990. Fish-marking techniques in New Zealand. American Fisheries Society Symposium 7:737–745.

Newman, K. B. 1990. Variance estimation for stock-contribution estimates based on sample recoveries of coded-wire-tagged fish. American Fisheries Society Symposium 7:677–683.

Palermo, R. V. 1990. Jeopardized estimates of the contribution of marked Pacific salmon to the sport fishery of the Strait of Georgia, British Columbia, due to awareness factor variability. American Fisheries Society Symposium 7:631–646.

Parker, N. C., A. E. Giorgi, R. C. Heidinger, D. B. Jester, Jr., E. D. Prince, and G. A. Winans, editors. 1990. Fish-marking techniques. American Fisheries Society Symposium 7, Bethesda, Maryland.

Perry, E. A., H. L. Blankenship, and R. V. Palermo. 1990. Comparison of two methods for replicating coded wire tag studies. American Fisheries Society Symposium 7:660–666.

Rexstad, E., K. P. Burnham, and D. R. Anderson. 1990. Design of survival experiments with marked animals: a case study. American Fisheries Society Symposium 7:581–587.

Ricker, W. E. 1975. Computation and interpretation of biological statistics of fish populations. Fisheries Research Board of Canada Bulletin 191.

Ryan, P. M. 1990. Sizes, structures, and movements of brook trout and Atlantic salmon populations inferred from Schnabel mark–recapture studies in two Newfoundland lakes. American Fisheries Society Symposium 7:725–735.

SAS Institute. 1985. SAS user's guide: statistics, version 5 edition. SAS Institute, Cary, North Carolina.

Schwarz, C. J., and A. N. Arnason. 1990. Use of tag-recovery information in migration and movement studies. American Fisheries Society Symposium 7:588–603.

Scott, E. L., E. D. Prince, and C. D. Goodyear. 1990. History of the Cooperative Game Fish Tagging Program in the Atlantic Ocean, Gulf of Mexico, and Caribbean Sea, 1954–1987. American Fisheries Society Symposium 7:841–853.

Seber, G. A. F. 1982. The estimation of animal abundance and related parameters. Macmillan, New York.

Shaul, L. D., and J. E. Clark. 1990. Use of coded wire tag data to estimate aggregate stock composition of salmon catches in multiple mixed-stock fisheries. American Fisheries Society Symposium 7:613–622.

Sheridan, P. F., and R. G. C. Melendez. 1990. Determining movement patterns in marine organisms: comparison of methods tested on penaeid shrimp. American Fisheries Society Symposium 7:604–612.

Snedecor, G. W., and W. C. Cochran. 1980. Statistical methods, 7th edition. Iowa State University Press, Ames.

Sokal, R. R., and F. J. Rohlf. 1981. Biometry, 2nd edition. Freeman, San Francisco.

Steel, R. G. D., and J. H. Torrie. 1980. Principles and procedures of statistics, 2nd edition. McGraw-Hill, New York.

Summerfelt, R. C., and L. S. Smith. 1990. Anesthesia, surgery, and related techniques. Pages 213–272 in C. B. Schreck and P. B. Moyle, editors. Methods for fish biology. American Fisheries Society, Bethesda, Maryland.

van der Elst, R. P. 1990. Marine fish tagging in South Africa. American Fisheries Society Symposium 7:854–862.

Vreeland, R. R. 1990. Random-sampling design to estimate hatchery contributions to fisheries. American Fisheries Society Symposium 7:691–707.

Wooley, C. M., N. C. Parker, B. M. Florence, and R. W. Miller. 1990. Striped bass restoration along the Atlantic Coast: a multistate and federal cooperative hatchery and tagging program. American Fisheries Society Symposium 7:775–781.

Zar, J. H. 1984. Biostatistical analysis, 2nd edition. Prentice-Hall, Englewood Cliffs, New Jersey.

Chapter 3

External Tags

3.1 INTRODUCTION

External tags are the oldest and most widely used devices to mark fish and other animals. The earliest records date to the 1600s, when naturalists tied wool threads around the tails of brown trout in European streams. Since then, fish taggers have never looked back, rivaling fishing lure designers in the sizes, shapes, materials, and colors of their inventions (Figure 3.1). In an exhaustive literature review, McFarlane et al. (1990) read more than 900 papers about marking and tagging; two-thirds were about external tags.

External tags have traveled everywhere, on all parts of all sorts of aquatic animals and in all variety of environments. They are more common for marine studies, but external tags are just as useful in fresh waters and estuaries. They have been applied in frigid Arctic waters and in the tropics. They adorn fish, crustaceans, and molluscs.

The enormous creativity devoted to inventing and modifying external tags has been necessary for a simple reason: every external tag has disadvantages. Because they make such radical intrusions into an animal's body, external tags designed for one species or one habitat are likely to be useless in another. The tag may fall off, may alter the animal's behavior, or may fatally injure it. Consequently, fisheries workers will continue to invent new external tags and refine existing models to meet their new needs.

The most commonly used external tags fall into three categories based on the way they attach to the animal. *Transbody tags* protrude through both sides of the animal's body. The tag generally includes a shaft (wire, thread, plastic strip, or tube) that passes through the body and is enlarged on both ends to prevent it from slipping off the animal. The enlargements include flat discs, beads or bubbles, and knots. Alternatively, the two ends of the shaft are tied together, forming a loop with one knot. Generally, the tag is attached just below the dorsal fin of a fish, with the shaft passing between the bones that support the fin or the vertebral spines.

Dart-style tags protrude through only one surface of the animal. As with transbody tags, the tag includes a shaft (plastic thread or thin wire). The protruding end of the shaft holds an enlarged device—a vinyl tube, flattened disc, or bead. The other end is embedded in the animal's body; it contains an anchor that prevents the tag from pulling out of the body. The two most common styles have an arrow-like head with one or two barbs (dart tag) or a T-shaped head like the tags used to attach price tags to clothing (T-bar or Floy® tag). Dart-style tags are also generally inserted on a fish just below the dorsal fin, with the anchor

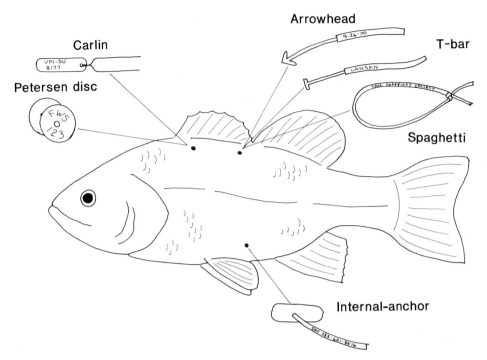

Figure 3.1 Examples of the variety modern of external tags.

embedded past the midline of the fish so that it is held in place by bones supporting the fin or by vertebral spines.

Internal-anchor tags also protrude through only one surface of the animal. The external portion of the tag is like a dart-style tag, but the anchoring device is much different. The anchor is a flat disc that lies against the inside wall of the fish's body cavity. The tag usually must be inserted through a small incision in the ventral surface of a fish.

The older literature contains descriptions of literally dozens of external tags. Although these tags are historically important and may still be applicable in special circumstances, most are not used widely in current studies. These tags are listed in Table 3.1 for reference, but will not be described further here.

External tags are popular because they are inexpensive and easily visible, and they allow most vital statistics of an animal population to be measured. Growth rates can be estimated because external tags identify individual animals whose size or weight can be measured at tagging and later at recapture. Because the tag identification can be read without sacrificing the animal, individuals can be captured, identified, and measured several times, allowing calculation of highly precise individual growth rates.

External tags also provide the fundamental tool for measuring fishing mortality. The tags are easily seen by anglers and commercial fishers, and instructions for their return can be printed on the enlarged area of the tags. Because a known number of tagged animals are at large, the proportion captured is a direct estimate of exploitation rate.

External tags are usually essential for behavioral studies. Researchers can

Table 3.1 Historically important external tags, based on Jones (1979), Wydoski and Emery (1983), and McFarlane et al. (1990).

Tag type	Name	Description
Transbody	Albrechtsen tag	Plastic loop with enlarged tabs on each end
	Alcathene tag	External disc carrying an internal tag
	Archer tag	Twin rectangular plates attached with two pins
	Atkins tag	Loop of wire or thread with a dangling disc
	Bachelor button	Paired discs attached through the operculum
	Flag tag	Thread loop with plastic disc attached
	Hydrostatic tag	Wire loop with a hollow plastic tube designed to be of neutral buoyancy
	Monel tag	V-shaped metal strip clamped onto operculum or jaw
	Strap tag	Similar to Monel tag
Dart-style	Sphyrion tag	Spring-loaded barbs, used mostly on crustaceans
Internal	Celluloid tag	Thin strip inserted into body cavity
	Subcutaneous	Rectangular disc inserted shallowly below skin

identify externally tagged animals individually and repeatedly from a distance (Matthews and Reavis 1990). This reduces the influence of the observer on behavior and allows more animals to be observed simultaneously.

External tags are especially useful for migration and movement studies. Because the tags can be applied easily (especially dart-style tags), many animals can be marked in a short time by many people in many locations. Multiple sightings of animals are also possible, allowing tracking of movements over several seasons and areas. Because the tags can carry detailed reporting instructions, anglers and commercial fishers can report tags without knowing about the tagging program beforehand.

Although many species have been tagged with external tags, their use is limited. External tags are generally restricted to juvenile or adult animals. Smaller animals may not survive the extensive handling during tagging, and even the smallest tags may add an unacceptably large metabolic burden to small animals. External tags are also best suited to open-water animals rather than to animals associated with physical habitat structure. Reclusive and cryptic animals, living in or near structures, may be prevented from free habitat choice or movement by the presence of a cumbersome tag (Moring 1990). Benthic animals may be irritated by tags that are pressed against their bodies by the substrate. Tags placed on benthic or cryptic animals may become entangled in habitat structures, increasing the likelihood of injury to the animal and loss of the tag.

3.2 ASSUMPTIONS FOR EXTERNAL TAGS

The fundamental assumption for using external tags is that the tag and the tagging process do not affect the animal in any way. Because scientists study tagged animals in order to understand untagged ones, this assumption is critical. Each step in the tagging process and each type of tag influence the truth of this assumption, so each tagging project requires complete and careful evaluation (McFarlane and Beamish 1990; Box 3.1). This overall assumption can be analyzed in terms of the more restricted assumptions described below. These assumptions

Box 3.1   Twenty Questions for a Valid Mark

Marking studies are useful only to the extent that marked animals are identical to unmarked animals. Because no mark is perfect, each marking project should be evaluated objectively and explicitly by answering the following questions.

A. Does marking affect mortality?

   (1) Do the handling and marking procedures cause acute mortality?
   (2) Do the handling and marking procedures produce chronic infection or wounding that cause delayed mortality?
   (3) Does the mark increase or decrease the likelihood of subsequent recapture?
   (4) Does the mark change the animal's visibility or swimming speed so that predation increases?
   (5) Is the likelihood of increased mortality uniform among sizes, sexes, and habitat types?

B. Does marking affect growth?

   (6) Does the mark interfere with capture, handling, or swallowing of food?
   (7) Does the mark slow the rate of digestion or assimilation of food?
   (8) Does the mark increase the metabolic cost of swimming or maintaining position in the water?
   (9) Will the mark constrain growth as the animal gets larger?
   (10) Is the likelihood of altered growth uniform among sizes, sexes, and habitat types?

C. Does marking affect behavior?

   (11) Does a marked animal react differently to the presence of other animals?
   (12) Do other animals react differently to the presence of a marked animal?
   (13) Does the marked animal avoid preferred habitats or habitat features?
   (14) Do animals react dramatically to the handling and marking process?
   (15) Can released marked animals return readily to their former habitats, home ranges, or territories?

D. Are marked animals identifiable?

   (16) Do marks remain on the animals for the length of time intended?
   (17) Can a natural color, shape, or morphological phenomenon be confused as a mark?
   (18) Are marks obvious to both a professional and a volunteer observer?
   (19) Are all observed marks reported?

And the final question:

   (20) What evidence exists to support the answers to questions 1–19?

are discussed in more detail here than in later chapters because most of the assumptions are common to all marking methods; use this as reference for later chapters as well.

Tagging should not increase the population's mortality. This assumption is absolutely critical if tagging is used for mark–recapture abundance estimates because the techniques depend on a constant proportion of marked to unmarked animals throughout the study period (Gutherz et al. 1990). It is less critical for movement studies, in which only comparative data from tagged animals are used. Even in movement studies, however, the death of many tagged animals reduces the probability of recapturing tagged animals and consequently reduces the quality of data.

Higher mortality of tagged animals often occurs because tagging is a complicated and stressful process. Haegele (1990), for example, reported that more than 50% of tagged Pacific herring may die just from the handling process, and Berg and Berg (1990) reported increased mortality of tagged Arctic char. Mortality is both acute, occurring during or soon after tagging, and delayed, occurring long after the animals have been released into the environment. Acute mortality is caused by the animal's trauma during capture, tagging, and release. Acute mortality can be reduced by handling animals gently and by choosing the appropriate tag for the species and size of animal. A sample of tagged animals should be held in captivity for at least 24 hours to assess acute mortality. If dead and dying animals are present, the appropriate proportion should be subtracted from the tagging records. High acute mortality usually indicates that the tags or some aspect of the tagging procedure must be changed.

Delayed mortality occurs if the tag (or the tagging procedure) harms the animal in direct or subtle ways. Tags may cause wounds that do not heal properly, may make swimming more difficult, and may make tagged animals more vulnerable to predation (Howe and Hoyt 1982; Matthews and Reavis 1990; Moring 1990). Delayed mortality is more difficult to assess than acute mortality because it occurs after the tagged animals have dispersed in the environment. When a new tag or procedure is used or a new species is being tagged, a long-term holding experiment should be conducted to evaluate delayed mortality.

The second assumption is that tagging does not reduce growth of tagged animals. This assumption is critical for virtually all studies because a reduction in nutritional status may influence all other population statistics. Malnourished animals will grow slowly, reproduce poorly, and exhibit physiological and behavioral abnormalities. Such animals may be more vulnerable to disease, predation, and harvest. Migration studies may be affected if physiologically stressed, tagged animals cannot travel as far or as fast as untagged animals. Reduced growth is generally a long-term problem, caused by the presence of the tag itself. McFarlane and Beamish (1990), for example, observed slower growth of tagged sablefish for 7 years after tagging.

Fortunately, problems with growth and related physiological conditions are relatively easy to observe. An animal's appearance and the difference between lengths, weights, and body condition of tagged and untagged animals indicate whether tagging has affected growth. Early fish tags often interfered with feeding (e.g., jaw tags), causing emaciation; such tags have been abandoned now except for special uses. Although modern tags are designed to reduce growth problems, many people still worry that tagging subtly affects growth by increasing the energetic costs of swimming and maintaining balance.

The third assumption is that tagging does not change behavior of tagged animals. This condition also is critical for almost every study because behavior affects all aspects of an animal's life history. Behavioral changes are expected because of the very presence of a tag. The size and color of the tag may encourage or discourage aggressive behavior by the tagged animal and by animals seeing it. The size and style of attachment may prevent animals from using a preferred habitat. For example, dangling tags may prevent cryptic animals from hiding in crevices, and cumbersome tags may impair the burrowing ability of shrimp. The tagging process also may affect behavior. Animals released at a place different than their place of capture will encounter different environmental conditions, making them more vulnerable to predation. This is particularly troublesome for animals captured in deep water, marked, and then released at the surface (Matthews and Reavis 1990). Captured and released animals may stop feeding, swim erratically or become especially aggressive for a period of time.

Scientists know little about the altered behavior of tagged aquatic animals. Understanding differences between behavior of tagged and untagged animals requires direct observation of untagged animals—but our inability to do that is precisely why we use tags! Observation is possible in laboratory tanks and in ideal natural settings (e.g., coral reefs, intertidal zones, headwater streams). Likely behavioral changes also can be deduced from knowledge of general behavior. Tagging probably affects the behavior of smaller animals, which are more susceptible to physical effects of tags; of animals living in clear water, where behavioral encounters are continuous forces in structuring animal communities; and of highly aggressive animals, which defend territories. As with all considerations, choosing the proper tag, based on specific experimental studies, can reduce behavioral impacts of tagging.

The last assumption is that all tagged animals can be identified as "tagged animals." This assumption has two aspects: that each tagged animal retains its tag, and that all recaptured, tagged animals are recognized and reported. This assumption is critical for studies based on knowing the number of marked animals at large, such as estimations of abundance and fishing mortality (Kallemeyn 1989). It is less critical for studies based on recaptured or observed animals only, like growth, migration, and behavior, except that efficiency declines if fewer tagged animals are available for recapture. Tag retention depends on several factors, including the tagging procedure, the attachment mechanism of the tag, and the species being tagged. Tag recognition and reporting depend on the visibility of the tag and the willingness of people to report the tag. Because many tagging studies rely on voluntary tag returns by commercial fishers or recreational anglers, reporting rates are unlikely to be perfect. Because both tag loss and underreporting usually occur, some adjustment of tagging data is often necessary (Chapter 2).

The rates of tag retention can be estimated through holding studies and double-tagging. Double-tagging involves adding a second mark to the animal (most commonly an adipose fin clip on salmonids; see Chapter 4) which alerts the observer that a tag should be present.

Tag retention rates can be increased by choosing the tag and attachment style most appropriate for the animal. The tag shape and color should make it highly visible in the recovery environment. Underwater observation, for example, requires tags that are easily visible in water; international orange or yellow are typically best. For animals observed out of the water, a tag that contrasts well with the animal's body color is needed; bright colors, like red, orange, and yellow, are usually appropriate. Reporting rates can be increased by publicizing the study widely and by offering rewards for returned tags (see Chapter 2).

3.3 TRANSBODY TAGS

3.3.1 General Description

Transbody tags are the oldest of modern tags. They were used as early as 1927 on red king crabs in Japan (Gray 1965). The oldest style still in use is the *Petersen disc tag,* which consists of a wire passed through an animal and attached to both sides with close-fitting circular discs (Figure 3.1). Identifying information is printed on the circular discs. The *disc-dangler tag* is attached by passing a long shaft (wire or plastic thread) through the body. One end is enlarged with an attachment device (knot, bubble, disc); attached to the other end is a flat plate printed with the identifying information. The *Carlin tag* is a popular disc-dangler that uses a U-shaped wire to attach the tag to the animal (Figure 3.1). The two ends of the U are both passed through one side of the animal and out the opposite side, then twisted together to complete a loop. The closed end of the U holds a plate with the identifying information. The *spaghetti tag* is also a loop, but made of thin plastic tubing that is passed through the animal and tied in a knot, forming a single loop; identifying information is printed on the tubing (Figure 3.1). The *streamer tag* is a simple plastic strip designed for tagging shrimp. The strip is wider at both ends than in the middle, to prevent it from slipping through the shrimp's body.

Modified transbody tags can be used on the gill covers of fish (Coombs et al. 1990) and on other thin tissues such as fins. Such tags, which include staple-like metal strips (Monel tags) and button tags similar to Petersen discs, are used only in special circumstances.

3.3.2 Advantages of Transbody Tags (Box 3.2)

Transbody tags are retained well by most aquatic animals (Table 3.2). Recent studies of shortnose sturgeon, for example, have demonstrated tag retention for up to 36 months (Smith et al. 1990). Because the tags are anchored externally, the tagger can easily tell if she has attached the tag correctly. The retention rate increases with the number of attachment sites, just like wearing a belt and suspenders increases pants retention. For example, moving from a Petersen disc with one shaft to an oval disc with two shafts (an Archer tag) increases the retention time (McFarlane et al. 1990). Tag retention of transbody tags is especially favorable on narrow-bodied fishes (herrings and flatfishes) and shrimp, for which dart-style and internal-anchor tags are less appropriate. Spaghetti tags and their modifications are especially useful for crabs because they can be attached through the musculature where the exoskeleton separates during molting or they can be wrapped around the flattened thorax like a harness (Gray 1965; Taylor et al. 1989).

Transbody tags fit animals of all sizes and are especially useful for small fishes. Tags for small fishes may consist of fine embroidery or plastic thread strung with

---

Box 3.2   Advantages and Disadvantages of Transbody Tags

Advantages

- High tag retention rates
- Long tag retention times
- Successful on narrow-bodied fishes
- Successful on shrimp, crabs
- Suitable for all sizes, including small animals
- Easily detected
- Large surface for printing information
- Remote reading of tag codes
- Individual identification possible
- Little drag on swimming animals

Disadvantages

- Difficult and extensive tagging procedures
- May inhibit growth
- May become entangled
- May accumulate algae

---

small, colored objects such as embroidery beads or drops of fingernail polish (Moring 1990). Anchoring such tags to small fishes is easy—heating the end of plastic thread, for example, causes a bubble which prevents it from slipping through an animal. Studies of small fishes have shown that appropriately sized tags had no effect on growth (Chapman and Bevan 1990).

Transbody tags are easy to detect and can carry much information. The tags can carry codes that identify animals individually or as members of groups, along with detailed instructions for reporting the tag's recapture. Because they protrude through two sides of an animal, they are seen readily by workers and anglers. This is especially helpful when a worker must scan large numbers of animals rapidly

Table 3.2 Comparison of characteristics for the three major styles of external tags.

Criterion	Transbody	Dart-style	Internal-anchor
Effects on			
Growth	Medium	Low	Low
Mortality	Medium	Low	Medium
Behavior	High	Medium	Medium
Tag retention rate	High	Medium	High
Tag retention time	Long	Medium	Long
Tagging rate	Slow	Fast	Slow
Recapture visibility	High	High	Medium
Recommended for	Narrow-bodied fishes	Most fishes	Wide-bodied fishes
	Shrimp, crabs	Lobsters	Lobsters
	Pelagic fishes	Large animals	Large animals
	Long-term studies	Large-scale studies	Long-term studies

(e.g., as commercial catches pass on a conveyor belt). Codes on disc-carrying tags can be read from a distance, which is especially useful for behavioral studies or for monitoring individuals with little handling (e.g., in an aquarium or for brood stock).

Transbody tags generally cause little drag on swimming animals. The tags either fit close to the animal (Petersen discs) or ride behind the animal when it is swimming. This is especially important for pelagic fishes like tunas that swim long distances daily at high speeds. Spaghetti tags are specifically recommended for pelagic fishes because the loop lies behind the fish's body and assumes a hydrodynamically efficient shape (McFarlane et al. 1990).

3.3.3   Disadvantages of Transbody Tags (Box 3.2)

The processes for attaching transbody tags are extensive. Nakashima and Winters (1984), for example, required three times longer to apply a transbody tag than a dart-style tag. Each tag produces at least two surface wounds, doubling the chance for infection compared with dart-style or internal-anchor tags; some tags, like the Carlin tag, produce four surface wounds. Therefore, transbody tags must be applied by skilled workers rather than by casual volunteers. The tagging process must be especially precise for crustaceans, because improper placement may cause the tag to shed during molting or may alter the animal's natural molting pattern.

Close-fitting tags may interfere with the growth of fish. This concern especially limits the use of Petersen discs and similar tags with plates that fit tightly against the animal's body. Such tags are best used for short-term studies or on adult animals—situations in which little growth is expected.

The protruding parts of transbody tags can become entangled with objects in the water. Because parts of the tag protrude from both sides of an animal, the risk of entanglement is greater than for dart-style or internal-anchor tags. This is particularly likely for tags tied in loops or with enlarged discs hanging on the end of long shafts. Tagged fish, therefore, may be more vulnerable to gill nets and other entangling fishing devices (Smith et al. 1990), violating the equal-mortality assumption needed for abundance and mortality studies. Tagged fish may also be entangled in natural habitat structures, increasing the likelihood of predation and injury.

Transbody tags generally have large surfaces where algae, fungus, or molluscs can grow and other materials can accumulate. Algae growth is especially likely for animals living near the surface or in clear water (Chapman and Bevan 1990), such as in coral reefs or hatchery raceways (Figure 3.2). Although algal accumulations sluff off after reaching a certain size, any accumulation increases the drag on swimming animals.

3.3.4   Attaching a Transbody Tag

3.3.4.1   Tagging Location

Fish.   Transbody tags are generally attached to fish just below the dorsal fin, far from the internal body organs and where the body is relatively thin (Figure 3.1). Spaghetti tags and other tags with dangling discs or plates are generally attached towards the rear of the dorsal fin area, allowing the tag to trail behind and

Figure 3.2   Growth of algae on a transbody tag attached to a trout living in a shallow hatchery raceway. Photo by author.

below the highest point of the back; this reduces the drag of the tag extension for fast-swimming fishes such as tunas.

Shrimp.   The preferred tag for shrimp is the streamer tag (Farmer 1981). The streamer is a thin, narrow, flexible piece of durable synthetic cloth (approximately 9 cm long and 3 mm wide). The streamer reduces drag on burrowing shrimp as well as tag loss due to snagging on habitat structure. The streamer should be inserted through the articular membrane between the first and second abdominal segments (Marullo et al. 1976), so that it does not interfere with molting. It should pass laterally through the body, centered along the body depth (Figure 3.3).

Crabs.   The diverse body shapes of crabs provide unique tagging locations and styles. The spaghetti tag has been successful on red king crabs (Gray 1965). The tag is attached through the isthmus, the soft tissue bridge joining the carapace to the abdomen. As with the streamer tag on shrimp, this tag does not inhibit molting.

Spaghetti-style tags and attachments also can be tied around the oval carapace of crabs. This tagging strategy works for short-term studies (within one molt

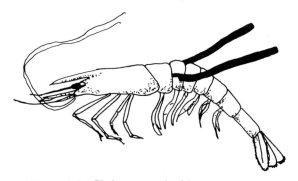

Figure 3.3   Shrimp tagged with a streamer tag.

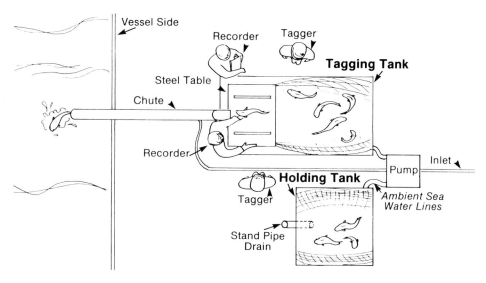

Figure 3.4 An example of an ideal tagging station, designed to minimize handling and tagging stress on animals. This particular system, reproduced from Clay (1990), can be adapted for small vessels or shoreline stations.

cycle) or for studies of nonmolting adults. Taylor et al. (1989) tied spaghetti tags around snow crabs' carapaces between the first and second pereiopods. Monan and Thorne (1973) secured sonic tags to king crabs by drilling holes through carapace, passing leads from the tag through the holes, and tying them together, much like a Carlin tag.

3.3.4.2 Tagging Environment

A critical part of the tagging operation is creating a favorable environment for animals before and during tagging. Reducing an animal's stress during tagging not only improves the likelihood of a successful project, it also expresses the respect that fisheries professionals have for the individual animals they study and manage. The American Fisheries Society's guidelines for handling live animals provide appropriate handling procedures (see Appendix, page 195). The premise of the AFS guidelines is that the environmental conditions for animals should be a primary concern during all scientific and management operations.

A generalized marking station appropriate for most marking operations was described by Clay (1990). It consists of a large holding tank, a smaller tagging tank, a submerged tagging surface, and a quick release chute (Figure 3.4). The holding tank is a large, deep reservoir fitted with a loose netting liner that can be raised to bring animals to the surface for transfer to the tagging tank. The loose netting is designed to avoid the stressful process of capturing animals with a dip net from a large tank. Fresh ambient water should be continuously pumped to the holding tank to maintain optimum conditions.

The tagging tank is a smaller tank designed to hold only a few animals at one time. It also is fitted with loose netting so that individual animals can be isolated gently for tagging. The tagging tank may be treated with an anesthetic if necessary for the tagging operation. If anesthetic is not used, the water in this tank also should be changed continuously. If an anesthetic is used, water quality should be monitored, and the water should be changed when conditions fall below established standards.

The tagging surface is a shallowly submerged area within the tagging tank. One worker isolates an animal and raises it to the surface with the loose netting and moves it—still underwater—to the tagging surface. The tagging surface itself should be customized for each species and tagging procedure. For example, a contoured pad or cradle that fits the animal's body and exposes the area to be tagged will improve tagging efficiency and reduce handling. A worker attaches the tag to the animal, under water if possible, and makes any auxiliary measurements or observations. A second worker records the data. The tagged animal is then released immediately to its natural environment or transferred to a recovery tank through a chute or trough. The chute is bathed continuously with water delivered through a hose at the top of the chute.

This tagging system is designed for large-vessel tagging, but the principles apply equally well to tagging aboard small boats or on shore. For small projects, the holding and tagging tanks may be the same and a two-person crew may be sufficient for the operation. The important considerations are to reduce the frequency and harshness of handling and to reduce the amount of time animals are out of the water.

In most cases, animals should be anesthetized to reduce the chance of injury and the handling stress during tagging (see Chapter 2). Anesthesia is not possible in some situations (e.g., tagging very large animals such as adult salmon or tuna), but it is generally desirable for complex tagging operations involving transbody tags.

Animals should be left in the anesthesia for the shortest possible time. Exposure should not last more than 2 minutes in any case, and animals showing abnormal behavior should be moved immediately to a recovery tank, even if tagging must be abandoned for some animals. Animals also should be released or moved from the recovery tank as soon as possible.

3.3.4.3   Tag Attachment

Tags should be attached according to the manufacturer's instructions. Because transbody tags are now established commercial products, manufacturers generally are eager to offer their substantial experience to novice workers.

In all cases, the critical step is passing the shaft through the animal's body. Techniques differ for different tags. For Carlin and other tags that have thin, flexible wires as shafts, a hollow applicator is inserted through the animal's body. The tag shaft is threaded through the hollow applicator, and the applicator is then pulled out backwards, leaving the tag shaft in place (Figure 3.5). The applicator is usually one or a pair of hypodermic needles. For spaghetti tags, the applicator is a pointed shaft that fits tightly inside the hollow spaghetti tube. The pointed shaft is pushed through the animal, pulling the tube with it. The shaft is then removed from the spaghetti tube, and the ends of the tube are tied together in a single knot. Some tags, such as shrimp streamer tags and spaghetti-style tags of thread, are inserted with a standard sewing needle. Some tags that have rigid stainless steel wires as shafts (Petersen discs) are inserted by pushing the tag shaft directly

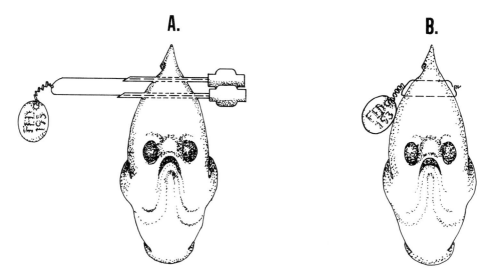

Figure 3.5 Attaching a Carlin tag to a fish by using two hypodermic needles that have been soldered together. (**A**) The needles are inserted through the fish and the ends of the tag shafts are threaded into the needles so they pass entirely through the body. (**B**) The needles are withdrawn, leaving the tag shafts in place and ready for connection. Reproduced from Wydoski and Emery (1983).

through the animal's body. For all transbody tags, the shaft should be inserted through the body perpendicular to the main body axis.

The second step is enlarging the end of the shaft so that the tag remains on the animal. Close-fitting tags, such as Petersen discs and Carlin tags, should be attached tightly to the body. This prevents abrasion around the tag shaft or disc caused by vibration of the tag when the animal is swimming or in fast water. Loose-fitting tags, such as spaghetti tags, must be securely tied or enlarged at the ends so that they do not slip from the animal. Spaghetti tags must be long enough that they form a tear-dropped shape behind the animal, the most favorable hydrodynamic shape for reducing drag and vibration.

Because each tag and each species is different, special techniques are often needed. Attaching a transbody tag to a crab, for example, may require no internal wound or may require drilling holes in the exoskeleton. The best advice is to consult with manufacturers and experienced users of a particular tag. Recent references that give detailed descriptions of specific tagging operations are listed in Table 3.3.

3.3.4.4 Posttagging Treatment

Tagged animals may be treated with an antibiotic to reduce the possibility of infection from the tagging wounds and from handling (see Chapter 2). Antibiotic treatment is not usually required for marine animals—seawater is a mild antibiotic solution—but it is recommended for many freshwater animals, particularly in warm waters.

Tagged animals should be inspected shortly after tagging for signs of continuing stress and improper tag attachment. Dead and dying animals and those with poorly attached tags should not be released, and they should be subtracted from

Table 3.3 References providing detailed instructions for some external tags and species. Also see Jones (1979) for various tagging types.

Tag type	Species	Reference
Transbody		
Carlin	Shortnose sturgeon	Smith et al. (1990)
	Nonspecific	Wydoski and Emery (1983)
Spaghetti	Molly[a]	Chapman and Bevan (1990)
	Red king crab	Gray (1965); Monan and Thorne (1973)
Petersen	Nonspecific	Wydoski and Emery (1983)
	Shrimp[b]	Lucas et al. (1972)
Streamer	Shrimp[b]	Marullo et al. (1976); Farmer (1981)
Dart-style		
Arrowhead	Scombrids	McFarlane et al. (1990)
T-bar	American lobster	Krouse and Nutting (1990)
	Blue crab	Fannaly (1978)
Sphyrion	American lobster	Cooper (1970)
Internal-anchor	Striped bass	Dunning et al. (1987); Mattson et al. (1990)
	Red drum	Gutherz et al. (1990)

[a]*Poecilia gillii.*   [b]Penaeidae.

the number tagged. If large numbers of animals must be tagged quickly and released immediately, a representative sample should be collected at randomly defined intervals and held to observe acute mortality and tag loss.

A sample of tagged animals also should be held for approximately 24 hours to assess the short-term effects of tagging. A large holding tank filled with ambient water or an enclosure placed in the water body is needed to simulate postrelease conditions. After each test, each animal should be externally inspected to determine its condition, and several animals should be sacrificed and examined internally. These examinations provide feedback for improving the handling and tagging procedures. A few tagged animals should be photographed and then preserved to show the placement and appearance of the tags and to compare with recaptured animals later. The proportion of live to dead animals should be used to adjust the estimated total number of tagged animals released into the environment. Tagged animals should be released as close to their capture location as possible, as described in Chapter 2.

3.4 DART-STYLE TAGS

3.4.1 General Description

Dart-style tags are miniature spears. The tag consists of a shaft with an enlarged head shaped like an arrow point or a T. The two commonly used styles differ in the shape of the head. The *arrowhead tag* has a pointed end with one or more barbs to anchor the tag (Figure 3.6). The *T-bar tag* has a plastic T-shaped head and often is called the Floy® tag, after one of its major commercial manufacturers (Figure 3.7). The external portion of the tag is generally a separate piece attached to the protruding shaft and containing the identification codes and message. In

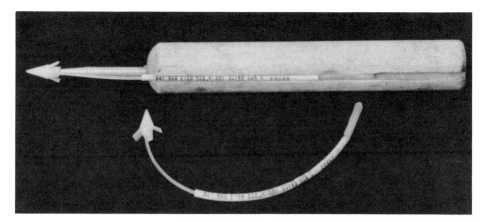

Figure 3.6 Arrowhead tag with two barbs and a custom-made tagging tool. Reprinted from Gutherz et al. (1990).

most cases, this is a plastic tube that slides over and is bonded to the shaft, but it may also be a flattened disc. Some tags have one-piece construction in which the shaft itself is enlarged or flattened to provide the printing surface.

Dart-style tags are attached to the animal by embedding the head inside the muscle mass of the animal. The barbs prevent the tag from pulling loose from the animal. Dart-style tags are generally attached to fish by inserting the tag into the body below the dorsal fin and past the mid-line so that the anchoring barbs are beyond the bones that support the dorsal fin and beyond axial extensions of the vertebrae. On crustaceans, the tag can be inserted shallowly, held in place by the rigid exoskeleton.

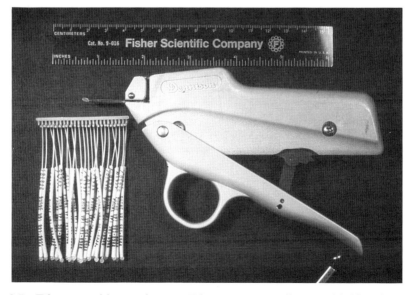

Figure 3.7 T-bar tags with a tagging gun. T-bar tags are usually assembled in a linear array for use in the semiautomated tagging gun. Photo by Louis Helfrich.

Box 3.3   Advantages and Disadvantages of Dart-Style Tags

Advantages

- High retention rates
- Little effect on tagged animals
- Successful on lobsters
- Successful on wide-bodied fishes
- Suitable for very large animals
- Easy and rapid application techniques
- Can be performed by volunteers
- Individual identification possible
- Large surface for printing information
- Easily detected

Disadvantages

- Not useful on smaller animals
- Quality of attachment is difficult to control
- Loss of tagging information from abrasion or separation of legend from shaft
- May produce abrasion or enlarged tagging wound
- May become entangled

Dart-style tags are undoubtedly the most popular external tags used today. A large commercial industry has developed to produce and service this style of tag, and extensive manufacturer support is available for the tagging customer. Tags are available in a kaleidoscopic array of sizes, shapes, and colors, with customized messages and semiautomated tag applicators. The plastic heads of modern dart-style tags are formulated to be compatible with biological tissues, an important consideration whenever something is to be placed into the body of an animal.

3.4.2   Advantages of Dart-Style Tags (Box 3.3)

Dart-style tags are retained well by fish and crustaceans in most cases (Table 3.2). Retention is best in wide-bodied fishes, such as largemouth bass and red drum (Gutherz et al. 1990; Weathers et al. 1990), and is lower for narrow-bodied fishes such as clupeids. Retention is often good for lobsters, especially if the molting frequency is low (Cooper 1970; Davis 1978; Ennis 1986).

Initial retention is achieved by anchoring the tag beyond the axial bones, but long-term retention is encouraged by incorporation of the tag head into the animal's tissues. This process is called encapsulation. Dissection of tagged fish has shown that connective tissue rapidly penetrates into the plastic anchor material, fusing the tag with the body. This is an advantage for fishes, which do not appear to suffer from the encapsulation (Gutherz et al. 1990), but may be a disadvantage for crustaceans, which sometimes suffer abnormal molting, loss of tagged appendages, and death as a result (Hurley et al. 1990).

Dart-style tags can be applied easily and quickly. Consequently, the tags can be

Table 3.4 Rates of tagging, relative survival, and relative return of Atlantic herring for various types of tags (modified from Nakashima and Winters 1984).

Type of tag	Tagging rate (number/hour)	Relative survival	Hypothetical return (number of animals) from 25 hours of tagging effort[a]
Carlin	24	1.00	36
Petersen disc	92	0.47	65
Disc-dangler	118	0.45	80
Streamer	167	—	—
Dart (one barb)	237	0.47	167
T-bar (short shaft)	273	—	—
T-bar (long shaft)	292	0.77	337

[a]Assume 6% return rate under best survival conditions (Carlin tag).

used in a wide variety of conditions that do not permit carefully controlled tagging. This characteristic is especially important for large marking projects (e.g., marking hatchery fish before release), for marking large fish (e.g., tuna that cannot be lifted into the boat), and for dispersed tagging by volunteers, anglers, or commercial fishers (Fable 1990). Homemade and commercially marketed tag applicators allow marking rates of several hundred animals per hour (Table 3.4).

Dart-style tags, like transbody tags, can identify individual animals as well as groups. The tag surface can contain extensive information, including identification codes, instructions for returning tags, and even reward values. Because tags are available in many sizes, styles, and colors, they can be adapted for virtually any kind of data collection. This is especially valuable for large, multijurisdictional projects, including internationally coordinated programs, which require a large range of tagging codes.

Dart-style tags generally cause little change in the growth or mortality of tagged animals. Recent studies have shown no effect of dart-style tags on growth of crustaceans (Hurley et al. 1990) and fish (Tranquilli and Childers 1982; Chapman and Bevan 1990). Although initial mortality may be relatively high because of extensive handling, long-term mortality is presumably low if tags are applied correctly and the tag size and style are well chosen for the species. Dart-style tags produce only one wound, considerably reducing the likelihood of trauma and infection to the marked animal relative to transbody tags.

3.4.3 Disadvantages of Dart-Style Tags (Box 3.3)

Dart-style tags are very successful on large animals but less so on small ones. The applicator needle and tag head cause a puncture wound larger than the tag shaft (Figure 3.6), and the associated trauma can be great for small animals. For example, dart-style tags work well on lobsters, but are not recommended for shrimp (Farmer 1981). Continual development of smaller tags and more delicate tagging instruments, however, is reducing the minimum size at which animals can be tagged.

Dart-style tags fall off animals more frequently than transbody tags. Haegele (1990), for example, observed a 50% loss of T-bar tags from Pacific herring within 2 weeks of tagging. Proper application of the tag is more difficult to assess because the anchor is buried in the animal. Tags inserted too shallowly in the body are shed quite rapidly. Like transbody tags, dart-style tags can become entangled in habitat structures and pull out of the animal's body. Consequently, dart-style tags are most useful in the short term for studies that require knowing the absolute numbers of tagged animals and in the long term for studies that only require having many tagged animals at large.

Early versions of dart-style tags (and internal-anchor tags) suffered two problems resulting in the loss of tagging legends. In some cases, the message-carrying tube separated from the tag shaft (Tranquilli and Childers 1982; McFarlane et al. 1990). In other cases, the printed message faded or wore off the tube (Mattson et al. 1990). Because dart-style tags are commercially valuable products, these problems are being conquered through improvements in materials, design, and manufacturing.

Dart-style tags protrude from one surface of an animal's body, lying against or near the body when the animal is swimming. Constant rubbing of the tag against the body can cause irritation and open sores in some cases (Gutherz et al. 1990). Although tagging wounds usually heal quickly, insertion of the tag at the wrong angle can cause vibration of the tag shaft, in turn causing erosion of an enlarged hole where the tag shaft leaves the body. This increases the risk, common to all external tags, that pathogens will invade or body fluids will be lost through the wound. If the tag is too large for the animal or has a large printed surface, the additional and uneven drag may cause disorientation and increased energy loss for swimming.

3.4.4   Attaching a Dart-Style Tag

3.4.4.1   Tagging Location

Fish.   Dart-style tags are generally attached dorsally to fish just below the dorsal fin. Because the tag protrudes from only one side of the fish, each tagging program must specify which side of the fish is to be tagged (generally the left side of the fish).

Tags should be inserted into white muscle tissue, rather than red muscle (Gutherz et al. 1990). White tissue has fewer blood vessels, so the tagging wound in white muscle causes less bleeding. The distribution of white muscle tissue must be determined for each species. The tagging location also should allow the tag applicator to pass across the mid-line so that the tag head is anchored beyond the axial bones. As with other tagging techniques, the tagging location should be precise and consistent with reference to a specified scale or other anatomical feature. Several applicators of different lengths and diameters may be needed to accommodate specimens in different size ranges. Tagging and dissection of practice specimens will help pinpoint the best tagging location and depth, thus assuring proper placement of the tag with a minimum of tissue disruption.

Crustaceans.   Researchers have applied tags to crustaceans at various body locations. The general principle, however, is to attach the tag at a location that allows normal molting and that allows the molted exoskeleton to break loose from the tag shaft.

T-bar and sphyrion tags are often recommended for lobsters and presumably would work well for larger crayfish. The best tagging location is in the dorsal muscle between the cephalothorax and the first abdominal segment (Cooper 1970; Davis 1978). Tags placed at this location often remain on the animal through successive molts (Figure 3.8).

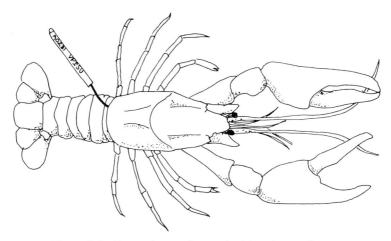

Figure 3.8   Large decapod tagged with a dart-style tag.

T-bar tags have also been tested successfully on crabs. The tagging locations
have been on the walking legs, along the molt suture (Fannaly 1978; Hurley et al.
1990). The tag should be inserted shallowly, to avoid shedding or deformation of
the appendage. Similar appendage locations have been attempted with lobsters,
with little success (Cooper 1970).

3.4.4.2   Tagging Environment

The tagging environment described earlier for transbody tagging is also appropriate for most dart-style tagging. However, because dart-style tags are used in a
wide variety of circumstances, a highly controlled tagging environment is often
unavailable. In such cases, the emphasis should be on efficient handling so the
animal is tagged and released to its natural environment quickly. The need for
anesthesia must be judged separately for each circumstance.

Dart-style tagging is especially useful for large animals that cannot be hauled
aboard a vessel or to a shore-based facility. In these circumstances, the captured
animal can only be brought alongside the vessel or cradled in shallow water. It
should be restrained as motionless as possible while the tag is inserted. For very
large animals alongside a vessel, the tag may need to be inserted with a
long-handled applicator (McFarlane et al. 1990). If the animal has been caught on
a hook, every effort should be made to remove the hook, or at least to cut the line
as near the hook as possible, before the animal is released.

3.4.4.3   Tag Attachment

As with transbody tags, dart-style tags should be attached according to the
manufacturer's instructions. The manufacturer may have previous experience
with the species being tagged and should be able to refer a novice to experienced
individuals who used similar tags, species, or techniques.

Dart-style tags should be inserted from behind at an acute angle to the body's
long axis (Figure 3.9). This allows the tag to lie next to the body when the animal
swims or holds in fast water, reducing drag and the probability of wound
enlargement.

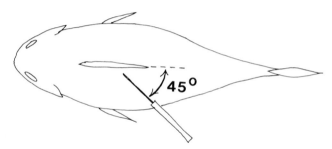

Figure 3.9 Angle of attachment for dart-tags.

Dart-style tags usually require an applicator for pushing the flexible tag into the body (Figure 3.6). Arrowhead tags are generally loaded singly into an open steel shaft with the arrowhead exposed. For use on large animals, some arrowhead tags fit atop long pins attached to wooden handles, operating like primitive harpoons. T-bar tags are generally applied with a continuously feeding tagging gun, also equipped with an open steel shaft (Figure 3.7).

If the fish has scales, the applicator point should be used to remove the defined scale at the point of insertion. The applicator is then pushed into the body so that the anchoring head travels beyond the mid-line. Choosing the proper applicator length is critical so that the tag is inserted sufficiently far, but does not penetrate the opposite body wall. Twisting the applicator slightly dislodges the tag, allowing the applicator to be withdrawn and leaving the tag in place.

A properly maintained tag applicator is essential. If a tagging needle is used, it must be sharpened regularly, especially when coarse-scaled or thick-skinned animals are tagged. Bent needles cause the tags to misfeed or stick in the applicator; they should be replaced. A variety of tag applicators should be available for different sizes or species of animals. A short-term study to determine recovery rate of fish in a rotenone survey, for example, will require several applicator sizes for different species. Consequently, a reserve supply of tag applicators and needles must be readily available.

Proper attachment of the tag should be tested by tugging gently on the tag. Any tag that feels loose or pulls free should not be counted as a viable tag. The animal should not be tagged again because the additional trauma may increase mortality; it should be released immediately after the appropriate posttagging treatment.

Tagging equipment need not be sterilized between animals, but the highest degree of cleanliness must be maintained throughout the process. All equipment should be washed and dipped in alcohol, peroxide, or other antibacterial solution before being stored.

3.4.4.4 Posttagging Treatment

Animals tagged with dart-style tags should be treated in the same manner described earlier for transbody tagging. Because of the less extensive tagging procedure and varied tagging situations, antibiotic treatment is used seldom. Although the effects of dart-style tagging may be less severe than those of transbody tagging, the extent of tag loss and short-term mortality will depend on the conditions in each tagging operation. Consequently, the responses of animals to tagging and tag retention rates should be checked whenever possible by monitoring samples for short periods.

For crustaceans, short-term mortality and tag loss may be substantial. Therefore, extra animals should be tagged in anticipation of these losses (Hurley et al. 1990). Careful statistical adjustments for crustacean data will be needed to account for estimated tag loss and mortality (see Chapter 2; Fable 1990).

3.5 INTERNAL-ANCHOR TAGS

3.5.1 General Description

Internal-anchor tags are similar to dart-style tags. Each has a shaft attached to a single anchoring device that is embedded in the animal's body. For internal-anchor tags, however, the anchor is a flattened rectangular or oval plate (about three times as long as wide) that is inserted into the body cavity of the animal and lies flush against the body wall (Figure 3.10). The anchor functions just like a washer that prevents the head of a bolt from passing through a drilled hole. The protruding part of the tag is essentially the same as a dart-style tag. The printed portion may be a tube or disc affixed to the shaft or an enlarged portion of the shaft itself.

Internal-anchor tags have been widely used on fish. They have been especially popular for marine tagging programs, perhaps because they are particularly useful for large animals. As with dart-style tags, a thriving industry has developed to manufacture internal-anchor tags and serve their users. Consequently, the quality and utility of these tags continue to improve.

3.5.2 Advantages of Internal-Anchor Tags (Box 3.4)

Internal-anchor tags offer excellent retention when placed on appropriate animals. They are particularly effective on wide-bodied fishes and on large specimens (Table 3.2). Recent studies have recorded high retention rates for many species (Table 3.5). For example, retention rates of internal-anchor tags were 8 times higher for king mackerel (Fable 1990) and 2 times higher for striped bass (Dunning et al. 1987) than retention rates of dart-style tags.

In general, internal-anchor tags have not demonstrably altered growth and mortality of fish (Dunning et al. 1987). When tags are applied correctly, the tagging

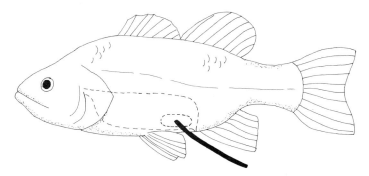

Figure 3.10 The common internal-anchor tagging location and orientation.

Box 3.4   Advantages and Disadvantages of Internal-Anchor Tags

Advantages

- High retention rates
- Long retention times
- Little effect on tagged animals
- Successful on wide-bodied fishes
- Suitable for large specimens
- Individual identification possible
- Large surface for printing information

Disadvantages

- Difficult and extensive tagging procedures
- Not useful on narrow-bodied fishes
- Not useful on small specimens
- Danger to internal organs
- Loss of tagging information from abrasion or separation of legend from shaft
- Less easily detected
- May become entangled

---

wounds usually heal completely (McFarlane et al. 1990). The progress of healing seems to be highly specific to the environment and the animal; for example, shortnose sturgeons healed better in fresh water than in salt water (Smith et al. 1990), whereas red drum healed better in salt water than in fresh water (Gutherz et al. 1990).

Like dart-style tags, internal-anchor tags can be used to identify animals individually or into groups. The large range of available sizes and colors allows these tags to be the basis of large-scale cooperative tagging programs.

3.5.3   Disadvantages of Internal-Anchor Tags (Box 3.4)

Internal-anchor tags work best on wide-bodied fishes rather than on narrow-bodied fishes. Movement or misalignment of the anchor can cause abrasion of the muscle tissue by the anchor and eventual protrusion of the anchor through the body wall. Experiments on young striped bass, for example, demonstrated the protrusion of the anchors from the body cavity (Mattson et al. 1990); similar results have been reported for herrings and spot (e.g., see Weathers et al. 1990).

Internal-anchor tags are inappropriate for small fishes. The insertion of the large anchor plate within a relatively small body cavity may cause considerable trauma in small animals. In general, successful reports of internal-anchor tags have involved either juvenile or adult animals.

The tagging procedure is difficult, requiring considerable experience and care. Because the anchor is placed within the body cavity, injury to internal organs is possible. Tag insertion requires an incision of precise depth, and the tag must be inserted below the muscle layers but above the internal organs (Krouse and Nutting 1990). Tagging is particularly risky before and during spawning because

Table 3.5 Retention and wounding rates for internal-anchor tags on various animals.

Taxon	Tag retention		Anchor wounds (%)	Reference
	Period (days)	Rate (%)		
Red drum	117	80	54	Gutherz et al. (1990)
Largemouth bass	30	100	0	Weathers et al. (1990)
Striped bass	210	—	16	Mattson et al. (1990)
	730	98	—	Dunning et al. (1987)
Shortnose sturgeon	130	100	—	Smith et al. (1990)
King mackerel	—	84	—	Fable (1990)
American lobster				
Small juveniles	365	97	—	Krouse and Nutting (1990)
Large juveniles	365	89	—	Krouse and Nutting (1990)

the body cavity of mature fish may be filled completely with enlarged reproductive organs. This risk of injury must be balanced against the excellent retention of internal-anchor tags, especially for long-term studies.

The external structure of internal-anchor tags is much like that of dart-style tags. Consequently, internal-anchor tags may suffer the same physical problems of legend loss and abrasion. The external shaft may become stiff after several months on the animal, bending into a fixed curvature and position. Mattson et al. (1990) reported substantial abrasion of the anterior portion of tag legends on striped bass, because the same spots on the tags had rubbed against the fish's lower body. The extended shaft may also entangle in netting or habitat structure.

Internal-anchor tags are more difficult to detect than transbody or dart-style tags because they are attached to the ventral surface of the fish's body (Fable 1990). This can be particularly problematic if fish are observed from above while they are swimming (for example, in a behavioral study).

3.5.4 Attaching an Internal-Anchor Tag

3.5.4.1 Tagging Location

Internal-anchor tags are inserted into fish on the ventral side so that the anchor rests within the body cavity. Because the tag protrudes from only one side, the tagging program must designate which side will be tagged (usually the left, as for dart-style tags).

The specific choice of tagging location is critical because injury to internal organs may otherwise occur during tagging. The choice should be guided by dissection of sample specimens of the same species, size, and condition as the animals to be tagged. The appropriate location is where the organs do not rest against the body cavity wall; this generally occurs low on the body and toward the rear. As with other external tags, but much more importantly with internal-anchor tags, a specific scale or other consistent reference point should be chosen as the site of insertion (Mattson et al. 1990).

The literature includes no reports of internal-anchor tags being used on crustaceans. Because of invertebrate anatomy, this style of tagging seems unlikely to be successful on invertebrates in general.

3.5.4.2   Tagging Environment

The tagging environment should be managed as described earlier for transbody tags. Unlike the earlier procedures, however, the area of the body that will be the tagging site should be kept out of the water so that water does not inadvertently enter the body cavity. A tagging cradle that holds the fish upside down with the ventral surface exposed or on its side with the left side exposed is highly desirable. Because inserting an internal-anchor tag is a surgical procedure, great care is needed in the treatment of tagged animals before, during, and after tagging. Summerfelt and Smith (1990) provided a detailed description of the facilities, equipment, supplies, and techniques for surgery.

3.5.4.3   Tag Attachment

The tag is inserted through a small incision in the body wall. The incision should be equal in length to the width of the tag anchor, generally less than 10 mm. The incision should be perpendicular to the long axis of the body cavity. The incision should be deep enough to cut through the skin and muscle, but not through the peritoneum surrounding the body cavity (Mattson et al. 1990). Tags should be dipped in a sterilizing solution before insertion; Summerfelt and Smith (1990) recommended a 1:1,000 solution of benzalkonium chloride. After sterilization, the tag should be rinsed in sterile water. The anchor then can be inserted into the incision and pushed through the peritoneum into the body cavity. The anchor must be pushed gently towards the fish's head and parallel to the body surface, so that it slides along the near wall of the body cavity. In some cases, the scalpel used for making the incision can be adapted to hold the tag, allowing the operation to be completed in one step (Fable 1990; Figure 3.11). The tag shaft should be pulled back so that the anchor is centered over the incision. Suturing of the incision is not needed in most cases.

3.5.4.4   Posttagging Treatment

Treatment of tagged fish should be the same as described earlier for transbody tagging. The exposure of the body cavity to the air and water, however, requires careful attention to reduce the possibility of infection. Although treating the incision with a topical antiseptic seems reasonable, Summerfelt and Smith (1990) suggested that antiseptics commonly used on mammals may damage fish tissue and are not satisfactory for fishery use.

3.6   NEW DEVELOPMENTS—AND TESTING THEM
IN PONDS

Recent developments in external tagging have been directed at providing materials that improve tag retention and expand the size range of taggable animals. Because external tags are so widely used, the tagging industry invests continually in the improvement of these techniques. Manufacturers often publish their own newsletters, which are valuable information sources for recent changes in tags and applicators and for results of novel applications.

The use of porous plastic for the anchor of dart-style tags is being investigated as a way to increase tag retention (McFarlane et al. 1990). As mentioned earlier,

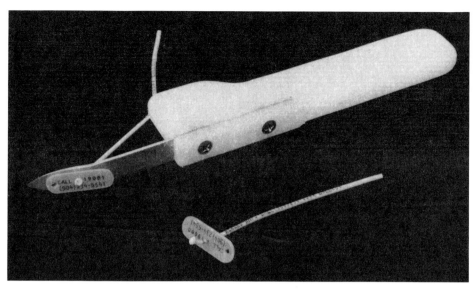

Figure 3.11 Tagging scalpel for inserting an internal-anchor tag. The scalpel blade has a small channel that allows the tag to slide off the scalpel as the scalpel is withdrawn. Reproduced from Gutherz et al. (1990).

the tag head may become encapsulated in an animal's body. By developing an anchor that encourages encapsulation, scientists are hoping to increase the speed of encapsulation and to assure that encapsulation will occur in all animal species.

Tag manufacturers are continually seeking ways to make external tags useful on smaller animals. These developments include thinner tagging shafts, smaller anchors, and more delicate tools for attaching tags. Anyone discouraged from using external tags because of the size constraints presented here should check with industry representatives to discuss recent advances in the miniaturization of tags and tagging tools.

Development of any new tag application must be accompanied by objective evidence that the tag is retained and does not affect the tagged animal. This requires extensive experimentation, especially before a large-scale tagging program is begun. McFarlane and Beamish (1990) demonstrated the value of long-term observation for establishing the effects of tagging on a fish population. By monitoring tagged and untagged sablefish for 9 years after tagging, they detected subtle differences in growth, age at maturity, and mortality. Although most projects cannot be followed for that long, all new projects can be evaluated in shorter pond or tank experiments. The following procedure, generalized and modified from Gutherz et al. (1990), can be used for conducting such an experiment in ponds.

A sample of the animals that are scheduled for tagging should be collected and stocked randomly into several small ponds (0.1 hectare or larger). The animals should be allowed to acclimate to the ponds for up to 1 month, but at least until all handling mortality ceases. A beach seine (or other collecting method) should be used to capture approximately half of the estimated animals remaining in the pond. Those animals not caught serve as an untagged, unhandled control. The captured animals should be divided randomly into two groups. Animals in one group should be tagged with the technique under study, given a temporary fin clip or other mark, and released. Animals in another group should be handled identically to the tagged group, except for the specific tagging operation (that is, incision or tag insertion); instead, the animals should receive just a different temporary fin clip or other mark (e.g., upper versus lower caudal fin clips). The fin-clipped-only group serves as an untagged, handled control. Dead animals found in the ponds should be removed and recorded once or twice daily. After approximately 1 month (or other period, as appropriate), all animals should be collected by draining the ponds or using another complete census technique. Differences in mean size and mortality among the three groups will distinguish the effects of handling and tagging on growth and mortality. Tag loss can be computed from the presence of fin-clipped fish without tags.

3.7 REFERENCES

Berg, O. K., and M. Berg. 1990. Effects of Carlin tagging on the mortality and growth of anadromous Arctic char, *Salvelinus arcticus* (L.). Aquaculture and Fisheries Management 21:221–227.

Chapman, L. J., and D. J. Bevan. 1990. Development and field evaluation of a mini-spaghetti tag for individual identification of small fishes. American Fisheries Society Symposium 7:101–108.

Clay, D. 1990. Tagging demersal marine fish in subzero temperatures along the Canadian Atlantic coast. American Fisheries Society Symposium 7:147–151.

Coombs, K. A., J. K. Bailey, C. M. Herbinger, and G. W. Friars. 1990. Evaluation of various external marking techniques for Atlantic salmon. American Fisheries Society Symposium 7:142–146.

Cooper, R. A. 1970. Retention of marks and their effects on growth, behavior, and migrations of the American lobster, *Homarus americanus*. Transactions of the American Fisheries Society 99:409–417.

Davis, G. E. 1978. Field evaluation of a tag for juvenile spiny lobsters, *Panilurus argus*. Transactions of the American Fisheries Society 107:100–103.

Dunning, D. J., O. E. Ross, J. R. Waldman, and M. T. Mattson. 1987. Tag retention by, and tagging mortality of, Hudson River striped bass. North American Journal of Fisheries Management 7:535–538.

Ennis, G. P. 1986. Sphyrion tag loss from the American lobster *Homarus americanus*. Transactions of the American Fisheries Society 115:914–917.

Fable, W. A., Jr. 1990. Summary of king mackerel tagging in southeastern USA: mark–recapture techniques and factors influencing tag returns. American Fisheries Society Symposium 7:161–167.

Fannaly, M. T. 1978. A method for tagging immature blue crabs (*Callinectes sapidus* Rathbun). Northeast Gulf Science 2:124–126.

Farmer, A. S. D. 1981. A review of crustacean marking methods with particular reference to penaeid shrimp. Kuwait Bulletin of Marine Science 2:167–183.

Gray, G. W., Jr. 1965. Tags for marking king crabs. Progressive Fish-Culturist 27:221–227.

Gutherz, E. J., B. A. Rohr, and R. V. Minton. 1990. Use of hydroscopic molded nylon dart tags and internal anchor tags on red drum. American Fisheries Society Symposium 7:152–160.

Haegele, C. W. 1990. Anchor tag return rates for Pacific herring in British Columbia. American Fisheries Society Symposium 7:127–133.

Howe, N. R., and P. R. Hoyt. 1982. Mortality of juvenile brown shrimp *Penaeus aztecus* associated with streamer tags. Transactions of the American Fisheries Society 111:317–325.

Hurley, G. V., R. W. Elner, D. M. Taylor, and R. F. J. Bailey. 1990. Evaluation of snow crab tags retainable through molting. American Fisheries Society Symposium 7:84–93.

Jones, R. 1979. Materials and methods used in marking experiments in fishery research. FAO (Food and Agriculture Organization of the United Nations) Fisheries Technical Paper 190.

Kallemeyn, L. W. 1989. Loss of Carlin tags from walleyes. North American Journal of Fisheries Management 9:112–115.

Krouse, J. S., and G. E. Nutting. 1990. Effectiveness of the Australian western rock lobster tag for marking juvenile American lobsters along the Maine coast. American Fisheries Society Symposium 7:94–100.

Lucas, C., P. C. Young, and J. K. Brundrit. 1972. Preliminary mortality rates of marked king prawns, *Penaeus plebejus*, in laboratory tanks. Australian Journal of Marine and Freshwater Research 23:143–149.

Marullo, F., D. A. Emiliani, C. W. Caillouet, and S. H. Clark. 1976. A vinyl streamer tag for shrimp (*Penaeus* spp.). Transactions of the American Fisheries Society 105:658–663.

Matthews, K. R., and R. H. Reavis. 1990. Underwater tagging and visual recapture as a technique for studying movement patterns of rockfish. American Fisheries Society Symposium 7:168–172.

Mattson, M. T., J. R. Waldman, D. J. Dunning, and Q. E. Ross. 1990. Abrasion and protrusion of internal anchor tags in Hudson River striped bass. American Fisheries Society Symposium 7:121–126.

McFarlane, G. A., and R. J. Beamish. 1990. Effect of an external tag on growth of sablefish (*Anoplopoma fimbria*), and consequences to mortality and age at maturity. Canadian Journal of Fisheries and Aquatic Sciences 47:1551–1557.

McFarlane, G. A., R. S. Wydoski, and E. D. Prince. 1990. Historical review of the development of external tags and marks. American Fisheries Society Symposium 7:9–29.

Monan, G. E. and D. L. Thorne. 1973. Sonic tags attached to Alaska king crabs. U.S. National Marine Fisheries Service Marine Fisheries Review 35(7):18–21.

Moring, J. R. 1990. Marking and tagging intertidal fishes: review of techniques. American Fisheries Society Symposium 7:109–116.

Nakashima, B. S. and G. H. Winters. 1984. Selection of external tags for marking Atlantic herring (*Clupea harengus harengus*). Canadian Journal of Fisheries and Aquatic Sciences 41:1341–1348.

Smith, T. I., S. D. Lamprecht, and J. W. Hall. 1990. Evaluation of tagging techniques for shortnose sturgeon and Atlantic sturgeon. American Fisheries Society Symposium 7:134–141.

Summerfelt, R. C. and L. S. Smith. 1990. Anesthesia, surgery, and related techniques. Pages 213–272 in C. B. Schreck, and P. B. Moyle, editors. Methods for fish biology. American Fisheries Society, Bethesda, Maryland.

Taylor, D. M., G. W. Marshall, and P. G. O'Keefe. 1989. Shell hardening in snow crabs, *Chionoecetes opilio*, tagged in soft-shelled condition. North American Journal of Fisheries Management 9:504–508.

Tranquilli, J. A. and W. F. Childers. 1982. Growth and survival of largemouth bass tagged with Floy anchor tags. North American Journal of Fisheries Management 2:184–187.

Weathers, K. C., S. L. Morse, M. B. Bain, and W. D. Davies. 1990. Effects of abdominally implanted anchor tags on largemouth bass. American Fisheries Society Symposium 7:117–120.

Wydoski, R., and L. Emery. 1983. Tagging and marking. Pages 215–237 in L. A. Nielsen and D. L. Johnson, editors. Fisheries techniques. American Fisheries Society, Bethesda, Maryland.

Chapter 4

External Marks

4.1 INTRODUCTION

An external mark alters an animal's appearance in order to make it identifiable. The widespread use of external marking is favored by the complex anatomy of aquatic animals. Because water supports the bodies of aquatic animals, they have evolved elaborate shapes and external structures. Fish fins, which are composed of hard and adipose tissues without nerves or blood flow, can be trimmed or removed with little trauma to the fish—like clipping fingernails or cutting hair. Other aquatic animals, including molluscs, crustaceans, and turtles, have hardened exoskeletons that can be notched or numbered. The variety of these hard tissues has provided a fertile marking environment for fisheries scientists. Of the 900 citations searched by McFarlane et al. (1990), nearly 350 referred to external marking techniques.

External marking includes three major techniques. *Fin clipping* is the process of removing all or part of one or more fins from a fish's body. Fisheries workers have clipped fins at least since the 1820s, and fin clipping is undoubtedly today's most basic marking technique. Entire fins can be removed, with the expectation that the fin will never grow back. Alternatively, only a part of the fin can be removed, by clipping the ends of the fin or a few fin rays; if the fin regenerates, it will be distorted and, therefore, still identifiable. Similar marking of nonfinned animals can be accomplished by removing or clipping other tissues, usually parts of the exoskeleton.

The second external marking technique is *branding*—the process of scarring the skin tissue in a distinctive pattern. Fish branding is analogous to the branding of livestock, except that modern fish wranglers usually use extremely cold temperatures to produce the brands, a technique called cold branding or freeze branding. Freeze branding for marking aquatic animals is a recent application, dating only to the late 1960s (McFarlane et al. 1990).

The third set of techniques is *pigment marking,* in which inert colored material is embedded in or just beneath the animal's skin or exoskeleton. Pigment marking covers a wide variety of materials and procedures, including tattooing, injecting colored latex, and spraying fluorescent pigment granules. Pigment-marking techniques are generally successful in very specific situations, depending on the animal being marked, the pigmented materials, and the marking situation. For this reason, pigment marking is difficult to describe or evaluate in universal terms.

External marks are most useful for identifying animals as members of groups. Although individually identifiable marks are sometimes possible (for example, individual numbers tattooed on large animals), the number of available fin clips, colors, or patterns is generally small (Box 4.1). Therefore, external marking is used generally for situations that require only the separation of animals into a few groups (Bryant et al. 1990; Table 4.1).

A major use of external marking is stock identification. Before modern internal tags became available (see Chapter 5), fin clipping was the primary method for distinguishing hatchery and wild fish and, hence, for determining how important hatchery-raised fish were to the subsequent spawning population and catch. External marks also have been used to differentiate groups of the same hatchery stock that were treated differently—fed different hatchery diets, stocked at different locations, or stocked at different times or ages, for example.

External marking is also useful for movement studies, which require data only about the presence or absence of marked animals. In movement studies, marking a large number of animals cheaply and efficiently is more important than distinctively marking each individual. Because external marking is a rapid process and requires few specialized materials or equipment for either marking or detection (Laufle et al. 1990), it is often ideal for movement and migration projects.

External marking, especially partial fin clipping, is often used for temporary marking. Whenever short-term studies are planned, external marks should be considered first as the appropriate marking technique. Most mark–recapture abundance estimates, for example, require only group identification of the animals between sampling times, generally several days to 1 year. Partial fin clips, brands, or fluorescent marks are ideal for such circumstances because of their easy application and the relatively minor physiological effects of the marking process or the mark itself.

An increasingly important use of external marking is to identify animals that also carry an internal tag. In such cases, a single obvious mark, such as absence of the adipose fin, signals that an internal tag may be present. The internal tag then contains more specific identifying information (see Chapter 5). Researchers also use fin clips to study retention rates for external and internal tags, as described in Chapter 3.

Short-term and special-purpose studies can often use marks that are not broadly applicable and, therefore, are not described in this book. A common need in research studies, for example, is determining the absolute rate of capture during a recovery process, such as retrieval of a cove rotenone sample. Another example is the release of animals so that researchers can observe their immediate response. These animals must be marked so they are distinguishable from wild animals—as they must be when the mortality of fish passing through a power turbine is assessed. Such studies can use a wide variety of techniques, and the researcher

---

Box 4.1   Marking Walleyes in Oneida Lake

John Forney and his colleagues at Cornell University monitored walleye populations in Oneida Lake, New York, for more than 20 years. Beginning in the late 1950s, they clipped fins on adult walleyes captured in trap nets for hatchery spawning. They recaptured the walleyes during summer and fall with gill nets, trawls, and electroshockers, producing annual mark–recapture abundance estimates (Forney 1967).

Continued.

Box 4.1   Continued.

Sustaining this monitoring program required careful planning so that the few available fin clips would be used efficiently. The marking program began with complete clips of the easily seen and clipped pelvic fins:

Year	Fin clipped	Number clipped
1957	Right pelvic	12,500
1958	Left pelvic	20,451
1959	Both pelvic	25,686

In the following years, workers used partial clips of the pelvic fins, even though this prevented re-marking of most fish that had been captured and marked in one of the previous years:

1960	1/2 right pelvic	13,109
1961	1/2 left pelvic	25,381

Following this pattern, the next clip would have been "1/2 both pelvic fins." However, none of the fish clipped in previous years would be available for reclipping because part of at least one fin would have been removed already—eliminating nearly 100,000 fish. Therefore, workers began clipping pectoral fins:

1962	1/2 right pectoral	25,733
1963	1/2 left pectoral	20,462

Pectoral fin clips proved unsatisfactory, however, because many unmarked fish had deformed fins. These deformities, presumably related to hatchery conditions, were difficult to distinguish from fins regenerated after partial clips.

After 1963, therefore, Forney decided to use only full and half clips of pelvic fins. To separate the use of the same clip by as many years as possible, they switched to alternate-year marking. A study of the survival of walleyes marked with a right-pelvic clip in 1957 showed that only about 600 of these fish would still be alive when the 20,000+ fish marked with the same clip in 1965 would first be recaptured. This 3% possible error was judged acceptable, and the marking program resumed the original order for a second and third time:

1965	Right pelvic	26,141
1967	Left pelvic	21,264
1970	1/2 right pelvic	22,472
1972	1/2 left pelvic	21,588
1974	Right pelvic	14,807
1976	Left pelvic	25,001
1978	1/2 right pelvic	19,803

Any long-term marking program involving external marks is likely to require similar decisions about the kind of mark, the specific sites, colors, or shapes used, and the frequency and longevity of the mark. (Thanks to John Forney for his description of the Oneida Lake project.)

Table 4.1 Data collected and taxa studied with external marks, based on review of interpretable titles in Emery and Wydoski (1987).

Data type or taxon	Number of studies involving			Total studies
	Fin clips	Brands	Pigments	
Data type				
Movement or distribution	22	8		30
Abundance estimate	18	2		20
Stock characteristics	5			5
Mortality rate	6			6
Growth rate	10			10
Life history	6			6
Individual identification	10	7		17
Tag evaluation	58	20	4	82
General techniques	27	39	4	70
Taxon				
Salmonids	67	22	2	91
Centrarchids	22	3	1	26
Ictalurids	2	7		9
Esocids	6			6
Cyprinids	1			1
Molluscs	10			10
Crustaceans	12	3		15
Reptiles	20	6		26
Marine mammals		8		8

should not be inhibited by the constraints described here. An expansive search of the primary literature may reveal a short-term technique ideal for the study. Emery and Wydoski (1987) provided a starting point, with their annotated bibliography of more than 1,400 references on marking and tagging!

4.2 ASSUMPTIONS FOR EXTERNAL MARKS

The primary assumption for external marking is that the mark does not alter an animal's physiology or behavior. Because livestock brands and human tattoos are harmless, fisheries workers have presumed that similar marks on aquatic animals will be similarly harmless. As described later, direct studies of brands and pigment marks have verified that presumption.

Many studies have examined the effects of fin clips on fish growth, survival, and behavior. As with other aspects of marking, the data about fin clipping are variable. Specific concerns about fin clips are described later, but in general the clipping of one pelvic fin or the adipose fin has relatively little effect on survival and virtually none on growth.

An important assumption is that all externally marked animals will be identified correctly. This assumption has two parts. First, all marks must be retained by the animals and observed by workers. External marks, however, may disappear—fins can regenerate, natural pigments can obscure brands and tattoos, and dyes can fade. Such problems become increasingly likely as time passes, reducing the effectiveness of external marks for long-term studies (Knight 1990). Furthermore, because most external marks are subtle, observers may have difficulty detecting them. Detection is particularly difficult when many animals are observed quickly or when the orientation of the animal may hide the mark. For example, fish marked with a left-pectoral fin clip must be turned so the left side is visible—virtually impossible if the fish are moving by continuously on a conveyor belt. Untrained and volunteer observers are especially likely to miss external marks.

Second, only marked animals should be classified as marked animals. Tissue mutilations and color variations also occur naturally; the absence or distortion of fins is especially common. Consequently, more animals may be identified as marked than were actually marked and released into the population. This is a particular problem when fin clips are used to indicate the presence of an internal tag. Therefore, the calculation of abundance and other statistics based on mark recovery must be very carefully assessed and often must be adjusted for misreading (see Chapter 2).

4.3 CLIPPING FINS AND OTHER TISSUES

4.3.1 General Description

Fin clipping includes either total or partial fin removal. Total fin removal usually prevents regeneration of the fin, thus producing a mark that lasts indefinitely. Partial fin removal provides a temporary mark until the fin regenerates. Regenerated fins often are deformed in some manner, however, so that a partial fin clip may be visible even after the fin regenerates (Figure 4.1). All fins have been used for marking at one time or another, but current preference is for clipping adipose, pelvic, or pectoral fins. Scientists often have clipped more than one fin per fish in order to increase the number of groups that could be distinguished.

Many modifications of full or partial fin clips have been used. These include punching holes or notches in fins, which causes sloughing of the fin tissue beyond the cut (Wydoski and Emery 1983); creating scars by severing individual fin rays (Welch and Mills 1981); and removing single prominent fin rays (Kohlhorst 1979).

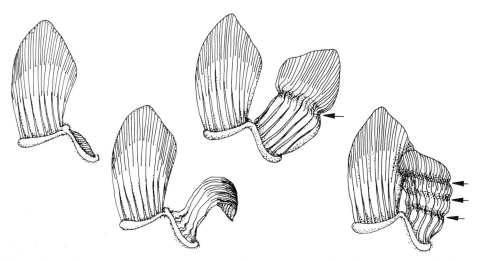

Figure 4.1 The appearance of regenerated fins after partial fin clips may show distinct distortions, allowing detection of the mark long after regeneration. Fins can be clipped successively at different distances from the base, producing more than one line of distortion (arrows). Reprinted from Wydoski and Emery (1983).

Box 4.2   Advantages and Disadvantages of Fin Clipping

Advantages

- Easy and rapid process
- No effect on growth
- Suitable for all fishes and many invertebrates
- Suitable for all sizes and life stages
- Adaptable for short- and long-term studies

Disadvantages

- Individual marks not available
- Limited number of group marks available
- Mortality depends on fish size, fin clip, and handling
- High error rate for recognizing and interpreting clips
- Negative public opinion

For invertebrates, this technique usually involves notching portions of the external skeleton, including the shells of molluscs (Neves and Moyer 1988) and the carapace, telson, and uropods of crustaceans.

4.3.2 Advantages of Fin Clipping (Box 4.2)

Clipping fins is easy. It generally requires only a pair of sharp shears or wire-cutters. Experienced workers can clip hundreds of fins per hour, the exact rate depending mostly on how fast fish can be delivered to the clipper. The logistics differ for each species and clipping environment, but once the particular assembly line process is set up, clipping each fin is a routine task. For this reason, managers often have used fin clips to mark huge numbers of hatchery fish before stocking, as a way to evaluate stocking success.

Fin clipping is applicable to virtually all fishes and many invertebrates. It has been used most frequently on salmonids, centrarchids, and percids and on decapod crustaceans because of their commercial or recreational importance (Coble 1967). Fins on all sizes of fish can be clipped, producing permanent marks. This capability is also important for stocking evaluations, because fish are generally stocked at a small size and evaluation occurs several years later when the fish are harvested.

Partial fin clips are most useful for short-term purposes. Partial fin clips are excellent, for example, for mark–recapture abundance estimates in which the interval between marking and recapture is only a few days or weeks. Regeneration of fins begins almost immediately, however, and complete regeneration of partially clipped fins may occur within a few months (Churchill 1963). Although regenerated fins often can be identified by deformities (Figure 4.1), several authors have reported difficulty recognizing regeneration (e.g., McNeil and Crossman 1979; Coombs et al. 1990).

Total fin clips are generally permanent, allowing their use for long-term purposes. Total fin clips, therefore, are used primarily for studies extending across several years, such as migration studies, assessments of relative mortality and harvest, and multiple mark–recapture abundance estimation. Because only a few fin-clipping sites are acceptable on any fish species and because total fin clips are permanent, only a few batches of marked fish can be distinguished in any water body. Careful coordination is necessary to assure that each study occurring on a water body uses a unique fin clip.

Fin clips generally do not alter the growth of fish. Studies comparing the growth of clipped and unclipped fish generally have shown no differences (e.g., Brynildson and Brynildson 1967). Wounds caused by fin clipping usually heal quickly, especially those caused by partial clips.

Mortality of fin-clipped fish, however, is highly variable. Some immediate mortality may occur during the marking process, especially if fish have been handled extensively for other purposes (e.g., stripping eggs at a hatchery, or stomach sampling). Delayed mortality depends on fish size. High mortality of small fishes has been reported repeatedly; Coble (1967) suggested that fish shorter than 90 mm are especially susceptible. Delayed mortality appears to be relatively high for salmonids, intermediate for centrarchids, and low for percids.

Mortality also depends on which fin is clipped (Table 4.2). Mortality is generally lower for clips of adipose and pelvic fins, which are used little by most fishes for movement or balance (McNeil and Crossman 1979). Mortality is generally higher for clips of the major median fins and pectoral fins. The preferred clips are adipose (if the species has one), left pelvic, and right pelvic. Mears and Hatch (1976) showed that clipping more than one fin may increase delayed mortality, but other studies have been less conclusive. Nevertheless, clipping more than one fin should be avoided if possible, unless the second clip is partial or temporary.

4.3.3 Disadvantages of Fin Clipping (Box 4.2)

Fin clips can be used only to identify groups. Although some researchers have developed complex schemes for producing individual codes based on the number and location of multiple clips on multiple fins, these systems are difficult to apply and to interpret at recapture. The small number of available fins also means that only a few groups at any time can be separated. The permanence of total fin clips can be a disadvantage in some situations if long-lived fish continue to carry clips that are needed to mark new fish in new studies.

Substantial errors are likely by observers of fin clips. Fin mutilation sometimes occurs in nature, producing fish with missing, partial, or deformed fins, and these can falsely increase the number of fish classified as marked. Adipose fins are especially prone to loss, presumably because they are bitten by predators in the wild or by aggressive individuals in hatcheries; Blankenship (1990) recorded loss rates of up to 2% in hatchery stocks of adult coho salmon. A one-time survey of fin aberrations in the unmarked population can be a helpful tool in choosing suitable fins for clipping, distinguishing natural from applied fin clips, and adjusting recapture data.

The underreporting of fin clips, however, is the more common problem. Unless fins are removed completely, by incision into the underlying tissue, the fins may regenerate (Johnsen and Ugedal 1988) and look like naturally deformed fins. Recognizing fins regenerated from partial clips requires experience and constant attention to detail. Fin clips also are more difficult to observe than external tags. Whereas most external tags are large, brightly colored, and located on the fish's

Table 4.2 Relative recovery rate of fin-clipped fingerlings compared to unclipped fingerlings in field and laboratory studies, as an index of survival. Data have been recalculated from the original sources in some cases.

Fin clipped	Species	Relative recovery (%)	Reference
Adipose	Rainbow trout	60	Nicola and Cordova (1973)
	Brook trout	95	Mears and Hatch (1976)
	Coho salmon	100	Stolte (1973)
Pelvic	Brook trout	40	Mears and Hatch (1976)
	Smallmouth bass	44	Coble (1971)
	Rainbow trout	52	Nicola and Cordova (1973)
	Brown trout	100	Brynildson and Brynildson (1967)
	Coho salmon	100	Stolte (1973)
	Yellow perch	100	Coble (1967)
	Walleye	100	Churchill (1963)
Pectoral	Rainbow trout	38	Nicola and Cordova (1973)
	Smallmouth bass	38	Coble (1971)
	Brook trout	56	Mears and Hatch (1976)
	Largemouth bass	83	Boxrucker (1982)
	Brown trout	100	Brynildson and Brynildson (1967)
	Yellow perch	100	Coble (1967)
	Walleye	100	Churchill (1963)
Dorsal	Rainbow trout	37	Nicola and Cordova (1973)
	Brook trout	10	Mears and Hatch (1976)
Anal	Smallmouth bass	33	Coble (1971)
	Rainbow trout	41	Nicola and Cordova (1973)
	Brown trout	44	Mears and Hatch (1976)
	Yellow perch	77	Coble (1967)

dorsal surface, fin clips are inconspicuous and often located on the fish's ventral surface.

The final disadvantage is a public relations problem. Anglers and other people do not like to see animals with clipped fins or other mutilations, and anglers become especially annoyed if their trophy fish are imperfect. Fin clipping should be limited to the fish actually needed for a study, and it should be conducted skillfully, with the proper equipment, to minimize trauma to the fish. Biologists and managers associated with the study should be prepared to explain the purpose and value of the clips to inquiring members of the public.

4.3.4   Clipping a Fin or Other Tissue

4.3.4.1   Clipping Environment

Because fins can be clipped very rapidly, fish are not usually anesthetized for fin clipping. Comparisons of subsequent growth and mortality have shown no difference between anesthetized and nonanesthetized fish (e.g., Nicola and Cordova 1973). If each fish must be extensively handled to collect many data, however, anesthesia may be needed.

Fish should be kept under water as much as possible during fin clipping. Holding a fish in shallow water or an immersed fabric cradle (see Chapter 3), the worker need expose to the air only the body area—usually the ventral or dorsal

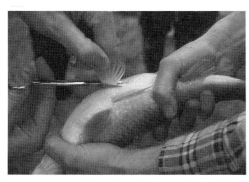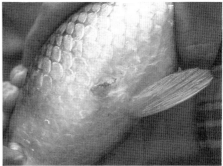

Figure 4.2 Total removal of a pelvic fin from common carp, showing clipping at the base of the fin. These photos were taken during a training class. Normally, only the fin area would be exposed above water. Photo by author.

surface—where the fin is located. If fish are exposed to bright sunlight, their eyes should be shaded.

Because many fish are generally fin-clipped at one time, they are often held in dense concentrations in the marking tank. Water quality in the tank should be checked regularly and the water should be replaced or treated if conditions deteriorate. The tank should be completely emptied of fish regularly to assure that no fish remain in the tank for an extended time.

4.3.4.2 Clipping a Fin

Fin clipping is a routine process, generally requiring only a pair of sharp, good-quality shears. Depending on the size and species of fish and the particular fin to be clipped, the shears may vary from curved surgical scissors (e.g., for the adipose fin of fingerling trout) to wire cutters (e.g., for the pelvic fins of yellow perch). The shears should be heavy enough and long enough to produce a clean cut in one motion. Practice on a few dead specimens will reveal the necessary size and ruggedness of the shears.

The worker should cradle the fish from below, exposing the fin to be clipped. A thumb or finger can be used to lift the fin slightly from the body surface so the shears can be inserted between the fin and body. For removal of an entire pelvic or pectoral fin, the cut must be made into the underlying tissue, so that the entire base of the fin is removed (Figure 4.2). The cutting axis of the shears should match the long axis of the fin's insertion into the body, assuring a complete and clean cut. All fin rays must be removed to discourage regeneration. For removal of the adipose fin, the tips of the shears should be used to raise the posterior portion of the fin slightly. Then the shears can be slipped under this loose portion, assuring complete removal. The fin should be clipped as close to the body as possible, but without rupturing the skin.

For partial removal of a pelvic or pectoral fin, the cut should be made perpendicular to the principal fin ray and no more than halfway from the base of the fin (Eipper and Forney 1965). For partial marking of the dorsal, caudal, or anal fins, the mark will be most recognizable if the corner of the fin is clipped at an angle to remove approximately equal lengths from adjacent edges of the fin (Figure 4.3).

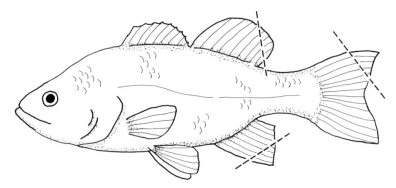

Figure 4.3 Temporary fin clips of dorsal, anal, or caudal fins should be oriented so the section of fin removed approximates an isosceles triangle, whose base is the cut line. Such a cut is the most recognizable before and after regeneration.

4.3.4.3   Clipping a Crustacean Appendage

Crustaceans can be identified by clipping one or more appendage. Some investigators have removed one of the two eye stalks, but this can cause mortality or alter the molt cycle. The more common technique is clipping the uropods and telson of the tail. Generally, partial clips are used, even though they will be obscured eventually through regeneration. The process is analogous to partial fin clipping, with the clip made perpendicular to the appendage's main axis and approximately halfway to the base (Barr 1971). The tail segments of crustaceans also can be notched in distinctive patterns. Unlike fin notches, uropod and telson notches retain their shape until regenerated or molted. Balazs (1973) described a system of uropod notching that can code up to 122 animals (Figure 4.4).

4.3.4.4   Notching a Mollusc Shell

Mollusc shells are often marked to validate the growth of shells in relation to supposed aging marks on or in the shell. Ropers et al. (1984) used an electric grinder fitted with a pair of thin carborundum discs separated by a narrow space to cut a pair of shallow parallel grooves at the edge of ocean quahog shells. The parallel lines distinguished the mark from natural scratches and better defined the edge of the notches. The marks were visible for more than 2 years. Similarly, Bretos (1980) sawed notches in the margin of limpet shells, producing marks that were detectable 18 months later.

Although mollusc shells are often considered as solid mineral structures, they do contain organic materials and are quite fragile at the margin. Therefore, the process of notching mollusc shells should be performed as carefully and sensitively as tissue alterations on fish and crustaceans.

4.3.4.5   Postclipping Treatment

Special treatment of the wound is generally not necessary. Boxrucker (1982), however, cauterized fin-clipping wounds with a cold brand, with no apparent harm to the fish. The same equipment and techniques used for cold branding (see section 4.4.4) can be used for cauterization, except that the contact of the brand to the fish should be extended to 5–6 seconds (Bourgeois et al. 1987).

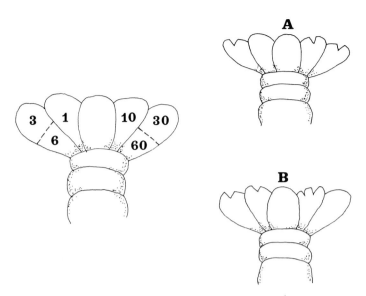

Figure 4.4 The shrimp uropod notching system of Balazs (1973). By numbering uropod sections as shown at left and cutting no more than two notches per uropod, one can individually code 122 animals. The animal's number is the sum of the value in each section times the number of notches in that section. Example A shows number 43 (3 + 10 + 30); example B shows number 24 (3 + 1 + 20).

If the animals are part of a massive marking project designed only to identify them into groups, they should be released immediately. If animals have been handled extensively, holding them in a tank with an antibiotic may be desirable to reduce the risk of infection (see Chapter 2). If the animals are part of a study in which knowing the precise number of released animals is important (e.g., mark–recapture abundance estimation), a sample should be held for 24 hours to assess short-term mortality.

Regardless of the taxon being marked, representative clips or notches should be photographed as a record of the appearance of marks at release. Photographs allow later workers to verify the precise marking location and style. Photographs of marked animals recaptured at later intervals will also allow analysis of the process of regeneration and general mark deterioration.

4.4 BRANDING

4.4.1 General Description

Branding creates a recognizable scar on the body of a fish or other animal. Although hot branding has been used for marking fish, cold branding is the preferred method. Cold branding is a simple process of touching a chilled metallic symbol to the body of the animal for a few seconds. In a few days, the slightly injured tissue forms a scar in the shape of the branding symbol.

A wide assortment of equipment and techniques is used for cold branding. The essential parts are a chilling apparatus to hold the coolant, a coolant that chills the brand, and the brand itself (Figure 4.5). Workers have used various coolants, but

Figure 4.5 A cold-branding apparatus that features a Dewar flask containing liquid nitrogen and a stationary branding symbol. The Atlantic salmon parr has just been marked with the symbol "⌐." Reprinted from Knight (1990).

the two most common are liquid nitrogen (N_2), dispensed from a Dewar flask (Knight 1990), and pressurized carbon dioxide (CO_2), which can be dispensed from a standard fire extinguisher (Bryant et al. 1990). The chilling apparatus delivers coolant to a heat-conducting shaft, usually copper or silver, which has the branding symbol mounted on one end. The branding symbol is sometimes fixed to the chilling apparatus, and the animal is pressed against the symbol. In other cases the brand is separate, just like the long-handled brands cowboys use, and is removed from the coolant to be pressed against the animal.

Branding has been used primarily on fish, reptiles, and marine mammals (Table 4.1). Other techniques designed to produce a visible pattern on the exoskeleton of invertebrates are described in this section, but they are like branding only in the appearance of the mark (e.g., a scratched or painted symbol).

4.4.2 Advantages of Cold Branding (Box 4.3)

Cold branding is a rapid process for marking large numbers of animals. Bryant et al. (1990) estimated that an efficiently working crew could brand up to 1,000 fish per hour. As with fin clipping, the marking rate is limited by the fish-handling process rather than by the marking itself.

This technique has little apparent effect on the marked animals. Short-term tests on salmonids have revealed no observable increases in mortality, decreases in growth, or changes in behavior (Bryant et al. 1990). Although long-term tests have not been reported, it seems reasonable that with a short marking time and no

---

Box 4.3   Advantages and Disadvantages of Cold Branding

Advantages

- Easy and rapid process
- Probably no effects on growth, survival, or behavior
- Suitable for all sizes of animals
- Suitable for remote locations

Disadvantages

- Suitable primarily for scaleless or fine-scaled fishes
- Individual marks not available
- Limited number of group marks available
- Limited to short-term studies
- Difficult to see and interpret
- Cold temperatures can burn workers

---

intrusion into the animal's body, cold branding would not cause substantial long-term physiological changes.

Cold-branding apparatus is very portable, well suited for use in remote marking locations. The marking implements are small and rugged. The major piece of equipment is the coolant container, usually a small fire extinguisher or liquid nitrogen tank. Although these tanks are bulky, Bryant et al. (1990) reported that a single 9-kg carbon dioxide tank could supply coolant for branding 3,500 fish.

Cold branding is useful for a wide range of fish sizes. Fish as small as 40 mm total length have been marked with brands as small as 1×5 mm. Large fish can be branded with large brands, providing better long-term recognition of the mark.

Brands provide excellent short-term marks for fish, and they may last for several years. In general, however, brands are particularly useful for short studies (e.g., short-term mark–recapture estimation or local movement studies). Brands become visible on fish within 2–3 days after marking (the time may vary with water temperature; Knight 1990) and last for weeks to months.

4.4.3   Disadvantages of Cold Branding (Box 4.3)

Cold branding is useful mainly for marking scaleless or fine-scaled fishes. Most successful cold branding reported in the literature has been used on salmonids or ictalurids; about 85% of studies compiled by Emery and Wydoski (1987) concerned these two taxa. Because branding requires scarring of the dermal tissue, coarsely scaled fishes are difficult to brand effectively. Although not documented, the use of brands on fine-scaled cyprinids and other small-bodied fishes may be useful. Branding has not been successful on invertebrates with exoskeletons, because brands are lost during molting (Farmer 1981).

Cold branding is useful primarily for group identification of animals, and usually only a few groups can be distinguished in a water body. Brand symbols must be simple and distinctively shaped so that recognition is easy. Because branding is generally a mass-marking technique and because individual fish vary in their reaction to the brand, the likelihood is low that subtle differences among brands will be uniformly applied to the fish or later visible by an observer. Bryant et al. (1990) recommended straight-line letters, such as T, I, V, and X. Although specific orientations and locations of brands (e.g., upside down, near the tail) can increase the number of identifiable groups (Coombs et al. 1990), the likelihood of missed or misread marks also increases.

Brands eventually disappear, but the rates of long-term retention are largely unknown. Brands become less recognizable as time passes, because the scars fade, the skin becomes more heavily pigmented, and fish continue to grow (Herbinger et al. 1990). Recognizing a brand on a rapidly growing fish can be very difficult; the process is like drawing a message on a deflated balloon, inflating the balloon, and trying to read the message (Bryant et al. 1990). Gunnes and Refstie (1980), for example, observed cold brands on salmonids 22–28 months after marking, correctly identifying more than 80% of the marks. In contrast, in a more recent study of cold branding on Atlantic salmon, only one recognizable brand was found among 140 returning adults known to have been marked the previous year (Bourgeois et al. 1987).

4.4.4   Branding a Fish

4.4.4.1   Branding Location

The brand should be created on the lightest part of the animal's body that is readily observable. This area will generally be along the side of a fish in the mid-body region. Knight (1990) recommended holding fish to be branded in a dark container; fish will then be observed in their darkest phase, showing the location where a light background is most likely to occur in any condition. Because fish often lose coloration during handling, this precaution is very important. As with other techniques, a specific branding location should be defined explicitly. To improve the visibility of brands on recaptured fish, Knight also recommended holding the fish in a light-colored container for maximum contrast between the body and the brand.

4.4.4.2   Branding Environment

Fish often are anesthetized before branding to prevent their movement during the branding operation (see Chapter 2). If the fish are to be marked with a hand-held brand, a group equal only to the number that can be branded in one cooling operation (5–30 fish) should be anesthetized together.

Fish must be removed from water for branding. Therefore, a highly efficient branding operation is necessary to minimize the exposure of fish to air. If a hand-held brand is used, the group of anesthetized fish must be treated as a batch. The fish should be arranged on a flat surface, blotted to remove excess water, branded, and returned to the water. If a fixed brand is used, anesthetized fish should be processed individually. That is, one fish should be removed from the anesthetic tank, blotted, branded, and immediately returned to the recovery tank before the next fish is removed from the anesthetic. As in all cases, the water quality in both anesthetic and recovery tanks should be monitored regularly and corrected if it falls below critical levels.

4.4.4.3 Brand Application

The cooling and branding equipment usually must be specially constructed for cold-branding purposes. Knight (1990) described a system cooled by liquid nitrogen ($-196°C$). A commercial Dewar flask is fitted with a threaded copper rod that protrudes from the flask a short distance and then bends 90° sideways. Brass or copper nuts, which can be threaded on the copper rod, are fitted with brass brands of necessary size and shape (Figure 4.5).

An alternative process has a carbon dioxide fire extinguisher as the cooling apparatus. The critical part of the system is the nozzle, which delivers coolant to the brand at -70 to $-80°C$. Bryant et al. (1990) recommended a 0.14-mm inside-diameter nozzle, which provided sufficient flow with little clogging in their studies. Their system used a brand attached to a straight silver rod; the rod was placed inside the nozzle of the fire extinguisher, where the escaping carbon dioxide cooled the brand.

The branding process is quite simple. The brand must be cold, clean, and dry. A hand-held brand can be used to mark as many as 30 fish before it is recooled, depending on the air temperature. If the brand sticks to the fish, it needs to be recooled. Pretesting with a sample of fish will reveal how many animals can be branded before the brand must be recooled, and slightly fewer than this number should be anesthetized together for each branding operation. Buildup of materials on the branding symbol will affect the completeness of contact and the shape of the eventual brand. Therefore, the brand should be cleaned regularly by flooding it with acetone and wiping with a dry rag. (Dipping the brand in acetone before an application also can help prevent sticking to the fish.) The brand symbol must be kept dry to avoid ice accumulation.

The brand should contact the fish for 1–2 seconds only; use the standard "one thousand one, one thousand two" to measure time. Experiments have shown that longer contact times do not improve the mark (Bryant et al. 1990). The brand should just touch the skin, not be embedded in it. Only gentle pressure is necessary to assure uniform contact of the brand symbol and the skin.

Workers applying the brands must be especially cautious because the coolants can seriously damage human tissue. Workers should learn the appropriate safety precautions and first-aid techniques for burns and frostbite before using the equipment. The coolant must be stored in containers that meet government safety standards; this is especially important for liquid nitrogen. Workers should wear insulated gloves with long cuffs and long-sleeved shirts to prevent cold damage to their hands and accidental contact of their lower arms with cold surfaces.

4.4.4.4 Postbranding Treatment

Anesthetized fish should be returned to a recovery tank immediately after branding. The tank can be treated with an antibiotic (see Chapter 2), especially if the handling has been extensive. Fish can be returned to the water after they have resumed normal swimming position and behavior. Fish that were not anesthetized for branding generally can be released immediately, without antibiotic treatment.

A sample of branded animals should be held for several days to assess marking-induced mortality and brand appearance. Because the brand may take several days to develop, a sample is needed so that workers can see the mark as it will appear on recaptured animals. The brands of several specimens should be

Figure 4.6 Etched and glued marks on the shells of molluscs. Specimens prepared by Richard Neves; photo by author.

photographed with color print film to produce a permanent record that can be used later for field reference. The photographed specimens should include large and small animals held in light and dark conditions.

4.4.5 "Branding" Invertebrates

Molluscs and some crustaceans can be marked in ways that produce brand-like marks. In these cases, however, the brands are made by scratching or painting a symbol on the animal's exoskeleton.

Exoskeleton marks are obviously useful for molluscs (Figure 4.6). The hard, thick shells provide a surface that can be etched with an engraver's tool or grinder when the shells are wet or dry (Miller and Nelson 1983). Because the outer surface of the shell is generally darker than the inside, the scratched symbols will be highly visible, especially after cleaning. Similar engraving of numbers has been used on the carapace of Atlantic rock crabs (Drummond-Davis et al. 1982). The technique is useful only on crustacean species with thick exoskeletons and then only until the next molt.

Painted marks are also commonly used for molluscs. If the shell is fairly smooth and light in color, an indelible ink can be applied directly to the shell (Fritz and Haven 1983; Peterson et al. 1983). The mark should be made on the posterior half of the shell, where shell erosion is lowest. The shell should be cleaned before painting by scrubbing it gently with a soft-bristled toothbrush, but harsh treatments (such as sanding to make a smooth surface) should be avoided. The shell must be dry for marking. To protect the mark from erosion, a thin layer of clear plastic cement can be applied on the top of the ink or paint (Brousseau 1979).

4.5 PIGMENT MARKS

4.5.1 General Description

Pigments of various kinds can be injected or embedded shallowly in the skin of fish and other aquatic animals, producing a simple, long-lasting mark. The range of pigments and techniques for applying them is great, but the primary techniques are injection of liquid pigment, tattooing of indelible inks, and high-pressure embedding of granular fluorescent pigment.

These techniques are sometimes grouped with chemical marks (e.g., Emery and Wydoski 1983). In this book, however, chemical marks are classified as those in which a chemical reaction occurs between an animal's tissues and the marking substance (see Chapter 9). Pigments, in contrast, are intended to be inert, not incorporated biologically. Thus, they are more closely related to branding and other physical alterations of the skin and appendages.

Marking animals with pigments is a common technique, but it has never become a standard process. The techniques originated mostly in the 1920s and enjoyed increasing popularity during the 1960s and early 1970s (McFarlane et al. 1990). As physical tags have become more sophisticated, however, pigment marking has declined. Pigment marking, therefore, is used mostly in special situations where the species or the setting make a particular technique advantageous.

4.5.2 Advantages of Pigment Marks (Box 4.4)

Pigment marks have negligible effects on aquatic organisms. Because the pigments themselves are inert, reactions between an animal and the pigment are generally minor. The processes of attaching the marks are generally unobtrusive, consisting of localized disruptions of the skin. The major trauma to the animal is the handling process, during which the animal usually must be removed from the water (Laufle et al. 1990).

Pigments can be applied to a wide variety of aquatic animals. As with other marks, pigments have been used primarily on commercially or recreationally important species like salmonids (Nielson 1990) and shrimp (Farmer 1981), but they are probably similarly appropriate on most species. They are particularly useful for animals that tend to shed physical tags, such as sturgeons (Bordner et al. 1990).

Pigments produce highly visible marks that may remain on an animal for long periods. Tattoos have been observed for up to 1 year (Bordner et al. 1990) and latex injections for 1–3.5 months (Fay and Pardue 1985; Laufle et al. 1990). Fluorescent granules, embedded in the skin under pressure and viewed under ultraviolet light, have been observed more than 4 years after marking in one study (Evenson and Ewing 1985) and up to 12 years in another (Nielson 1990). Most pigment marks have been used for short periods of time, so long-term assessments of retention are rare.

Marking animals with pigments is a quick and technologically simple process. Tattoos are applied with standard tattooing equipment, available from disreputable supply stores, or with hand-held dental inoculators (Laufle et al. 1990). Latex marks are injected with modified syringes (Kelly 1967; Farmer 1981). Fluorescent pigments are generally applied to batches of animals at one time. The pigmented granules are sprayed with sandblasting equipment onto the sides of fish or shrimp held in a single layer in a basket or similar device (Phinney et al. 1967; Farmer

---

Box 4.4   Advantages and Disadvantages of Pigment Marking

Advantages

- Easy and simple procedures
- Negligible effects on marked animals
- Suitable for many fishes and crustaceans
- Highly visible marks
- Probably suitable for long-term marking
- Tattoos allow individual identification

Disadvantages

- Individual marks not generally available
- Detection may require special equipment and facilities
- Suitable for special conditions only
- Detection difficulty increases with time
- Less suitable for small animals
- Marks on head lost if specimens are decapitated

1981; Nielson 1990). Depending on the particular pigment-marking process, marking rates range from several hundred to several thousand animals per hour.

4.5.3   Disadvantages of Pigment Marks (Box 4.4)

Pigment marks are generally useful only to identify animals into groups because the colors and marking locations are limited (tattoos are the exception because individual symbols can be used). Although large ranges of colors are available from pigment manufacturers, the consistency of the dye colors may be poor, and the ability to distinguish among similar colors becomes difficult as time passes. The detection of fluorescent granules of two colors on the same fish, for example, a marking strategy that would allow more groups to be distinguished, is more difficult than the detection of a single color (Evenson and Ewing 1985).

Special conditions are required for observation of fluorescent pigment marks. Because the pigment granules are broadcast across an animal's body during marking, granules may appear anywhere on the animal. The highest concentrations of pigment granules on fish, however, are found in the transparent tissue around the eyes and in the caudal peduncle (Evenson and Ewing 1985). Because the pigments are only visible under ultraviolet light, animals must be observed in a darkened location equipped with ultraviolet lamps. Often animals must be examined carefully by trained personnel because only a few granules will be present.

Detection of pigment marks also becomes more difficult as more time passes between marking and recapture. Natural pigmentation of fish skin increases with size, obscuring marks. Skin thickness also increases as fish mature, further obscuring the pigmented marks (Evenson and Ewing 1985; Nielson 1990). For these reasons, pigments have usually been applied to larger fish for studies of adult movements, short-term mark–recapture estimates of abundance and mortality, or identification of spawning stocks.

A minor problem associated with pigment marks is the loss of marks when fish are decapitated. The head is often the best site for pigment marking, either because fluorescent pigments are likely to lodge around the eye or because the light-colored, bony structures beneath the jaws are good sites for latex injections. If fish are frequently decapitated before observation—by anglers who have cleaned their catches, for example—many marks will be lost. A public information program might turn this liability into an opportunity to recover heads, however.

4.5.4 Applying a Pigment Mark

4.5.4.1 Marking Environment

The extent of premarking treatment depends on the marking technique. For tattoos and injections, animals must be anesthetized before marking (see Chapter 2). Animals should be held in a small anesthetic tank and removed singly for marking.

Fluorescent granule marking is a batch-marking process that requires large numbers of animals to be available at all times. The general procedure is to spread a group of animals into a single layer that can be sprayed effectively with fluorescent granules. Anesthesia is not practical in these circumstances. Consequently, the animals must be retained in a large holding tank (e.g., a hatchery raceway) and then concentrated into a smaller area. Subsequently, animals may be netted and spread inside a shallow holding box (Nielson 1990) or passed across a conveyor system (Evenson and Ewing 1985).

4.5.4.2 Tattooing

Tattoos are applied by injecting ink below the skin. Fish must be removed from the water and the marking surface dried (Laufle et al. 1990). A standard marking location should be chosen, preferably where a relatively flat and light-colored surface occurs. The ventral surface of the body, adjacent to the points of fin insertion, generally provides a good tattooing location (Bordner et al. 1990; Laufle et al. 1990). Tattooing can take up to 3 minutes per animal, depending on the size and detail of the tattoo. If the process is long, a marking tank should be constructed that will allow most of the animal to be submerged except for the surface to be tattooed.

The tattooing pigment is a suspension of ink in water. The solution should be as concentrated as possible without clogging the injection device. Many colors are available, but blue, black, red, and green are the most visible. Because blue and black may look similar (Black 1963), they should not be used in the same study.

Various devices have been used for tattooing. For large animals, a standard tattooing tool is appropriate. It has a set of short, fine needles that rapidly and repeatedly penetrate the skin (Figure 4.7; Bordner et al. 1990). For smaller fish, Laufle et al. (1990) used a dental inoculator. By holding the instrument on or near (2–3 cm) the skin, they were able to produce a round tattoo 3–5 mm in diameter. Similarly, Herbinger et al. (1990) applied blue dots to the fins of Atlantic salmon fingerlings with a dental inoculator. Black (1963) injected ink with a syringe into the epidermis of shrimp, producing a readily recognizable colored spot.

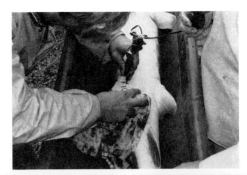

Figure 4.7 Workers tattooing an adult white sturgeon with a commercial tattooing instrument. The lower left shows the mark just after tattooing; the lower right shows the same tattoo 1 year later. Reprinted from Bordner et al. (1990).

4.5.4.3 Latex Injection

Latex marks are usually made by injecting colored latex pigments through a modified syringe. The best tagging sites are those where bone lies shallowly below the skin and where the skin is not pigmented. The ventral side of the jaw is the most common marking site (Kelly 1967; Fay and Pardue 1985). Kelly (1967) recommended using a 12-gauge syringe, fitted with a plunger, to push the pigment into the tissue. The needle should be inserted shallowly under the skin; Kelly (1967) suggested that insertion is at the correct depth if the needle is visible as a dark line below the skin. The latex is then injected into the tissue as the needle is withdrawn, forming a broad line (Figure 4.8).

A variation used on shrimp is the injection of fluorescent colored granules suspended in petroleum jelly (Farmer 1981). Small quantities of material (less than 0.1 mL) injected into abdominal muscle have remained in place for several weeks, with no apparent harm to the animals. Farmer (1981) recommended this technique over all others for marking small shrimp.

4.5.4.4 Fluorescent Marking

Fluorescent marks are made by embedding pigment granules in an animal's skin. Many colors of granules are available, but red, yellow, and dark green have been used successfully (Brandt and Schreck 1975; Nielson 1990). For maximum retention, the pigment should be in the form of granules (not powder) between 30 and 350 μm in diameter (Phinney et al. 1967). The technique requires a pressur-

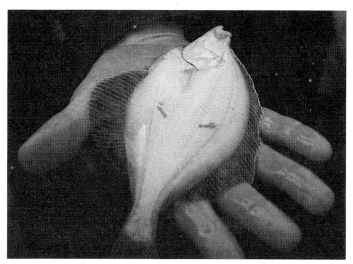

Figure 4.8   Latex pigments injected on the bottom side of flatfish where little natural skin pigmentation occurs. The marks appear as broad lines following the track of the injecting needle. Photo by author.

ized spraying apparatus, usually sandblasting equipment. The sprayer should produce a pressure of between 80 and 160 pounds per square inch at the nozzle, a range that allows penetration of the granules into the skin but presumably does not injure delicate eye tissue (Phinney et al. 1967). The nozzle should be held approximately 40 cm from the animal (Nielson 1990), and two passes of the sandblaster should be made across each batch of animals (Evenson and Ewing 1985). Smaller organisms, such as crayfish, are tumbled by the air stream, exposing all body surfaces to the marking process (Brandt and Schreck 1975).

People who conduct spraying operations should wear protective clothing, goggles, and masks. Bystanders should be kept at a distance.

4.5.4.5   Postmarking Treatment

For both tattooing and pigment injecting, which require anesthesia and which break the skin, the animals may be placed in a recovery tank treated with antibiotics after marking and held for a suitable time to assure recovery (see Chapter 2). As with other external marks, a photographic record of sample specimens is valuable for later comparison with recaptured animals.

Animals marked with fluorescent pigments do not require special postmarking treatment. Examination of a sample of marked fish is desirable to determine the effectiveness of the pigment-spraying procedure and to provide experience for the recapture team (Evenson and Ewing 1985).

4.5.4.6   Fluorescent Mark Detection

Detection of fluorescent pigments requires special equipment and conditions. A darkened area is needed; in the field, a temporary tent is necessary to exclude visible light. Ultraviolet lighting, placed behind the worker, is needed to excite the fluorescent pigments. Evenson and Ewing (1985) recommended a two-bulb system and at least 40-watt bulbs. Workers should be familiar with the dangers of ultraviolet radiation and take appropriate measures to protect their eyes and skin.

Careful examination is needed to detect the pigmented granules, because only a few granules may be present on each animal. Extra attention should be directed at the eyes and the caudal peduncle of fish, where granules are more frequently embedded. On invertebrates, most granules will be lost after molting. Careful examination, however, may reveal a few granules at the joints between body and appendage segments (Brandt and Schreck 1975). Workers should attempt to brush or wash away any granules seen, to be sure that the granules are actually embedded in the skin (Nielson 1990).

4.6   NEW AND SPECIAL CIRCUMSTANCES

External marking includes a large variety of techniques. Only a few commonly applied techniques are covered in this chapter. The range of possible external marks seems almost limitless, given the diversity of modern materials and equipment developed for other uses but applicable to fisheries.

Nonetheless, external marking has not enjoyed widespread commercial development like that given to tagging methods. Consequently, external marking is much like a hobby, with the techniques largely homegrown and locally perfected for specific projects. External marking has been only sparingly documented in the recent literature, presumably because fin clipping is considered too routine and other techniques are considered too anecdotal.

The real value of external marking lies in special circumstances that tagging cannot accommodate. Small, isolated, and brief studies may not warrant the extensive time or monetary investment needed for tagging systems. Studies using unusual, unstudied, or valuable animals may require less intrusive or more visible marks than are provided by tags.

Investigators who are faced with unique marking problems or opportunities should consider external marks as a first option because they are easy, simple, and benign. If an external mark is successful, the developer of the technique or application also should take the extra time to test the technique in a statistically valid way and report it in the technical literature.

4.7   REFERENCES

Balazs, G. H. 1973. A simplified method for identifying experimental shrimp. Progressive Fish-Culturist 35:27.

Barr, L. 1971. Methods of estimating the abundance of juvenile spot shrimp in a shallow nursery area. Transactions of the American Fisheries Society 100:781–787.

Black, J. B. 1963. Observations on the home range of stream dwelling crawfishes. Ecology 44:592–595.

Blackenship, H. L. 1990. Effects of time and fish size on coded wire tag loss from chinook and coho salmon. American Fisheries Symposium 7:237–243.

Bordner, C. E., S. I. Doroshov, D. E. Hinton, R. E. Pipkin, R. B. Fridley, and F. Haw. 1990. Evaluation of marking techniques for juvenile and adult white sturgeons reared in captivity. American Fisheries Society Symposium 7:293–303.

Bourgeois, C. E., M. F. O'Connell, and D. C. Scott. 1987. Cold-branding and fin-clipping Atlantic salmon smolts on the Exploits River, Newfoundland. North American Journal of Fisheries Management 7:154–156.

Boxrucker, J. C. 1982. Mass marking of fingerling largemouth bass by fin-clipping followed by freeze-cauterization of the wound. North American Journal of Fisheries Management 2:94–96.

Brandt, T. M., and C. B. Schreck. 1975. Crayfish marking with fluorescent pigment. American Midland Naturalist 94:494–499.

Bretos, M. 1980. Age determination in the keyhole limpet *Fissurella crassa* Lamarck (Archaeogastropode: Fissurellidae), based on shell growth rings. Biological Bulletin (Woods Hole) 159:606–612.

Brousseau, D. J. 1979. Analysis of growth rate in *Mya arenaria* using the von Bertalanffy equation. Marine Biology 51:221–227.

Bryant, M. D., C. A. Dolloff, P. E. Porter, and B. E. Wright. 1990. Freeze branding with CO_2: an effective and easy-to-use field method to mark fish. American Fisheries Society Symposium 7:30–35.

Brynildson, O. M., and C. L. Brynildson. 1967. The effect of pectoral and ventral fin removal on survival and growth of wild brown trout in a Wisconsin stream. Transactions of the American Fisheries Society 96:353–355.

Churchill, W. S. 1963. The effect of fin removal on survival, growth, and vulnerability to capture of stocked walleye fingerlings. Transactions of the American Fisheries Society 92:298–300.

Coble, D. W. 1967. Effects of fin-clipping on mortality and growth of yellow perch with a review of similar investigations. Journal of Wildlife Management 31:173–180.

Coble, D. W. 1971. Effects of fin clipping and other factors on survival and growth of smallmouth bass. Transactions of the American Fisheries Society 100:460–473.

Coombs, K. A., J. K. Bailey, C. M. Herbinger, and G. W. Friars. 1990. Evaluation of various external marking techniques for Atlantic salmon. American Fisheries Society Symposium 7:142–146.

Drummond-Davis, N. C., K. H. Mann, and R. A. Pottle. 1982. Some estimates of population density and feeding habits of the rock crab, *Cancer irroratus,* in a kelp bed in Nova Scotia. Canadian Journal of Fisheries and Aquatic Sciences 39:636–639.

Eipper, A. W., and J. L. Forney. 1965. Evaluation of partial fin clips for marking largemouth bass, walleyes and rainbow trout. New York Fish and Game Journal 12:233–240.

Emery, L., and R. Wydoski. 1987. Marking and tagging of aquatic animals: an indexed bibliography. U.S. Fish and Wildlife Service Resource Publication 165.

Evenson, M. D., and R. D. Ewing. 1985. Long-term retention of fluorescent pigment marks by spring chinook salmon and summer steelhead. North American Journal of Fisheries Management 5:26–32.

Farmer, A. S. D. 1981. A review of crustacean marking methods with particular reference to penaeid shrimp. Kuwait Bulletin of Marine Science 2:167–183.

Fay, C. W., and G. B. Pardue. 1985. Freeze brands and submandibular latex injections as identifying marks on rainbow trout. North American Journal of Fisheries Management 5:248–251.

Forney, J. L. 1967. Estimates of biomass and mortality rates in a walleye population. New York Fish and Game Journal 14:176–192.

Fritz, L. W., and D. S. Haven. 1983. Hard clam, *Mercenaria mercenaria*: shell growth patterns in Chesapeake Bay. U.S. National Marine Fisheries Service Fishery Bulletin 81:697–708.

Gunnes, K., and T. Refstie. 1980. Cold branding and fin-clipping for marking of salmonids. Aquaculture 19:295–299.

Herbinger, C. M., G. F. Newkirk, and S. T. Lanes. 1990. Individual marking of Atlantic salmon: evaluations of cold branding and jet injection of Alcian Blue in several fin locations. Journal of Fish Biology 36:99–101.

Johnsen, B. O., and O. Ugedal. 1988. Effects of different kinds of fin-clipping on over-winter survival and growth of fingerling brown trout, *Salmo trutta* L., stocked in small streams in Norway. Aquaculture and Fisheries Management 19:305–311.

Kelly, W. H. 1967. Marking freshwater and a marine fish by injected dyes. Transactions of the American Fisheries Society 96:163–175.

Knight, A. E. 1990. Cold-branding techniques for estimating Atlantic salmon parr densities. American Fisheries Society Symposium 7:36–37.

Kohlhorst, D. W. 1979. Effect of first pectoral fin ray removal on survival and estimated harvest rate of white sturgeon in the Sacramento–San Joaquin estuary. California Fish and Game 65:173–177.

Laufle, J. C., L. Johnson, and C. L. Monk. 1990. Tattoo-ink marking method for batch-identification of fish. American Fisheries Society Symposium 7:38–41.

McFarlane, G. A., R. S. Wydoski, and E. D. Prince. 1990. Historical review of the development of external tags and marks. American Fisheries Society Symposium 7:9–29.

McNeil, F. I., and E. J. Crossman. 1979. Fin clips in the evaluation of stocking programs for muskellunge, *Esox masquinongy*. Transactions of the American Fisheries Society 108:335–343.

Mears, H. C., and R. W. Hatch. 1976. Overwinter survival of fingerling brook trout with single and multiple fin clips. Transactions of the American Fisheries Society 105:669–674.

Miller, A. C., and D. A. Nelson. 1983. An instruction report on freshwater mussels. U.S. Army, Corps of Engineers, Waterways Experiment Station, Instruction Report EL-83-2, Vicksburg, Mississippi.

Neves, R. J., and S. N. Moyer. 1988. Evaluation of techniques for age determination of freshwater mussels (Unionidae). American Malacological Bulletin 6:179–188.

Nicola, S. J., and A. J. Cordova. 1973. Effects of fin removal on survival and growth of rainbow trout (*Salmo gairdneri*) in a natural environment. Transactions of the American Fisheries Society 102:753–758.

Nielson, B. R. 1990. Twelve-year overview of fluorescent grit marking of cutthroat trout in Bear Lake, Utah–Idaho. American Fisheries Society Symposium 7:42–46.

Peterson, C. H., P. B. Duncan, H. C. Summerson, and G. W. Safrit, Jr. 1983. A mark–recapture test of annual periodicity of internal growth band deposition in shells of hard clams, *Mercenaria mercenaria*, from a population along the southeastern United States. U.S. National Marine Fisheries Service Fishery Bulletin 81:765–779.

Phinney, D. E., D. M. Miller, and M. L. Dahlberg. 1967. Mass-marking young salmonids with fluorescent pigment. Transactions of the American Fisheries Society 96:157–162.

Ropers, J. W., D. S. Jones, S. A. Murawski, F. M. Serchuk, and A. Jearld, Jr. 1984. Documentation of annual growth lines in ocean quahogs, *Arctica islandica* Linne. U.S. National Marine Fisheries Service Fishery Bulletin 82:1–19.

Stolte, L. W. 1973. Differences in survival and growth of marked and unmarked coho salmon. Progressive Fish-Culturist 35:229–230.

Welch, H. E., and K. H. Mills. 1981. Marking fish by scarring soft fin rays. Canadian Journal of Fisheries and Aquatic Sciences 38:1168–1170.

Wydoski, R., and L. Emery. 1983. Tagging and marking. Pages 215–237 *in* L. A. Nielsen and D. L. Johnson, editors. Fisheries techniques. American Fisheries Society, Bethesda, Maryland.

Chapter 5

Internal Tags

5.1 INTRODUCTION

The internal tag is a shrinking resource—literally. During the several decades that internal tags (tags completely embedded in the animal's body) have been used, the tags have become smaller and smaller. The most popular internal tag, and no doubt the most frequently applied tag in the world, is the coded wire tag, a tiny piece of thin wire barely visible to the human eye.

Early internal tags were much larger, consisting of rectangular metal or plastic plates several centimeters long and wide (McFarlane et al. 1990). The tags were inserted into the body cavity or embedded shallowly between the skin and musculature, avoiding many problems caused by early external tags. For example, internal tags were highly successful for tagging herrings, a group that does not react well to many traditional external tags (Jacobsson 1970). They have decreased in popularity due to changes in tagging needs and to the increased availability of other specialized tags. Recent reviews of tagging methods, for example, have covered traditional internal tags only superficially (Jones 1979; Wydoski and Emery 1983); this review will do the same.

Scientists, however, have continued to believe in the fundamental advantages of internal tags. Their faith has been rewarded by the invention of miniature internal tags that have succeeded or appear likely to succeed in many situations. Although internal tags all share the feature of being totally embedded within the animal, their other characteristics vary widely depending on the size, structure, and location of the tag.

The market for small internal tags is dominated today by the *coded wire tag,* a magnetized, stainless-steel wire bearing distinctive notches (Figure 5.1). Traditionally, animals known to contain coded wire tags had to be sacrificed, but today tags can be dissected from some tissue without loss of the animals. The codes are then deciphered under a microscope.

Two other types of miniature internal tags are gaining popularity because they can be read without sacrificing the animal. The *passive integrated transponder* (PIT) is so small and electronically sophisticated that it would please even James Bond's gadget maker. It contains an antenna and a preprogrammed computer chip. When activated by an external energy source, the transponder emits a radio signal that is translated into a unique code for the tagged animal.

The *visible implant* tag is an elegant invention. The tag is a small rectangular disk, usually plastic, printed with a unique code. It is embedded in transparent tissue on the animal's body, so that it can be read by an observer with no special tools other than keen eyesight.

These modern tags reveal the revolution currently underway in tagging technology. Sophisticated electronic and materials technologies have arrived in fisheries, with extraordinary results. This revolution is likely to continue. Without question, miniaturized tags like these represent the future of animal marking. Smaller, more informative, and more versatile internal tags will be invented and improved regularly in coming decades.

5.2   ASSUMPTIONS FOR MODERN INTERNAL TAGS

A basic assumption underlying use of any tag is that the tag does not affect an animal's growth, survival, or behavior. This is probably valid for modern miniaturized tags. Although some danger exists that the tagging process will injure the animal or that the embedded tag will irritate the surrounding tissues, these concerns are surely less serious with internal tags than with external tags. As the tags have become smaller, the negative effects have also presumably become smaller. Internal tagging should be performed as carefully and conscientiously as other tagging, however, because all tagging processes can be traumatic to the animals and because an improperly inserted tag can damage internal organs. Also, because the character of internal tags, the techniques of their insertion, the range of species with which they can be used, and the number of animals that can be marked per unit time all are changing rapidly, the normal caution in applying tags and monitoring their effects should be heightened during the internal-tagging revolution. Learn from the experiences of others, but take nothing for granted.

The principal operational assumption is that all tagged animals will be identified as such. This involves two separate conditions—that all tags will be retained and that all retained tags will be identified. Tag retention is described below in detail, but it varies depending on the species, age, and stage of maturation of the animal and on where the tag is located in the body. As new versions of internal tags are developed and applied to an increasing array of taxa, tag retention also must be evaluated and reported continuously.

The second condition is that all animals retaining tags will be properly identified as such. This assumption is likely to be violated to some extent for internal tags simply because most of them are not externally visible and all of them are purposefully small. For this reason, the presence of an internal tag is usually indicated indirectly, via a secondary mark or an automated detection device. Most studies have used fin clips as secondary marks, but the regeneration of clipped fins and the natural loss of fins can cause errors in the detection of internally tagged fish (see Chapter 4). Automatic detection devices, such as magnets, also have expected failure rates, which often change capriciously under field conditions. The methods for tag detection, therefore, must be carefully chosen and scrupulously monitored.

5.3   CODED WIRE TAGS

5.3.1   General Description

Coded wire tagging was invented in the early 1960s to monitor returns of hatchery-raised salmonids to the fishery several years later (Jefferts et al. 1963). It

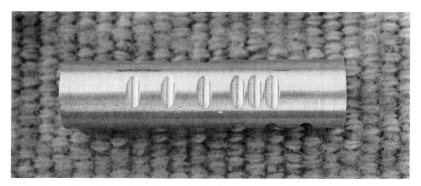

Figure 5.1 An enlarged model of a coded wire tag, showing the information-carrying notches on the wire. Each tag contains a standard marker (the "master word") that signifies the starting point for reading the code.

represents one of the more sophisticated and capital-intensive techniques in use today. Coded wire tags are used widely because of their assumed negligible effects on the tagged animals and their relatively low cost in large tagging programs.

The coded-wire-tagging system is most commonly used for assembly-line marking of small animals. Tags are intended to remain within the animal indefinitely, allowing identification of the animal at any time in the life cycle. Consequently, coded wire tags are ideal for long-term population-level assessments such as stock identification, recruitment success, and migration patterns. Large-scale releases of hatchery salmonids, primarily in the Pacific Northwest, routinely include millions of fish tagged with coded wires. More than 400 million fish have been tagged with coded wires in the past 25 years.

5.3.2 Advantages of Coded Wire Tags (Box 5.1)

A major advantage of coded wire tags is their minor effect on the biological condition or response of tagged animals. The tag itself is very small (usually 1.1 mm long and 0.25 mm in diameter; Figure 5.1), and its injection into the animal causes little direct tissue damage (Bergman et al. 1968; Bordner et al. 1990). The tagging wound is also small and heals rapidly (Buckley and Blankenship 1990). The absence of a protruding and visible tag eliminates effects on swimming, behavioral interactions with other animals, predator avoidance, and ability to use preferred habitat. The absence of a protrusion also means no increased mortality from tangling in nets.

Tagging-related immediate mortality is generally low, and few effects on growth have been reported. The typical placement of the tag in the snout of a fish has the potential to increase mortality, reduce growth, and damage olfactory tissue if the tag is implanted too deeply (Fletcher et al. 1987; Peltz and Miller 1990); this may be problematic for salmonids, which use olfactory clues to guide their spawning migrations (Morrison and Zajac 1987). Responses of crustaceans to coded wire tags have varied, apparently in response to tagging site and molting stage. For example, Prentice and Rensel (1977) showed no difference in growth, survival, or molting frequency of tagged and untagged spot shrimp. Hurley et al. (1990) also reported no short-term effects of tagging in the walking leg of snow crabs, but noted higher frequency of deformity and leg loss after molting.

Box 5.1   Advantages and Disadvantages of Coded Wire Tags

Advantages

- Little effect on growth, behavior, or mortality
- Absence of protruding tag
- Suitable for long-term studies
- Suitable for all sizes and life stages
- Suitable for most fishes and crustaceans
- High tag retention
- Designed for large-scale marking
- Strong commercial service and technical advice

Disadvantages

- Variable immediate tagging mortality
- Variable effect on crustacean molting and appendage deformation
- Tagging location must be determined for each taxon
- Customized tagging equipment and routine needed for each taxon
- Detailed training and supervision of taggers needed
- Extensive tag detection process
- Animals usually must be sacrificed
- Individual marks not generally available
- Capital- and labor-intensive

Coded wire tags are especially useful on small animals. Because the tag is small, both the tag and the tagging process make minor intrusions into the body. Tags are available in a half-length size (0.5 mm long), allowing their use on even smaller animals (but reducing the coding area of the tag). Blankenship (1990) recommended that half-length tags be used for fish smaller than 2.1 g; pink salmon as small as 0.25 g have been tagged successfully (Thrower and Smoker 1984). Tagging very small fish requires extra care, however, because damage to the olfactory tissue is more likely (Morrison and Zajac 1987). Nevertheless, coded wire tags are appropriate for early-life studies, which are particularly needed in fisheries management.

Coded wire tags are especially useful for long-term studies. The tags can be placed on animals early in the life span, they do not interfere with subsequent growth of the animals, and they remain readable indefinitely. Thus, coded wires can be used to trace recruitment, migration, and distribution patterns.

Coded wire tagging has been reported as successful on more than 20 genera of fishes (Buckley and Blankenship 1990) and on various macroinvertebrates (Krouse and Nutting 1990; Table 5.1). No doubt the technique has been used successfully on many more taxa than are listed in Table 5.1. As large-scale hatchery programs become more common, coded wire tagging will become more widely practiced (e.g., Bumguardner et al. 1990; Dunning et al. 1990; Morrison 1990). Although the optimum location for tag placement must be determined for each taxon, there is no reason why coded wire tags should not be tried on all fishes and crustaceans, and on other vertebrates and invertebrates.

Table 5.1 Taxa successfully tagged with implanted coded wire tags, modified from Fletcher et al. (1987), Buckley and Blankenship (1990), and Krouse and Nutting (1990).

Taxon	Tag location
Fishes	
Anchovies (*Stolephorus*)	Nasal cartilage
Catfishes (*Ictalurus*)	Nasal cartilage, opercular muscle, nape muscle
Chars (*Salvelinus*)	Nasal cartilage
Cichlids (*Tilapia*)	Nasal cartilage, body muscle
Codfishes (*Gadus, Theragra*)	Opercular muscle
Drums (*Sciaenops*)	Opercular muscle
Goatfishes (*Mulloidichthys*)	Opercular muscle, adipose eyelid
Graylings (*Thymallus*)	Nasal cartilage
Greenlings (*Ophiodon*)	Nasal cartilage
Herrings (*Clupea*)	Nape muscle
Jacks (*Caranx*)	Opercular muscle, adipose eyelid
Minnows (*Notemigonus, Ptychocheilus*)	Nasal cartilage, opercular muscle, nape muscle
Paddlefishes (*Polyodon*)	Rostrum
Perches (*Stizostedion*)	Nasal cartilage, opercular muscle
Pikes (*Esox*)	Opercular muscle
Salmon (*Oncorhynchus, Salmo*)	Nasal cartilage
Scorpionfishes (*Sebastes*)	Opercular muscle
Snappers (*Lutjanus*)	Opercular muscle, adipose eyelid, cornea
Snooks (*Centropomus*)	Opercular muscle
Sturgeons (*Acipenser*)	Nasal cartilage, first dorsal scute
Sunfishes (*Lepomis, Micropterus*)	Interorbital dermis, opercular muscle
Temperate basses (*Morone*)	Nasal cartilage, body muscle
Whitefishes (*Coregonus*)	Nasal cartilage
Invertebrates	
Snow crab	Walking leg
Lobsters (*Homarus*)	Walking leg
Spot shrimp	Thoracic sinus

Tag retention rates are generally high. Short-term retention has generally exceeded 90% in reported studies (Table 5.2). Most tag loss occurs soon after tagging, presumably because of improper tagging technique (Bailey and Dufour 1987) or poor choice of tagging location. Sequential surveys of tag loss generally show the most rapid loss in the first 3–4 weeks after tagging; later, tag loss is very low (Blankenship 1990). Proper selection of the tagging location and orientation, and continuous attention to the quality of tagging rather than to the speed, are important factors in reducing tag loss (see below).

Coded wire tagging is an integrated, efficient system for mass-marking large numbers of fish. Tagging rates of 1,000 animals per hour at one station are possible if an experienced crew and sufficient crew members are available to supply and process the animals. Equipment, supplies, and experience exist for a growing number of taxa and data needs. Because the coded wire tag is a highly successful commercial product, technical advice and service are readily available from tag manufacturers and their representatives.

5.3.3 Disadvantages of Coded Wire Tags (Box 5.1)

As with all taggings, the success of a coded-wire-tagging program depends on assuring high rates of tag retention. Retention of coded wire tags depends on two factors—the tagging site and the tagging routine.

Table 5.2 Examples of tag retention rates for coded wire tags in various fishes and crustaceans.

Species	Tag location	Short term Interval (days)	Short term Retention rate (%)	Long term Interval (days)	Long term Retention rate (%)	Reference
White sturgeon	Snout (shallow)	5	81	180	61	Bordner et al. (1990)
	Snout (deep)	5	100	180	100	
	Dorsal muscle	5	100	180	100	
Channel catfish	Snout			180	97	Cook et al. (1990)
Bluegill	Snout			180	97	Cook et al. (1990)
Walleye	Snout			180	98	Cook et al. (1990)
Largemouth bass	Snout			180	97	Cook et al. (1990)
	Cheek (vertical)			63	100	Fletcher et al. (1987)
Striped bass	Snout	14	98	≥63	65	Dunning et al. (1990)
	Cheek (horizontal)	14	30	≥63	30	
	Cheek (vertical)	14	91	≥63	91	
	Dorsal muscle	14	99	≥49	99	
Red drum	Cheek	1	67	91	44	Bumguardner et al. (1990)
Atlantic herring	Dorsal muscle			180	93	Morrison (1990)
Coho salmon	Snout			≥121	96	Blankenship (1990)
Chinook salmon	Snout			≥178	98	Blankenship (1990)
Pink salmon	Snout	≥20	95	≥365	65	Kaill et al. (1990)
Spot shrimp	Thoracic sinus			180	95	Prentice and Rensel (1977)
Snow crab	Walking leg	≥29	95			Bailey and Dufour (1987)

The standard tagging sites for fish are the tissues of the snout and cheek. The snout location was perfected for salmonids, which have dense cartilaginous, muscle and connective tissue in this region, providing a solid matrix for the embedded tag. Thus, salmonids generally have very high tag retention rates. Snout tissue is less acceptable for other taxa that have large sinuses or other characteristics that may allow movement of the tags (Fletcher et al. 1987). Cheek and nape muscles have been tested most often as alternative tagging sites, with variable results depending on the orientation (vertical or horizontal), angle of insertion, and species (Bumguardner et al. 1990; Dunning et al. 1990). A microanatomical examination of the tissues at candidate tagging sites is desirable, therefore, before a tagging site is chosen. Current experiments with inserting coded wires in adipose eye tissue, fin rays, and adipose fins suggest that potential tagging sites on fishes have not been exhausted.

The tagging routine also affects tag retention rates. Although tagging itself is a repetitive mechanical process, its success depends on careful attention to several details. Head molds, for example, may be used to hold the fish in position as the tagging needle enters the animal and inserts the tag. Custom molds are needed for each species and each size range of fish. Using head molds that are too large, too small, or the wrong shape will cause higher tag loss rates (Cook et al. 1990). Consequently, several head molds may be needed if fish vary in size, and fish must be graded. Also, when crustaceans are tagged, the wire may be pulled out of the animal as the tagging needle is withdrawn (Prentice and Rensel 1977; Bailey and Dufour 1987). The routine nature of the operation itself, designed for marking many animals quickly, can impair quality and subsequent retention. If the tagging machines are not kept clean and carefully adjusted, the tags may be inserted at improper depths and angles.

Detecting coded wire tags is an involved process because the tags are internal. Two primary tag detection systems are used. First, an external mark may be placed on the animal. An adipose fin clip is the standard mark on salmonids, and barbel clips have been used on sturgeons (Bordner et al. 1990). Because some clipped fins regenerate and because natural loss of fins and other structures occurs, external marks may introduce error into estimates of tag retention and into estimates of biological statistics based on tag return rates (Blankenship 1990).

The second method of tag detection uses magnetic field detectors to scan each captured animal in the field. The detecting sensor can be used either on captured animals or on animals passing a fixed station, such as a weir or fishway. The sensor detects the magnetic field associated with the tag to indicate its presence. With captured animals, this is a time-consuming process and, in the field, it is prone to errors. Older tag detectors have varying sensitivities that are affected by position in the boat, vibrations, and nearby magnetic objects (Mattson et al. 1990). Other objects embedded in animals, such as fish hooks, also cause false positive readings. Conversely, the angle of the tag to the sensor may cause false negative readings. Care must be taken to assure proper adjustment of electronic tag detection systems used in the field—by testing magnetized standards in the system at regular intervals, for example (Morrison 1990).

Reading the code on a wire tag usually requires sacrificing the animal. Although this is not a significant problem for analysis of commercial or recreational catches, it typically precludes the use of these tags in studies of rare species or valuable animals such as brood stock. Buckley and Blankenship (1990) and Haw et al. (1990) suggested that coded wire tags can be placed shallowly in muscle tissue so the tags can be removed surgically without sacrificing the animal, but this method is new and not commonly practiced.

Coded wire tags generally allow group identification only. Hence, they are most useful for stock- or population-level studies, not for studies of individual animals. Because many agencies use coded wire tags, especially in the Pacific Northwest, tagging programs must be carefully coordinated so that all tag codes are unique to one group at large at a time (see Chapter 2). Furthermore, the specialized handling of wire tags for decoding and data processing in large-scale programs often means that results will not be available until long after field collection.

As commonly practiced, coded wire tagging requires capital-intensive, technology-intensive, and knowledge-intensive systems. An injector for high-speed tagging, with electronic quality control, and a field sampling detector cost about US $16,000 in 1992. Consequently, coded wire tagging usually must be performed on a large scale to be economically efficient. For large programs, temporary tagging crews must be trained and supervised by experienced permanent personnel; volunteer programs are unlikely to be effective. In the state of Washington, where millions of salmonids are tagged annually, tagging units are built into portable trailers which can be moved among hatcheries (Schurman and Thompson

1990). Well-organized tagging units like those increase tagging rates and reduce tag loss and fish stress.

Coded wire tagging also can be used for smaller projects, with correspondingly lower costs. Hand-held tag injectors and rented detectors make coded wire tags accessible for short-term projects. As with most commercial products enjoying an expanding market, the relative price of coded wire tags continues to decline and their applicability continues to broaden with time.

5.3.4   Applying and Reading a Coded Wire Tag (Figure 5.2)

5.3.4.1   Tagging Environment (Large-Scale Projects)

The tagging process for mass marking depends on an efficient and effective physical facility. The facility must include holding tanks, anesthetic tanks, marking machines, quality control devices, and recovery tanks. Tagging trailers like those of Schurman and Thompson (1990), shown in Figure 5.3, are designed for rapid and low-stress tagging. Although such elaborate settings are not available everywhere, careful attention always must be given to reducing the number of times each animal is handled and the time it is out of water. Because this technique is usually used with young, small individuals, handling can be particularly traumatic. Holding water must be monitored to assure that it exceeds minimum standards at all times and must be changed as needed.

Because tag retention depends on skillful application of the tags, tagging crew members require specific training (Kaill et al. 1990). Experience has shown that tagging skills are quickly gained, but that the crew supervisor must constantly control tagging quality. Because coded wire tagging is a mass-marking process, taggers may subconsciously quicken their pace, with considerable loss of quality. Tagging crews also may compete for speed.

Variation in skill and technique among taggers is inevitable, and this variation can bias results if it is ignored. Therefore, animals should be delivered to taggers in a random way (or taggers should move among stations) to assure that all animals of one species, size, raceway, or experimental treatment are not all tagged by the same person.

Fish usually must be anesthetized before tagging (see Chapter 2). If extensive pretagging treatment is needed—for example, to clip the adipose fin or to grade the fish precisely into size groups—double anesthesia may be needed. In such cases, fish are anesthetized for the first operations, allowed to recover while awaiting tagging, and then anesthetized a second time for tagging (Schurman and Thompson 1990). The numbers of fish anesthetized should be matched to the rate of tagging so fish are not held in anesthesia longer than is necessary.

The tagging process works efficiently if all elements of the tagging equipment (tags, head molds, etc.) are in place and tested. Because coded wire tagging is a complex process, considerable set-up time and repeated practice runs are needed before actual tagging begins. During tagging, efficiency requires a continuous supply of fish to the tagging station. Taggers must monitor the supply and condition of the fish and instruct the other crew members to increase or decrease their speeds.

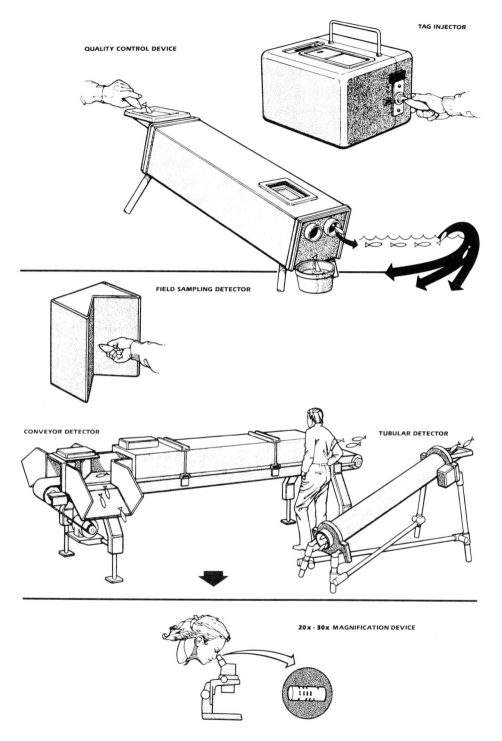

Figure 5.2 The binary-coded-wire tagging system includes a tag injector and a quality control device, used before the fish are released, and detection and sorting devices for recovered fish. Tags are read with a microscope. Illustration courtesy of Northwest Marine Technology.

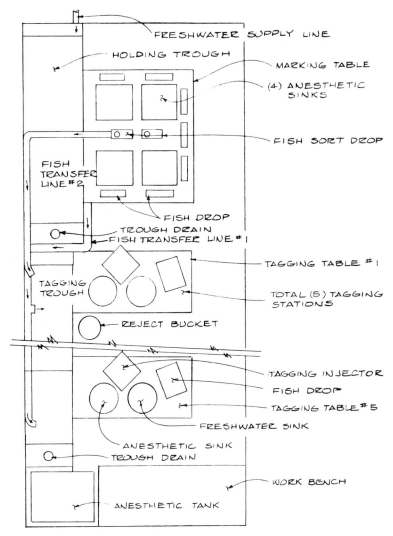

Figure 5.3 Floor plan for a portable tagging trailer, reprinted from Schurman and Thompson (1990). Marking tables are places where fish are anesthetized, fin-clipped, sorted to size, and then routed to the tagging station fitted with proper size head mold. Fish are tagged at the tagging tables, and pass through a quality control device before being returned to the hatchery raceway or other holding tank.

5.3.4.2 Tag Injection

The coded wire tag is injected into the fish by a slender needle attached to a machine that feeds a continuous supply of tags to the needle (Figure 5.4). The worker positions the fish as desired and triggers a switch to activate the needle, injecting the tag. The manufacturer's directions for operating, adjusting, and maintaining the tagging apparatus should be followed precisely. As mentioned earlier, hand-held injectors also are available, designed for single or semiautomatic tagging.

The best injection site should be determined experimentally for those species

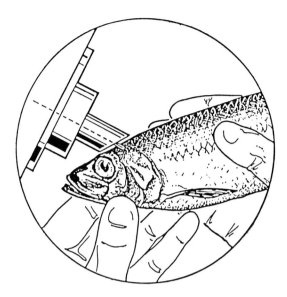

Figure 5.4 Tagging needle entering the nape muscle of an Atlantic herring. Reprinted from Morrison (1990).

without well-accepted standard sites. Although the snout is the most common site for salmonids, many other locations have been used, including cheek and nape muscles (Dunning et al. 1990). For species eaten by humans, tags usually are placed in locations not likely to be consumed. Crustaceans with massive legs, like snow crabs and lobsters, can be tagged effectively in the dactylus of the walking legs (Bailey and Dufour 1987; Krouse and Nutting 1990). Bailey and Dufour (1987) used different legs as tagging sites for different groups of animals, increasing the number of groups that could be distinguished with the same tagging code. Prentice and Rensel (1977) placed tags in the thoracic sinus of spot shrimp.

Holding the fish in the proper position relative to the path and depth of the injecting needle is essential for good tag retention and minimal tissue damage to the fish. Most tagging programs, therefore, use molds that guide the fish into position for tagging. The mold must be the correct size and shape for the particular species and size of fish being tagged. Duke (1980), for example, recommended creating head molds for three size ranges of salmonids (50–90, 70–140, and 110–300 mm); if 98% of the fish to be tagged fell within one of the size ranges, then no grading was necessary. Generally, the mold should be as small and nonrestricting as possible, reducing the extent of contact between the fish and the mold (Cook et al. 1990; Figure 5.5). An alternative for cheek or nape tagging is to use a fixed needle fitted with a collar that assures proper depth of tag injection (Fletcher et al. 1987).

For fish tagged in cheek muscle (e.g., centrarchids, percichthyids, cyprinids), the tag should be injected parallel to the muscle striations. For crustaceans, the tag should be injected sufficiently deep that it is embedded well below the molting membrane. If possible, crustaceans should be tagged early in the molt cycle, assuring that the tag is not placed accidentally in the enlarging space between the existing and the developing exoskeleton (Krouse and Nutting 1990).

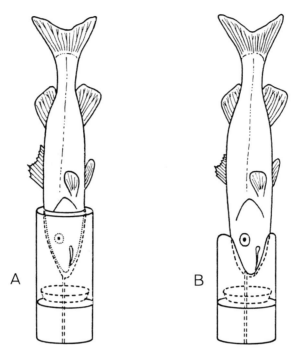

Figure 5.5 Alternative styles of head molds. (**A**) The head mold surrounds the fish's head completely; (**B**) the head mold is cut away to reduce contact with the fish and to accommodate a larger size range of specimens. Other head molds are designed to hold the fish with its mouth open. Reprinted from Cook et al. (1990).

5.3.4.3   Posttagging Treatment

After being tagged, each animal should be passed through a quality control device or field sampling detector that indicates if a tag is in place and is magnetized. Animals failing this test can be retagged or removed from the sample. Alternatively, a sample can be tested at frequent and regular intervals to check quality control and to determine data adjustment rates (if needed). Treatment with an antibiotic solution in the recovery tank may be also desirable (see Chapter 2), depending on the extent of handling.

Periodically during tagging, a sample of animals should be sacrificed for histological or X-ray examination to determine the placement of tags. A sample of animals should be held overnight and rechecked the following day to determine immediate tag retention rates. Although most tag loss occurs within a few days after tagging, a sample of several hundred fish should be retained for 3–4 weeks to test the long-term retention of tags (Duke 1980). These tests are particularly important when new species, sizes, tagging sites, equipment, and techniques are being used.

Large-scale operations involving hatchery stocks require thorough disinfection of tagging facilities and equipment after each tagging operation (Duke 1980).

5.3.4.4   Tag Detection

Tags are detected in two ways. First, an external mark can be placed on the tagged animal (e.g., an adipose fin clip). Marked animals can be separated from a

SALMON FISHERMEN!

HELP IMPROVE SALMON FISHING AND EARN UP TO $50.00 FOR THE HEAD OF AN <u>ADIPOSE</u> <u>FIN</u> <u>MARKED</u> <u>AND</u> <u>TAGGED</u> <u>COHO</u> (silver) SALMON, or <u>CHINOOK</u> (blackmouth, king) SALMON.

Several million experimental salmon have been released in Washington, each with a tiny wire tag implanted in the head and the adipose fin removed. Heads of tagged salmon qualify for a share of a monthly reward. <u>Do not</u> attempt to remove the tiny tag from the head of a marked fish. Each tag, although only the size of a fragment of hair, bears a coded "message" that identifies one of many test groups.

COHO (SILVER) SALMON

CODED WIRE TAG

IDENTIFIES TEST GROUP

MISSING ADIPOSE FIN IDENTIFIES TAGGED SALMON

CHINOOK (BLACKMOUTH, KING) SALMON

IF YOUR SALMON IS MISSING THE ADIPOSE FIN—
1. REMOVE THE FISH'S HEAD
2. TURN IN THE HEAD AT:_____

Figure 5.6 Poster asking anglers to leave fish heads and information about their catch. Such signs at major marinas can greatly increase the recapture sample of fish tagged with coded wires.

catch, the heads (or other tagged body part) removed and saved, and the rest of the animals returned to the angler or commercial fisher. Anglers are often asked to leave heads of fin-clipped fish at a central collection point so the coded wire tags can be removed later (Figure 5.6). Reward systems generally increase the return of tagged animals by fishers (see Chapter 2).

Second, if no external mark is used, then all captured animals must be passed through a tag detector. Because tag orientation varies and because tags may move during the life of the animal, each animal should be passed through older style

Box 5.2   Decoding a Coded Wire Tag

Coded wire tags contain information in the form of notches arranged in rows along the wire. The notches represent a binary code—the same kind used by digital computers. Although some variation in the coding occurs, most coded wire tags now use a standard "six-bit word."

The binary code represents numbers, but in a different format from the familiar decimal system. In decimal format, each place can have 10 different values (0 to 9) and, consequently, each place increases in value by an order of 10. Thus, the symbol "402" is really a code like this:

Place	100s	10s	1s
Number	4	0	2

In binary code, the places are called "bits," and each bit can have only two values (0 or 1). Therefore, each bit increases in value by an order of two. For a six-bit word (that is, one with six places), the successive bits represent values like this:

Bit	32s	16s	8s	4s	2s	1s

On coded wire tags, the absence of a notch represents 0 and the presence of a notch represents 1. Thus, a six-bit word with notches in this pattern

Bit	32s	16s	8s	4s	2s	1s
Notch	1	1		1	1	1

would equal the sum of 32, 16, 4, 2, and 1, or 55. The different notching patterns using six bits can represent numbers from 1 (with a single notch in the 1s bit) to 63 (with a notch in each bit).

On a coded wire tag, seven bits are actually present. The first bit is the "check," which does not represent a numerical value but serves a quality control function. By convention, each word must have an odd number of notches. If the numerical value represented uses an even number of notches, then the required extra notch is placed in the check bit.

Each coded wire tag contains four different six-bit words. Each word is arrayed down the length of the wire, repeating continuously. These four strings of notches are spaced 90° apart, as shown here in cross section:

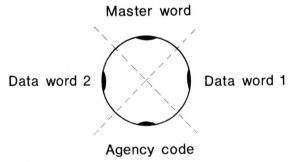

Master word

Data word 2   Data word 1

Agency code

As tags are injected into an animal, they are cut to standard lengths from a continuous wire. Each tag is long enough to contain the entire code, but the starting place is not necessarily the same on each tag. A reference is needed,

Continued.

Box 5.2 Continued.

therefore, on each tag. The reference is the "master word." The master word has the same code on all tags and also has an extra notch between the 2s and 1s bit. The master word always has this notch code:

Bit	ck	32s	16s	8s	4s	2s	1s
Notch		1	1	1	1	1	1

This distinctive pattern (especially the extra notch) allows the master word to be instantly identified. The rest is easy. The tag is oriented so the master word is readable from left to right, as shown above. Rotating the tag upward then reveals successively the three other rows. The first row contains data word 1, the second row contains the agency code, and the third row contains data word 2. The complete code for a tag, therefore, might look like this:

Bit	ck	32s	16s	8s	4s	2s	1s		
Master word			1	1	1	1	1	1		
Data word 1	1		1			1			=	18
Agency code		1		1	1				=	44
Data word 2			1	1	1	1	1		=	31

The agency code identifies which organization has tagged the animal. Data words 1 and 2 represent specific data about the animal as chosen by the tagging agency for the particular study. For example, data word 1 might tell the tagging year, and data word 2 might identify the animal's stock origin.

detectors in several positions (Bordner et al. 1990); newer detectors are more sensitive and can detect tags regardless of orientation. For some large-scale fisheries, automatic detection and sorting devices may be necessary. These systems can be compatible with the speed needed for commercial fish processing, but the rate of tag detection will be substantially below 100% (Morrison 1990).

Regardless of the detection method, a sample of animals in which a tag was not detected should be saved to determine error rate. This will generally require laboratory analysis, to determine if some tags are not detected in the field. Rates of nondetection can be high; Mattson et al. (1990) found as many as 7% undetected tags using a field detector.

5.3.4.5 Tag Recovery and Reading

In the laboratory, tags must be removed from the animal for analysis. Even if the only datum needed is presence or absence of a tag, the tag must be removed and identified. Researchers cannot assume that the embedded metal piece is one of their tags because fish hooks and other metallic particles can trigger the detection device and because fish may have been tagged by other researchers (Mattson et al. 1990).

The tag can be found by dividing the tissue sequentially into two pieces. Both are passed through the detector; the piece indicating presence of the tag is retained, the other is discarded. Repeating this process several times will produce a small tissue sample from which the tag can be dissected. The tag should be rolled with a finger on a piece of paper to remove clinging tissue. The tag must be handled carefully at this stage because it can be lost easily.

The identifying information is encoded in the notches on the tag. People reading the codes should be thoroughly trained in the decoding process. Although the technique is fundamentally easy with practice (Box 5.2), it is not intuitive, and a large number of codes may be possible. Dissecting a tag, reading the code under a dissecting microscope, and recording the data take a well-trained technician about 4 minutes (Buckley and Blankenship 1990). Multiple readings of at least some tags by different technicians provides quality control of decoding accuracy.

5.4 PASSIVE INTEGRATED TRANSPONDER TAGS

5.4.1 General Description

The passive integrated transponder, or PIT tag, is a recent invention that uses electronic circuitry to create a unique tagging system. The PIT tag is actually a miniature signal-relay station. The tiny PIT tag (12 mm long × 2.1 mm in diameter) carries no power source, but is energized by a strong external signal, similar to the way radio signals are sent from one signal tower to the next or from a ground station to a satellite and back again.

The system components include the tag, the energizing system, and the signal-receiving and -processing unit. The tag has an antenna of copper wire wound approximately 1,200 times around a cylindrical, ferromagnetic core (Figure 5.7). The coiled antenna is connected to an electronic chip, which produces the unique, preprogrammed signal when supplied with energy. The tag components are enclosed in a glass tube. The energizing system delivers energy to the tag by producing a magnetic field in the air or water. When the tag enters the magnetic field, its antenna induces an electric current in the core, which activates the chip and causes it to emit a signal in the 40–50 kHz range. A radio receiver hears the signal and transforms it into a unique, 10-digit, alphanumeric code (Prentice et al. 1990a).

Passive integrated transponders allow identification of animals without disturbing them, much like biotelemetric tags (see Chapter 7). Thus, PIT tags are especially useful for identifying individual animals with little or no handling. Such data are valuable for migration and movement studies, in which PIT-tagged animals can be monitored as they pass fixed receiving stations. They are also

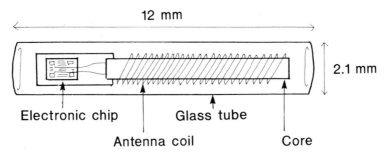

Figure 5.7 A passive integrated transponder (PIT) tag.

Box 5.3 Advantages and Disadvantages of PIT Tags

Advantages

- Probably little effect on growth, mortality, or behavior
- Suitable for many species
- Suitable on all sizes
- High retention rates
- Individual identification available
- Suitable for long-term studies
- No handling needed to identify animal
- Strong commercial interest

Disadvantages

- Limited documented experience available yet
- Short signal detection range
- Expert personnel needed
- Tags expensive

---

useful to identify important animals, such as research specimens whose behavior, growth, or other features must not be changed by the marking system. In breeding experiments, for example, where individual animals must be identified, PIT tags can allow all the animals to be kept in the same tank without external tags.

5.4.2 Advantages of PIT Tags (Box 5.3)

The small size and unobtrusive nature of PIT tags makes them usable on many species and sizes of animals. Although larger than coded wire tags, PIT tags are still much smaller than other conventional tags. They have been used successfully on salmon as small as 50 mm (Prentice et al. 1990a). Passive integrated transponder tags were first developed for salmonids, but they have been used successfully on crustaceans and other fishes (Prentice 1990). Medical researchers are beginning to use similar tags in their studies with rodents and other laboratory animals.

The tags generally are embedded totally within the animal, as are coded wire tags. Hence, the likelihood for substantial effects on an animal's life processes is low. The few reported studies of PIT tags have shown no effect on growth or survival (Prentice et al. 1987, 1990a; Jenkins and Smith 1990; Prentice 1990). The tagging wound heals quickly, with no unusual tissue damage at the tagging site (Prentice 1990).

Retention rates for PIT tags have been very high. The principal use of PIT tags has been on salmonids in the Pacific Northwest, where the tags have been inserted within the body cavities of fish as small as 2 g. Retention has been near 100% in these tests (Prentice et al. 1987, 1990a; Harvey and Campbell 1989; Prentice 1990). Retention rates for red drum and striped bass brood stock, tagged in the dorsal musculature, exceeded 97% (Jenkins and Smith 1990).

The greatest advantage of PIT tags is the ability to identify individual animals without sacrificing, or even touching, the animal. Current PIT circuitry allows 34 billion codes. Because the tags emit a code that is received remotely, the presence and identity of tagged animals are detected as the animals swim freely in tanks or natural environments. Because PIT tags have no batteries, the tags function until some component breaks. How long this may be is still unknown, but Prentice et al. (1990a) speculated that PIT tags may work beyond 10 years. Thus, a PIT tag can provide information from the tagged animal at many times and places during the animal's life. If the animal dies (and can be recovered), the tag can be extracted and used again.

Like coded wire tags, PIT tags have considerable commercial promise. Therefore, manufacturers are interested in improving the system based on user experience. Advances in PIT-tagging equipment and supplies are likely in coming years, along with reliable service and technical advice from manufacturers and representatives.

5.4.3 Disadvantages of PIT Tags (Box 5.3)

The principal disadvantages of PIT tags are their cost and the scarcity of reported experience about their use. The tags were introduced to fisheries in the early 1980s, and their use has been restricted mainly to the large-scale salmonid tagging programs in the Pacific Northwest. Many smaller-scale projects are using PIT tags throughout North America and in Europe and Asia. If these studies will corroborate the positive results reported for salmonids, PIT tagging will become increasingly common in future years. The unit cost of tags should decrease as a result.

The operational disadvantage of PIT tags is the small detection range of the signal. Because the tags are small, the emitted signals are weak and are currently detectable under optimal conditions at a maximum distance of 18 cm from the tag (Prentice et al. 1990b). Hand-held detectors used in the field have an even smaller range, currently about 7.6 cm. Consequently, the detection device must be quite close to the animals, requiring that the animals be herded into a shallow or narrow passageway. Detection systems at dams, for example, have been placed in narrow flumes or pipes through which migrating salmonids must pass (Prentice et al. 1990b).

Trained and experienced personnel are needed for both tagging and tag detection. Therefore, volunteers cannot operate a PIT-tagging program. A permanent tagging crew is probably desirable for any agency contemplating a large-scale program.

Like coded-wire-tagging systems, PIT tagging can be expensive. The basic equipment for a large-scale tagging and monitoring system costs about US $20,000, but simpler systems for smaller projects are available for about $2,000. The tags themselves are expensive because each is a complete electronic signalling unit. Depending on the quantity of tags purchased, tags can cost several dollars each. At this cost, PIT tags are generally most appropriate for tagging animals that are extremely valuable (for example, brood stock or endangered species), that provide extremely valuable data (for example, experimental animals), that have high posttagging survival rates, or that will be monitored repeatedly.

5.4.4 Inserting and Detecting a PIT Tag

5.4.4.1 Tagging Environment

The conditions for applying a PIT tag are similar to those for applying a coded wire tag. The environment must provide for high-quality water, anesthesia, quality control checking, and return to a holding environment. Given the substantial investment in each tagged animal, however, the emphasis must be on careful insertion of each tag and careful treatment of each tagged animal rather than on the assembly-line approaches typical of coded wire tagging.

If the tag will be placed in a fish's body cavity, the fish should be held without feeding for 2 days before tagging. This collapses the alimentary tract, reducing the danger of internal damage and reducing the possibility that internal pressure may force the tag back out through the path of the tagging needle.

5.4.4.2 Tag Insertion

Passive integrated transponders are inserted into an animal's body with a modified syringe fitted with a 12-gauge hypodermic needle. The needle is adapted with a plunger to inject the tag and with a terminal air hole to avoid injecting air into the body cavity or musculature (Prentice et al. 1990c). Alternatively, semiautomatic tag injectors, available commercially, can be used.

If the tag is to be inserted in the body cavity, Prentice et al. (1990c) suggested that the needle be inserted just off the midventral line of the body, posterior of the pectoral fin insertion. The needle should be inserted toward the posterior and at a 45° angle to the long axis of the body (Figure 5.8). When the needle penetrates the body musculature, it should be positioned parallel to the long axis of the body. The tag is then pushed into the body cavity via the plunger or tag injector. The needle then is removed. The tag should lie just anterior of the pelvic girdle after insertion. Practice tagging and subsequent dissection of several specimens will be necessary to perfect the optimum tagging location and insertion procedure. With this technique, Prentice et al. (1990c) reported tagging 150 fish per hour with hand-held needles and 300 fish per hour with semiautomatic tagging machines.

For intramusculature tagging, Jenkins and Smith (1990) inserted the tag in the dorsal muscles, posterior of the dorsal fin, of red drums. They chose that site because of the small size of scales and the low likelihood of damage to internal organs.

5.4.4.3 Posttagging Treatment

Immediately after tagging, the animal must be passed through the tag detection system to assure that a tag is present and functioning properly and to record the specific code for that tag. Treatment of tagged fish with an antibiotic may be desirable (see Chapter 2).

Fish tagged in the body cavity should be held on a maintenance diet for 3 days in order to prevent dislodging of the tag by an expanded stomach or intestine (Prentice et al. 1990c). Before release, the fish can be passed through the detection unit again to assure that a functioning tag is present.

As mentioned for coded wire tagging, the equipment and facilities used for PIT tagging should be thoroughly disinfected between tagging operations. This is particularly important for hatchery-based tagging, because transmission of pathogens between hatcheries can be catastrophic.

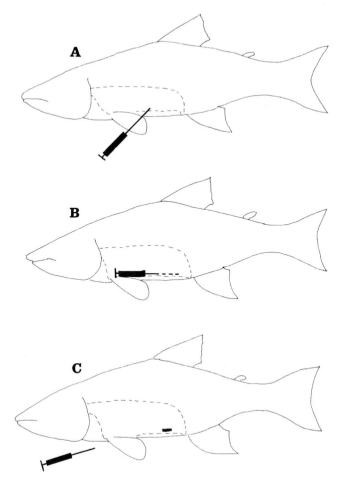

Figure 5.8 Proper placement of a PIT tag into a fish's body cavity involves **(A)** inserting the tagging needle into the body musculature at a 45° angle, **(B)** positioning the needle parallel to the fish's long body axis, and **(C)** pushing the tag from the needle as the needle is removed.

5.4.4.4 Tag Detection

Detecting a PIT tag is a simple process, but one that depends on a properly functioning detection system (often called the interrogation system). Fixed interrogation systems require a physical setting in which the animals pass near the detector, moving no faster than 4 m per second. Construction and operation of appropriate facilities require the advice of persons experienced in PIT-tagging operations.

Small-scale projects use a portable wand, containing both the energizing system (which emits a 400 kHz signal), and the receiver and processor. The signal can be seen directly as a 10-digit alphanumeric displayed on the portable wand, or it can be transferred to a printer and digital computer for later processing (Prentice et al. 1990c). Detection rates over 95% have been reported with these units. As stated earlier, the wand must be passed within 7.6 cm of the animal, to stimulate and

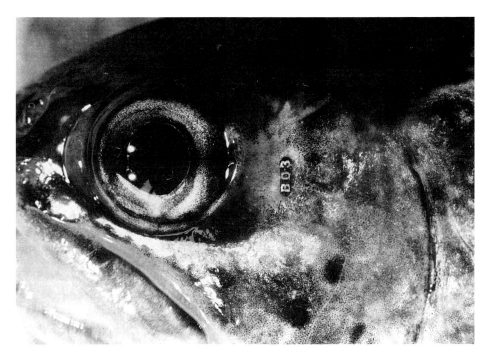

Figure 5.9 A visible implant tag embedded in the transparent tissues around the eye of a rainbow trout. Reprinted from Haw et al. (1990).

detect the signal. As with all equipment, regular quality control checks are necessary to assure proper performance.

5.5 NEW DEVELOPMENTS: VISIBLE IMPLANT TAGS

Most efforts to improve tagging in the near future will involve increasing the capabilities of internal tags. The advantages of internal tags over external tags are many, and improvements in detection ability will make internal tags more widely useful and less expensive.

The visible implant tag is a newly developed tag that attempts to combine the advantages of internal and external tags. The tag is placed entirely within the animal, like an internal tag, but is readable outside the animal, like an external tag. This seeming paradox is achieved by embedding the tag shallowly in transparent tissue (Figure 5.9).

Visible implant tags are usually small, flat rectangles, approximately 2–4 mm long, 0.5–2 mm wide, and 0.1 mm thick. They are coded with colors and a multidigit alphanumeric code, allowing individual identification of several thousand tagged animals in any single study. Fluorescent tags for group-only identification are also available. Although still in development, the tags appear to have little effect on the tagged animals, have a high retention rate, and remain readable for long periods (Haw et al. 1990).

The principal advantage of visible implant tags is that they can be read without sacrificing the animal, as can PIT tags. The tags were developed for salmonids, which have abundant transparent tissue around their eyes. Suitable tissues are present in other species as well, especially the thin and relatively unpigmented tissues of the head and adipose fins (Haw et al. 1990). The tagging system is not capital-intensive, and tags are inexpensive (between coded wire and PIT tags in price). The tags are inserted with a flattened needle adapted to hold a tag. Inserting the needle into the tissue creates a space for the tag, which is pushed into the space as the needle is withdrawn. Insertion is easy, although some experience is needed to assure that the tag is implanted at the right depth in the tissue. Tag detection requires only keen eyesight.

The principal disadvantage now is the preliminary nature of published information about visible implant tags. The range of applicability among species is unknown, and species-by-species testing will be necessary to determine the best tissues for tag implantation, inertness, retention, and readability over time. The techniques for applying the tags are still experimental, and new descriptions and equipment are made available regularly by the manufacturer. The tags themselves will undoubtedly undergo considerable evolution before optimal designs are created. Rapid development of the visible implant tag is likely, however, because of the conceptual advantages of a small externally readable tag that eliminates the disadvantages of traditional external tags.

5.6 REFERENCES

Bailey, R. F. J., and R. Dufour. 1987. Field use of an injected ferromagnetic tag on the snow crab (*Chionoecetes apilis o.* Fab.). Journal du Conseil, Conseil International pour l'Exploration de la Mer 43:237–244.

Bergman, P. K., K. B. Jefferts, H. F. Fiscus, and R. C. Hager. 1968. A preliminary evaluation of an implanted, coded wire fish tag. Washington Department of Fisheries, Fisheries Research Papers 3(1):63–84.

Blankenship, H. L. 1990. Effects of time and fish size on coded wire tag loss from chinook and coho salmon. American Fisheries Society Symposium 7:237–243.

Bordner, C. E., S. I. Doroshov, D. E. Hinton, R. E. Pipkin, R. B. Fridley, and Frank Haw. 1990. Evaluation of marking techniques for juvenile and adult white sturgeons reared in captivity. American Fisheries Society Symposium 7:293–303.

Buckley, R. M., and H. L. Blankenship. 1990. Internal extrinsic identification systems: overview of implanted wire tags, otolith marks, and parasites. American Fisheries Society Symposium 7:173–182.

Bumguardner, B. W., R. L. Colura, A. F. Maciorowski, and G. C. Matlock. 1990. Tag retention, survival, and growth of red drum fingerlings marked with coded wire tags. American Fisheries Society Symposium 7:286–292.

Cook, S. B., W. T. Davin, Jr., and R. C. Heidinger. 1990. Head mold design for coded wire tagging of selected spiny-rayed fingerling fishes. American Fisheries Society Symposium 7:281–285.

Duke, R. C. 1980. Fish tagging mobile unit: operation, repair, and service manual. Idaho Department of Fish and Game, Boise.

Dunning, D. J., Q. E. Ross, B. R. Friedmann, and K. L. Marcellus. 1990. Coded wire tag retention by, and tagging mortality of, striped bass reared at the Hudson River hatchery. American Fisheries Society Symposium 7:262–266.

Fletcher, D. H., F. Haw, and P. K. Bergman. 1987. Retention of coded-wire tags implanted into cheek musculature of largemouth bass. North American Journal of Fisheries Management 7:436–439.

Harvey, W. D., and D. L. Campbell. 1989. Retention of passive integrated transponder tags in largemouth bass brood fish. Progressive Fish-Culturist 51:164–166.

Haw, F., P. K. Bergman, R. D. Fralick, R. M. Buckley, and H. L. Blankenship. 1990. Visible implanted fish tag. American Fisheries Society Symposium 7:311–315.

Hurley, G. V., R. W. Elner, D. M. Taylor, and R. F. J. Bailey. 1990. Evaluation of snow crab tags retainable through molting. American Fisheries Society Symposium 7:84–93.

Jacobsson, J. 1970. On fish tags and tagging. Oceanography and Marine Biology: An Annual Review 8:457–499.

Jefferts, K. B., P. K. Bergman, and H. F. Fiscus. 1963. A coded wire identification system for macro-organisms. Nature (London) 198:460–462.

Jenkins, W. E., and T. I. J. Smith. 1990. Use of PIT tags to individually identify striped bass and red drum brood stocks. American Fisheries Society Symposium 7:341–345.

Jones, R. 1979. Materials and methods used in marking experiments in fishery research. FAO (Food and Agriculture Organization of the United Nations) Fisheries Technical Paper 190.

Kaill, W. M., K. Rawson, and T. Joyce. 1990. Retention rates of half-length coded wire tags implanted in emergent pink salmon. American Fisheries Society Symposium 7:253–258.

Krouse, J. S., and G. E. Nutting. 1990. Evaluation of coded microwire tags inserted in legs of small juvenile American lobsters. American Fisheries Society Symposium 7:304–310.

Mattson, M. T., B. R. Friedman, D. J. Dunning, and Q. E. Ross. 1990. Magnetic tag detection efficiency for Hudson River striped bass. American Fisheries Society Symposium 7:267–271.

McFarlane, G. A., R. S. Wydoski, and E. D. Prince. 1990. Historical review of the development of external tags and marks. American Fisheries Society Symposium 7:9–29.

Morrison, J., and D. Zajac. 1987. Histologic effect of coded wire tagging in chum salmon. North American Journal of Fisheries Management 7:439–441.

Morrison, J. A. 1990. Insertion and detection of magnetic microwire tags in Atlantic herring. American Fisheries Society Symposium 7:272–280.

Peltz, L., and J. Miller. 1990. Performance of half-length coded wire tags in a pink salmon hatchery marking program. American Fisheries Society Symposium 7:244–252.

Prentice, E. F. 1990. A new internal telemetry tag for fish and crustaceans. NOAA (National Oceanic and Atmospheric Administration) Technical Report NMFS (National Marine Fisheries Service) 85:1–9.

Prentice, E. F., T. A. Flagg, and S. McCutcheon. 1987. A study to determine the biological feasibility of a new fish tagging system, 1986–1987. Bonneville Power Administration, Portland, Oregon.

Prentice, E. F., T. A. Flagg, and C. S. McCutcheon. 1990a. Feasibility of using implantable passive integrated transponder (PIT) tags in salmonids. American Fisheries Society Symposium 7:317–322.

Prentice, E. F., T. A. Flagg, C. S. McCutcheon, and D. F. Brastow. 1990b. PIT-tag monitoring systems for hydroelectric dams and fish hatcheries. American Fisheries Society Symposium 7:323–334.

Prentice, E. F., T. A. Flagg, C. S. McCutcheon, D. F. Brastow, and D. C. Cross. 1990c. Equipment, methods, and an automated data-entry station for PIT tagging. American Fisheries Society Symposium 7:335–340.

Prentice, E. F., and J. E. Rensel. 1977. Tag retention of the spot prawn, *Pandalus platyceros,* injected with coded wire tags. Canadian Journal of Fisheries and Aquatic Sciences 34:2199–2203.

Schurman, G. C., and D. A. Thompson. 1990. Washington Department of Fisheries' mobile tagging units: construction and operation. American Fisheries Society Symposium 7:232–236.

Thrower, F. P., and W. W. Smoker. 1984. First adult return of pink salmon tagged as emergents with binary-coded wires. Transactions of the American Fisheries Society 113:803–804.

Wydoski, R., and L. Emery. 1983. Tagging and marking. Pages 215–237 *in* L. A. Nielsen and D. L. Johnson, editors. Fisheries techniques. American Fisheries Society, Bethesda, Maryland.

Chapter 6

Natural Marks

6.1 INTRODUCTION

Researchers have always sought natural ways to identify aquatic animals, spurred by the difficulties and expense of using artificial marks and tags. The existence of natural marks seems logical. After all, each of us can identify thousands of individual humans based on their appearance, and experts can distinguish among millions of humans based on fingerprints, dental patterns, and bumps on the head (well, maybe not bumps on the head).

Many natural features have been used as marks, but they can be divided into three basic groups. First, *morphometric marks* are those based on the shape, color, or markings of body features. The earliest and most successful morphometric marks have been scale patterns. Growing from work by Hjort on herrings in the 1910s, scale patterns have been used increasingly to identify Pacific salmon populations (McFarlane et al. 1990). Most of this chapter describes the use of scales and otoliths as natural morphometric marks.

Second, *meristic marks* are those based on intraspecific differences in the numbers of repeated tissue features, such as vertebrae, gill rakers, and fin rays. Third, *parasitic marks* are those based on the presence or absence of macroparasites in animals from different areas. Both meristic and parasitic marks are useful only in serendipitous situations, where the biological and environmental conditions create unique features coinciding with a management need. Consequently, neither type can be used as a common technique. Differences in the chemical composition of animal tissue also can be considered natural marks; these are covered in Chapter 9, Chemical Marks.

The primary value of natural marks is to distinguish among groups of animals. Except for unique color and scar patterns identifiable in special circumstances (e.g., on large marine mammals and intensively observed animals in small research populations), natural marks cannot readily distinguish individual animals. Thus, they have been used principally to assess the composition of mixtures of fish from different stocks, particularly for anadromous species (Wydoski and Emery 1983). Natural marks also can be used to distinguish hatchery fish from naturally spawned fish if the environments within the hatchery and the natural environment are sufficiently different to cause a consistent, recognizable mark.

The hatchery environment can be purposefully manipulated to create identifiable otolith or scale patterns that are unique for a specific hatchery, raceway, or treatment (chemical changes are also possible; see Chapter 9). Such marks may become highly useful for testing whether differences in hatchery practices produce beneficial outcomes, such as greater harvest rates for sport fishes or faster recovery times for endangered species.

6.2   ASSUMPTIONS FOR NATURAL MARKS

The assumptions for appropriate use of natural marks differ substantially from those for external and internal tags or marks. Most concerns about changes in growth, survival, and behavior because of tag insertion or presence are irrelevant, because the animal marks itself. The process of holding and handling animals in a hatchery can affect these characteristics, of course, so constant attention to treatment conditions is essential. The critical assumptions for natural marks, however, relate to the reliability of the natural feature used as a mark and to the statistical treatment of the mark-generated data.

First, natural marks must be present and stable throughout the time period under study. For example, if the mathematical ratio between length and girth is used as a morphometric mark, the ratio must remain constant across a wide range of sizes, seasons, and years. Similarly, a parasite used as a mark must be present throughout the time mark recoveries are made, rather than switching to an alternate host or becoming free-living during part of the year.

Most natural marks, however, lead inconsistent lives. Morphometric features are seldom consistent because genetic, environmental, and physiological factors affect them (Strauss and Bond 1990). As environmental conditions (such as water temperature and food supply) vary during the year and among years, ratios of morphometric measurements are likely to change. Furthermore, natural marks often become more difficult to identify on older animals as the mass of surrounding tissues increases and ages. For this reason, the stability of a natural mark must be verified for each species and environment before being accepted. This process may require several years, and even then unanticipated future conditions may negate the mark's reliability.

The second assumption is that a natural mark provides an unambiguous way to identify animals among groups. That is, the feature selected as a natural mark should have unique characteristics in different groups, providing a nonoverlapping rule for deciding in which group an animal belongs. If the mark is parasitic, for example, the parasite should be present in every individual for one group and in no individuals from all other groups. If the mark is meristic, such as vertebral count, every animal from one group should have more vertebrae than every animal from another.

Natural marks usually fail on this assumption also. As most taxonomic keys reveal, even the morphometric and meristic features used to separate species frequently overlap; success in identifying species often requires comparison of several features rather than one feature—and then an interpretation by an experienced taxonomist. The same situation exists for natural marks. Most marks rely on differences in the proportion of animals with a specific characteristic. For example, a parasite that occurred in 90% of animals in one stock and 10% of animals in another might be used as a natural mark.

The identification process for most natural marks, therefore, becomes statistical as well as observational. Individual animals often cannot be identified absolutely to one group or another, but groups of animals can be assigned proportionately to stocks, just as with genetic marks (see example in Chapter 8). Elaborate statistical processes have been developed for natural identification programs, involving discriminant analysis and other multivariate techniques (e.g., Cook and Lord 1978; Cook 1982; Myers et al. 1987). Consequently, the choice of statistical methods becomes critical to success, and the entire set of assumptions associated with those methods become assumptions of the natural-mark identification process. For a project using natural marks, therefore, a biostatistician is an essential team member.

6.3 MEASUREMENT OF NATURAL SCALE AND OTOLITH FEATURES

6.3.1 General Description

Fisheries workers have long recognized that scales and otoliths look different, not only among species, but also among fish of the same species living in different locations. In some situations, those differences may be so distinctive that they can be used as natural marks. These marks are truly natural, developing through genetic variation among populations, differences in life history patterns, or environmental variation among habitats.

The process for using scale and otolith measurements as marks (or for using any natural mark) has three basic steps (Figure 6.1). First, structures from fish of known origins must be collected, measured, and compared to determine if sufficient differences exist and to set up the discriminating criteria for the various groups. Second, structures from more fish of known origin must be evaluated according to the criteria and assigned to the various groups, as validation of the mark's reliability. Third, the process finally may be used to analyze a set of structures from fish of unknown origins and to assign the fish to groups according to the established criteria.

In some cases, the differences in scale and otolith features may be so distinctive that gross visual examination can separate animals. In most cases, however, more subtle differences will require more elaborate procedures. Scale shape, circulus number, and circulus spacing can now be measured precisely and relatively efficiently with computerized optical scanning devices. Scale shape can be described explicitly using an analytic method called Fourier series expansion. Discriminant analysis has developed as the standard statistical technique for creating separation criteria and for judging the composition of mixed-stock samples. With these improved analytic tools, scale and otolith marks are increasingly interesting to fisheries analysts.

6.3.2 Advantages of Scale and Otolith Measurements (Box 6.1)

The advantages of scale and otolith morphometry for fish identification stem mostly from the naturalness of the marks—they are unobtrusive and ubiquitous.

Because fish mark themselves, no individual handling or injury of the fish is needed to produce the mark. The entire marking step is eliminated, thereby also eliminating the physiological stress of capture and handling, as well as the long-term injury and metabolic costs associated with carrying an external tag. Furthermore, the marking process is free, and scale collection is also virtually free, given that fisheries workers normally collect scales as part of most projects.

Every fish within a group presumably carries the group's mark on its scales or otoliths. This greatly reduces the number of animals that must be recaptured to acquire a reliable sample for analysis. Because each fish is marked, the recapture

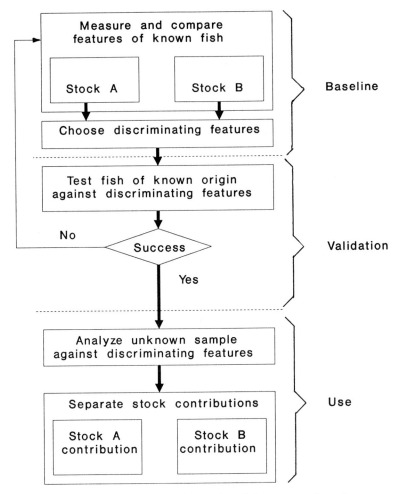

Figure 6.1 Steps in designing and applying a natural mark.

sample needs to be only as large as the statistical criteria demand. In general, experts agree that about 200 fish must be examined as the baseline sample for characterizing the unique scale or otolith shape of a single group (Myers et al. 1987). Fewer fish, around 100, are needed thereafter to identify the composition of a mixed sample.

6.3.3 Disadvantages of Scale and Otolith Measurements (Box 6.1)

Although scale characteristics are natural, their analysis requires removing scales from the fish. This process is not normally problematic, but it can affect fish, especially if performed by inexperienced persons or under difficult conditions. Scale removal disrupts the mucous coating and slightly breaks the skin surface. As with all marking, the process must be conducted carefully to minimize trauma to the fish. Removal of otoliths, however, requires sacrificing the animal. Otolith removal can require considerable experience because the structures are often deeply embedded in cranial tissues and because location varies among

---

Box 6.1   Advantages and Disadvantages of Natural Scale and Otolith Marks

Advantages

- No marking process required
- No effect on growth, survival, or behavior
- Small recapture sample required
- Field procedures routine

Disadvantages

- Individual marks not available
- Otolith marks require sacrificing the fish
- Extensive sample preparation
- Mark feature may change as fish grow or age
- Only statistical data are provided
- Validation required for each study

---

species. Subsequent preparation of otoliths (sectioning, grinding, and mounting) may be needed before the otoliths can be analyzed.

Fish scale characteristics may not be permanent. Scale morphology changes as fish grow and pass through various life stages (e.g., freshwater versus marine stages of diadromous fishes). Therefore, scale measurements must be compared for fish of the same age and size only. Fish also often lose scales and regenerate replacements. The regenerated scales lack the circulus banding contained near the focus of a normal scale and often are deformed. Because the critical measurements are usually near the scale focus, regenerated scales are useless. If regeneration rates differ among stocks, the analysis of a mixed-stock sample will be badly biased in favor of the stock with the lower rate of scale loss and regeneration (Knudsen 1990).

The analysis of scale and otolith measurements is almost always a statistical process. Fish are not uniquely identified as members of a particular group based on the known presence of an observable tag or mark, but are assigned to groups depending on how closely their scales or otoliths match those of the baseline statistical description of a particular group. Thus, scale characteristics are useful for stock assessment studies, such as determining the proportions of fish from various stocks captured in a mixed-stock fishery (Myers and Rogers 1988) or the proportions of hatchery versus wild fish caught (Humphreys et al. 1990).

The accuracy with which fish can be assigned to various groups depends on how different the mark features are among groups and how uniform they are within each group. In most reported studies, the accuracy of assigning fish to the correct stock ranged above 70% (Myers et al. 1987; Humphreys et al. 1990; Ross and Pickard 1990).

Because morphometric marks are statistical abstractions rather than real marks, their utility must be established in each study. This requires much time to collect scales or otoliths from known individuals of the appropriate groups, define and measure a large number of morphometric features, analyze the differences in

---

Box 6.2 Handling Scales

Jearld (1983) provided a detailed account of collection, handling, and storage procedures for scales, otoliths, and other hard body tissues useful for aging and marking. A summary of his suggested techniques for scales is as follows.

(1) Select the best place to collect scales after systematic examination of scales from all body areas. Choose scales that are uniformly large and symmetric.

(2) Remove mucus, dirt, and epidermis from the area by wiping toward the tail with a blunt-edged knife.

(3) Loosen scales with a quick, firm scraping motion towards the head with the edge of the knife.

(4) Pick up the loosened scales with the blade of the knife.

(5) Insert the blade into an opened scale envelope, press the envelope sides against the blade, and pull the blade out, leaving the scales in the envelope.

(6) In the laboratory, place several scales in a row on a plastic slide, sculpted side up, all in the same orientation.

(7) Place another plastic slide on top of the scales and roll through a scale press.

---

features among groups, select features that seem useful, and finally test whether those features allow accurate group separation. Although this process has proven reliable for salmonids and a few other species, it probably has been examined and rejected (but not reported) for other species and situations.

6.3.4 Performing a Scale or Otolith Analysis

6.3.4.1 Sample Collection

The scale collection process is generally the same as used in routine fisheries work. Because scale measurements vary with the location of the scales on the fish, the specific scales used must be identified precisely before the study, and the process must be recorded precisely during the study (Myers et al. 1987). Scales should be cleaned and stored according to Jearld (1983; Box 6.2). Regenerated scales cannot be used; therefore, several scales should be collected from each fish, both to increase the number of useful fish in the sample and to reduce the bias that may occur if stocks have different regeneration rates (Knudsen 1990). Impressions of several scales should be made for projection and measurement. If possible, measurements should be made directly into a computerized digitizer or optical scanning device.

Otoliths are collected by sectioning the head of a fish at the appropriate location so that the otoliths are exposed. In general, the larger otoliths, called sagittae, are used for all analyses, including aging and identification. Special care is necessary

Anterior

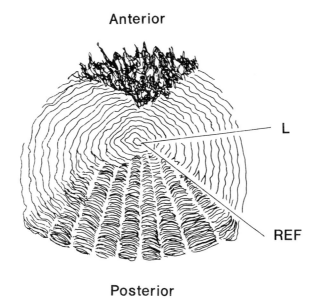

L

REF

Posterior

Figure 6.2 Stylized striped bass scale showing recommended reference radius (REF) and central point (L) for measuring scale features. Modified from Ross and Pickard (1990).

because the sagittae crack easily during dissection and later processing. The general techniques and advice of Jearld (1983) and Secor et al. (1991) should be followed, recognizing that the specific techniques for each species will need to be defined through experience. Therefore, a substantial experimental study will be needed before most otolith marking projects.

6.3.4.2 Measurement

Two sets of measurements generally are used to characterize scales and otoliths. The first is a series of measures relating to circuli (the rings around a scale) and radii (the clear lines running from the focus to the scale edge). If possible, measurements should be made on areas of the scales that formed during the part of the life cycle when the groups were separated, because this is when environmental differences may have produced the greatest differences in scale morphology. Commonly used measurements for both salmonids and striped bass include total numbers of circuli, average spacing between circuli for all circuli, average spacing between circuli for a selected group of circuli (usually the first 3–5), total length of a chosen radius, and ratios of radius length for the freshwater or marine portion of the scale to total radius length (Myers et al. 1987; Ross and Pickard 1990). Measuring these features requires a standardized location on each scale; Ross and Pickard (1990) recommended measuring along a radius where the circuli change from narrowly spaced to widely spaced in the dorsolateral field (Figure 6.2). Similar measurements of rings and ring spacing on otoliths are also appropriate.

The second set of measurements concern scale and otolith shape. The standard technique now incorporates a geometric analysis called Fourier series expansion. The process basically unrolls the perimeter of a shape, representing it first as an

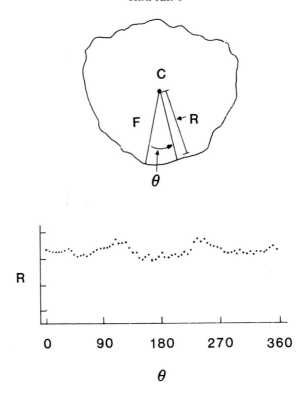

Figure 6.3 Example of scale measurements for use in Fourier series expansion. The outlined scale shows center (C), reference radius (F), angle of measurement (θ), and radius length (R). The graph plots R against θ. Units of R vary with magnification of the scale during measurement. Redrawn from Jarvis et al. (1978).

undulating line on a graph and then as a series of mathematical equations (Jarvis et al. 1978). Specifically, the process is as follows (Figure 6.3).

(1) An arbitrary point is designated as the center of the scale. The geometric center of the scale is usually selected, but any approximately central point is suitable (Bird et al. 1986). If the focus of the scale is central, it serves well as the designated center. Designating a central point that can be consistently located on all scales is important because the technique depends on having comparable data from scale to scale.

(2) An arbitrary reference radius is drawn, running from the scale center to the scale edge. This line serves as the base for measuring the angles at which other radii will be drawn. If the designated central point of the scale is not the focus, then the radius drawn from the central point through the focus serves as an easily located reference radius. If the central point is the focus, then a dominant radius on the scale should be used as the reference radius.

(3) A series of radial lines is drawn around the scale at a constant angular interval (e.g., every 5° from the reference line). The lengths of these radii are measured from center to scale edge. The lengths are plotted as the dependent variable (Y-axis) against the angles at which they were measured

Table 6.1 Classification accuracy for stock identification based on scale shape for age 2.2 sockeye salmon. After Cook and Lord (1978).

| Known stock origin | Sample size | Identified as | | | Percent correct classification |
		Bristol Bay	Gulf of Alaska	Kamchatka	
Bristol Bay	125	103	14	8	82.4
Gulf of Alaska	124	17	75	32	60.5
Kamchatka	128	5	35	88	68.8

(X-axis). Drawing more radii produces more points and a more detailed curve on the graph; 5° intervals produce 72 points—more than adequate to characterize a typical scale or otolith shape.

(4) This plot can then be modeled with the Fourier series expansion, which is the summation of a series of cosine wave functions; see Jarvis et al. (1978) for the mathematical treatment. Each cosine wave is defined by two measures—an amplitude and a phase angle. The amplitudes and phase angles for the waves needed to describe accurately a shape (usually around 10 waves, producing a list of 10 amplitudes and 10 angles) then become the descriptive measures of the scale shape. These measures are used in subsequent multivariate analysis, just like the measures of scale circuli and radii described earlier.

6.3.4.3 Analysis

The process of identifying fish to different stocks requires three steps, the first two involving fish of known origin and the last involving the unknown sample. For the first step, scales or otoliths are collected and characterized (as described above) for a sample of at least 200 fish from each group being studied. A discriminant analysis, a multivariate statistical technique, is then performed to determine which scale measurements are most useful for separating the groups. Cook and Lord (1978) and Cook (1982) described the technique in more detail for scale analysis, and advanced statistics books provide general coverage (see Chapter 2).

In the second step, the accuracy of the identification process is tested by subjecting another sample of fish from known groups to the discriminant analysis. To be valid, this test must be performed by someone who was not involved in the first step of creating the discriminant criteria. Step two produces a table showing the proportions of fish from each stock that were correctly and incorrectly classified (Table 6.1). No standards exist for judging whether or not given classification accuracy is high enough to be acceptable; that decision depends on the objective of the study and the accuracy and cost relative to other identification methods.

The third step is the actual identification process. Fish of mixed or unknown origin are assigned to groups by subjecting the scales or otoliths from a sample of fish to the discrimination process. The result is a proportional allocation of the fish among the stocks. Several biases may develop in this process, however, which must be corrected through various computational adjustments (Cook and Lord 1978; Cook 1982).

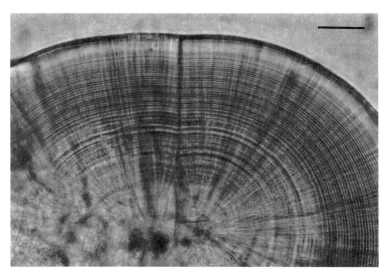

Figure 6.4 Daily growth rings on an otolith of a 56-day-old juvenile chum salmon held at relatively constant temperature. Scale bar = 100 μm. Reprinted from Volk et al. (1990).

6.4 INDUCED OTOLITH MARKS

6.4.1 General Description

Otoliths (literally, "ear stones") first attracted interest as a method of aging adult fish at the turn of the century. As their fine microstructure became apparent in the 1970s, otoliths became useful as a way to age larval fish in terms of days. Otoliths are the first calcified structures formed by a fish, often even before hatching. Otolith growth results from an accretion cycle, which tends to vary in a daily pattern because of cyclical differences in temperature, food availability, and other environmental cues. Each day's growth is recorded as one opaque and one translucent zone. These zones accumulate as concentric rings of increasing diameter, similar to the circulus patterns on scales. The daily rings are clearly visible when viewed microscopically in thin section with transmitted light (Figure 6.4).

Our growing knowledge about the formation and structure of fish otoliths has allowed the invention of a new marking technique—otolith patterning. Although these marks are not strictly natural in the sense of being a natural product of the fish's environment, they are natural in the sense that manipulation of a controlled environment induces the fish to produce the marks themselves.

By controlling the environment of captive fish, workers can alter the pace of otolith development, producing unique and recognizable patterns of otolith rings. For example, maintaining young fish at a rising or uniformly high temperature for several days produces rapid, constant growth and a broad translucent band on their otoliths. Conversely, maintaining the fish at a declining or uniformly cold temperature produces an opaque band. Varying the temperature in specific cycles can produce alternating translucent and opaque zones on the otoliths (Figure 6.5). In this way, unique codes can be formed. To illustrate the capability of this technique, Brothers (1990) coded salmonids with the Morse Code symbols for "GLFC," representing the Great Lakes Fishery Commission, sponsor of his

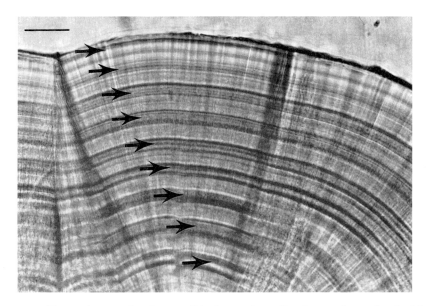

Figure 6.5 Photomicrograph of an otolith from a juvenile chum salmon that had been subjected to alternating 3-day periods in cold and warm water, showing uniform pattern of opaque zones (formed in cold water: arrows) and translucent zones. Scale bar = 100 μm. Reprinted from Volk et al. (1990).

study. Such thermal manipulations have been applied successfully to salmonid embryos, fry (alevins), and juveniles (Volk et al. 1990).

6.4.2   Advantages of Induced Otolith Marks (Box 6.3)

Otolith marks are useful primarily to mark fish raised in hatcheries and then released into natural waters. The marks can be induced during incubation or soon after hatching—earlier and at smaller fish sizes than is possible with other marking techniques. Otolith marks are also permanent. Unlike scales, which are sometimes shed, eroded, resorbed, and regenerated, otoliths retain their original size, shape, and markings regardless of the fish's nutritional or physiological state. Otolith marks, therefore, cover the entire life span. Consequently, they are well suited to stock-level research, including studies of movement, long-term survival, and contribution to fishery harvest.

Otolith marks do not harm fish, and the process of producing the marks also appears harmless. For example, studies of short-term mortality associated with manipulation of temperature levels have shown no significant effects (Bergstedt et al. 1990; Volk et al. 1990). In general, relatively small temperature changes, in the range of 5–10°C, are needed to produce the desired banding patterns. As with any captive animal, however, the treatment environment can cause subtle differences in performance, which must be evaluated as part of the marking process.

Otolith marking is inexpensive because large groups of fish are marked simultaneously. The major expenses associated with marking are the capital costs of plumbing modifications that allow mixing of water sources and the operational costs of heating or cooling the water. Because the fish are marked at an early stage when they occupy small water volumes, small quantities of water can serve large

---

Box 6.3   Advantages and Disadvantages of Induced Otolith Marks

Advantages

- No effect on growth, survival, or behavior
- Suitable for larval fish
- Suitable for mass marking
- Permanent marks for long-term studies
- Small recapture sample required

Disadvantages

- Individual marks not available
- Fish must be sacrificed to obtain otolith
- Primarily useful for hatchery-raised fish
- Requires precisely controlled environment
- Plumbing renovations may be required
- Extensive sample preparation
- Technique still experimental
- Pilot projects needed to establish necessary procedures to induce desired mark

---

numbers of fish. Marking rates are not comparable to other techniques, however, because the entire marking process will require enough days (maybe weeks) in the hatchery to produce the desired banding patterns. In essence, millions of fish can be marked within a several-day period.

Because all fish in a hatchery stock can be marked, the recovery process is also more efficient. No external mark is needed to identify an internally marked individual. The sample size needed to assure the recovery of enough marked fish is also much lower than with other techniques, again because every fish can be marked. This is particularly beneficial for multistock, international fisheries, for which the sample size is politically sensitive.

6.4.3 Disadvantages of Induced Otolith Marks (Box 6.3)

Otolith marking is a mass-production process. Consequently, individual fish cannot be marked uniquely, and the number of groups that can be marked is limited by the plumbing and holding capacities of the hatchery. However, the variety of patterns is large, allowing the technique to be used to distinguish fish from many locations in any one year or among years.

The production of clear and consistent otolith marks requires a precisely controlled environment. Because the banding pattern results from rapid changes in temperature interspersed with extended periods of uniform or uniformly changing temperatures, the temperature regime in the hatchery must be monitored and adjusted continuously and precisely. The basic criterion for clear banding is that the changes used in the treatment regime be substantially greater than the background variations. For example, if the normal variation in daily water temperature in a hatchery is 4°C, then a much larger temperature change (around 10°C) will be needed to produce marking patterns that are clearly distinguishable from bands produced before and after the treatment. Hatcheries using springs, deep-well water, or other water sources of uniform temperature are obviously the ideal locations for inducing otolith marks. Controlling the environmental conditions will require the ability to manipulate water sources and the presence of sophisticated monitoring equipment. These conditions are standard in large, modern hatcheries, but they may not be available in smaller and older hatcheries, requiring extensive modification before marking can occur.

Otoliths require extensive preparation before their microstructure can be seen. Otoliths from very young fish often can be observed without preparation, but otoliths of older, recaptured fish must be cut or ground into thin sections, a process that generally requires several steps of mounting, sectioning, grinding, and polishing (Jearld 1983; Secor et al. 1991). Considerable skill is required to prepare otoliths successfully. The sagittal plane must be included in the cross section to assure that all bands are intersected, at least in the central regions of the otolith, where the mark was produced.

Coupled with the difficulty of preparing otoliths is the uncertainty whether patterns will be visible in older fish. Studies to date have been largely experimental, successfully showing the ability of researchers to classify fish correctly during the first growing season. Even in these cases, some patterns are hard to distinguish. With more testing and with sophisticated microscopic equipment, this disadvantage is likely to become less problematic.

6.4.4 Inducing Otolith Marks

6.4.4.1 Marking Environment

The marking environment is the critical aspect of otolith marking, because environmental manipulation induces the fish to mark themselves. Control of the environment depends on two conditions: stability of the ambient environment, and precise manipulation of the treatment environment.

The base environment must be uniform at all times except during treatments. Water quality must be constant; water from wells or springs or from recirculation is the most desirable. Other conditions that may affect growth, such as food availability and light cycles, also must be kept on a constant daily cycle. This undoubtedly requires more frequent monitoring and precise control than are used in routine hatchery operations.

Conversely, the treatment environment must be capable of rapid changes in the conditions used to induce otolith patterning. Temperature manipulation has been used in most cases, but food availability and light cycles are also possible treatment variables. Because of the need to make rapid changes in temperature, reliable sources of warm and cool water are essential. If springs or deep wells are not available, then storage tanks of heated and cooled water may be necessary to create the needed temperature changes. Special plumbing is also needed to mix water and to move water to and from the treatment tanks. Alternatively, the fish may be moved to and from treatment tanks containing water held at the desired temperature. In either case, the fish being marked must be monitored closely so that handling or environmental stresses do not cause mortality.

6.4.4.2 Mark Induction

A unique banding pattern must be selected and a treatment regime designed to produce that pattern. Generally, the marking period should begin and end with several days of uniformly warm or increasing temperatures to produce broad uniform bands that border the mark pattern. The water temperatures should be monitored continuously during the marking period to provide a record of the precise thermal environment that produced the resulting pattern.

Several pilot studies will be needed before reliable large-scale marking can be attempted. Several small batches of fish should be subjected to various temperature treatments so that the relation between treatment and banding pattern can be verified. This process also will help identify treatments that produce clearly distinguishable patterns. This set of experiments must occur generally at least one cohort before actual marking is conducted, unless a related species or earlier-spawning population can be used. In any case, prior planning and experimentation will be needed to verify that the technique works with a given species and hatchery facility.

6.4.4.3   Postmarking Treatment

No special treatment is needed after this process, except the return of the fish to ambient hatchery conditions. The fish should be monitored closely for several days after treatment to detect any changes in growth, mortality or behavior.

A sample of the marked fish should be sacrificed a week or so after the treatment period. The week interval allows more material to form on the otolith margins, both defining the last treatment bands for easier interpretation and protecting them from damage during otolith preparation. The otoliths from these fish should be removed and held as a reference collection for comparison to fish recovered later. A sample of marked fish also should be maintained alive in the hatchery for several weeks or months. Marking these fish with a secondary external mark or tag is desirable to avoid later misidentification. These fish should be sacrificed at appropriate times, serving as an additional reference collection and verifying that workers can read and correctly identify the mark pattern.

6.5   OTHER NATURAL MARKS

The popularity of natural marks has risen and fallen through time. Their desirability has stimulated the search for ways to distinguish among groups based on naturally occurring features. As analytic and statistical methods have improved, our ability to use natural marks has also improved. One major style of natural identification is genetic marking, which has become so popular that it is covered separately in Chapter 8. However, artificial tags are becoming so versatile, inexpensive, and benign that traditional natural marks have become of limited importance in recent years. Consequently, this portion of the chapter will include only a brief review of other natural identification techniques.

The basic uses, advantages, and disadvantages of these marks are similar to those for natural scale and otolith marks (see section 6.3). The essential condition for the use of natural marks, however, is simply the presence of a feature or set of features that differs recognizably and consistently among the groups to be separated. Discovering those differences requires extensive study and observation of animals from the groups, a unique process for each situation. The most likely team to identify suitable features for testing as natural marks includes at least (1) an experienced taxonomist, familiar with the features that normally

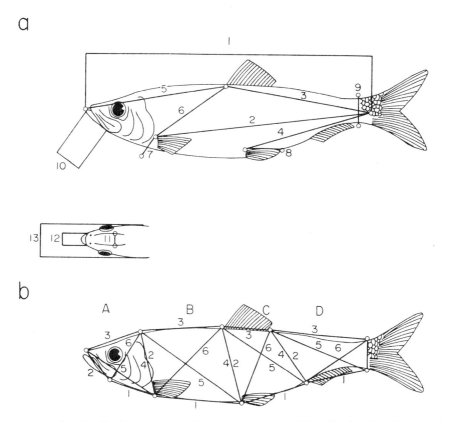

Figure 6.6 Standardized morphometric measurements of Pacific herring. In (**a**), the numbers refer to specific measurements. In (**b**), the numbers define elements in a specialized type of morphometry called truss analysis. Reprinted from Schweigert (1990).

distinguish similar species, (2) an experienced fish biologist, familiar with the particular groups under study, and (3) a biostatistician, familiar with the techniques of multivariate analysis.

6.5.1 Morphometry

Morphometric marks usually are based on differences in the relative measurements of particular body dimensions, such as the depth:length ratio (Strauss and Bond 1990; Figure 6.6). They also may be based on coloration patterns, such as the presence or absence of spots (McFarlane et al. 1990). Marine mammals, for example, can sometimes be identified individually by color patterns on their tail flukes, and Bachman (1984) identified individual brown trout in a study stream by their spot patterns. In an elaboration of simpler morphometric measurements, Strauss and Bookstein (1982) developed a multipoint "truss" grid for characterizing body shape and for separating body shape based on discriminant analysis. Truss analysis has been applied to several species (e.g., Schweigert 1990).

Morphometric marks are difficult to discover and use because body shape and color are so variable in aquatic species. Schweigert (1990) reported that large sample sizes are needed to ensure the necessary statistical reliability to separate stocks. Even then, the discriminating capacity of the technique may be low, and the likelihood of consistency from year to year seems modest at best. In general, morphometric marks (other than those of scales and otoliths) are likely to be useful only when major differences in shape or coloration exist among groups.

6.5.2 Meristic Counts

As described earlier, meristic counts are based on differences in the number of repeated skeletal features, such as the vertebrae, gill rakers, and fin rays of fish or the exoskeletal spines and segments of invertebrates (Wydoski and Emery 1983). The presence of such differences among groups of animals may be the result of genetic, physiological, and environmental factors, especially those that affect growth during early life periods. Meristic counts are often investigated as ways to separate subspecies or races of fish, as well as populations or stocks (Strauss and Bond 1990). These techniques have been applied most successfully on clupeids, which have highly variable development responses during early life. Like morphometric marks, meristic marks can be useful in unique circumstances. In general, however, meristic differences seem unlikely to be reliable marks.

6.5.3 Parasites

Because parasites sometimes have very restricted distributions, their presence on aquatic animals from particular locations can occasionally be used as natural marks. For example, the brain parasite *Myxobolus neurobius* occurs in sockeye salmon from southeast Alaska at a very high frequency, but in fish from British Columbia at a very low frequency (Moles et al. 1990). Frequencies of parasitic infection in mixed stocks can then be used to compute relative stock composition, just as with genetic frequencies (Chapter 8). The list of assumptions for appropriate use of a parasitic mark is quite long and restrictive (Wydoski and Emery 1983). The parasite should be ubiquitous in one group and absent in all others; in reality, parasitic marks are used when common in one group and rare in another. In the sockeye salmon example, infection rates were generally above 85% in Alaskan stocks and below 10% in Canadian stocks (Moles et al. 1990). The parasite should remain on the animal host throughout the host's and the parasite's life span. Also, the parasite should use no other hosts, so that it is present continuously on the animal group under study. *Myxobolus neurobius* infects only fish; the spores are released from the carcasses of dead adults and consumed by fry the following spring (Moles et al. 1990). When parasites fit these criteria, they are especially useful as marks. That situation is quite rare, however, making the utility of parasites marks greatly limited. Like other natural marks, parasites must be extensively evaluated before they are used for this purpose.

6.6 REFERENCES

Bachman, R. A. 1984. Foraging behavior of free-ranging wild and hatchery brown trout in a stream. Transactions of the American Fisheries Society 113:1–32.

Bergstedt, R. A., R. L. Eshenroder, C. Bowen II, J. G. Seelye, and J. C. Locke. 1990. Mass-marking of otoliths of lake trout sac fry by temperature manipulation. American Fisheries Society Symposium 7:216–223.

Bird, J. L., D. T. Eppler, and D. M. Checkley, Jr. 1986. Comparisons of herring otoliths using Fourier series shape analysis. Canadian Journal of Fisheries and Aquatic Sciences 43:1228–1234.

Brothers, E. B. 1990. Otolith marking. American Fisheries Society Symposium 7:183–202.

Cook, R. C. 1982. Stock identification of sockeye salmon (*Oncorhynchus nerka*) with scale pattern recognition. Canadian Journal of Fisheries and Aquatic Sciences 39:611–617.

Cook, R. C., and G. E. Lord. 1978. Identification of stocks of Bristol Bay sockeye salmon, *Oncorhynchus nerka,* by evaluating scale patterns with a polynomial discriminant method. U.S. National Marine Fisheries Service Fishery Bulletin 76:415–423.

Humphreys, M., R. E. Park, J. J. Reichle, M. T. Mattson, D. J. Dunning, and Q. E. Ross. 1990. Stocking checks on scales as marks for identifying hatchery striped bass in the Hudson River. American Fisheries Society Symposium 7:78–83.

Jarvis, R. S., H. F. Klodowski, and S. P. Sheldon. 1978. New method of quantifying scale shape and an application to stock identification in walleye (*Stizostedion vitreum vitreum*). Transactions of the American Fisheries Society 107:528–534.

Jearld, A., Jr. 1983. Age determination. Pages 301–324 *in* L. A. Nielsen and D. L. Johnson, editors. Fisheries techniques. American Fisheries Society, Bethesda, Maryland.

Knudsen, C. M. 1990. Bias and variation in stock composition estimates due to scale regeneration. American Fisheries Society Symposium 7:63–70.

McFarlane, G. A., R. S. Wydoski, and E. D. Prince. 1990. Historical review of the development of external tags and marks. American Fisheries Society Symposium 7:9–29.

Moles, A., P. Rounds, and C. Kondzela. 1990. Use of the brain parasite *Myxobolus neurobius* in separating mixed stocks of sockeye salmon. American Fisheries Society Symposium 7:224–231.

Myers, K. W., C. K. Harris, C. M. Knudsen, R. V. Walker, N. D. Davis, and D. E. Rogers. 1987. Stock origins of chinook salmon in the area of the Japanese mothership salmon fishery. North American Journal of Fisheries Management 7:459–474.

Myers, K. W., and D. E. Rogers. 1988. Stock origins of chinook salmon in incidental catches by groundfish fisheries in the eastern Bering Sea. North American Journal of Fisheries Management 8:162–171.

Ross, W. R., and A. Pickard. 1990. Use of scale patterns and shape as discriminators between wild and hatchery striped bass stocks in California. American Fisheries Society Symposium 7:71–77.

Schweigert, J. F. 1990. Comparison of morphometric and meristic data against truss networks for describing Pacific herring stocks. American Fisheries Society Symposium 7:47–62.

Secor, D. H., J. M. Dean, and E. H. Laban. 1991. Manual for otolith removal and preparation for microstructural examination. Belle W. Baruch Institute for Marine Biology and Coastal Research, University of South Carolina, Columbia.

Strauss, R. E., and C. E. Bond. 1990. Taxonomic methods: morphology. Pages 109–140 *in* C. B. Schreck and P. B. Moyle, editors. Methods for fish biology. American Fisheries Society, Bethesda, Maryland.

Strauss, R. E., and F. L. Bookstein. 1982. The truss: body form reconstructions in morphometrics. Systematic Zoology 31:113–135.

Volk, E. C., S. L. Schroder, and K. L. Fresh. 1990. Inducement of unique otolith banding patterns as a practical means to mass-mark juvenile Pacific salmon. American Fisheries Society Symposium 7:203–215.

Wydoski, R., and L. Emery. 1983. Tagging and marking. Pages 215–238 *in* L. A. Nielsen and D. L. Johnson, editors. Fisheries techniques. American Fisheries Society, Bethesda, Maryland.

Chapter 7

Biotelemetry

7.1 INTRODUCTION

Biotelemetry is entirely different from the marking methods described in previous chapters. Biotelemetric tags are miniature, wave-generating devices that broadcast signals into the water or air. A biotelemetric tag contains a battery that produces electrical energy that is converted into waves of selected wavelengths, frequencies, and other characteristics. The signals are detected by a receiver at a remote location—sometimes kilometers away from the tagged animal. A listener (human or electronic) can locate the tag based on the loudness of the signal and the direction from which it comes (Figure 7.1).

Like other miniaturized tagging systems, biotelemetry is a recent invention. Biologists first placed biotelemetric tags on salmon in 1956 (Stasko and Pincock 1977), about the same time that wildlife researchers were trying similar devices on birds and mammals (Kenward 1987). Biotelemetry became popular rapidly and had become commonplace by the mid-1970s. Although biotelemetry departs from the characteristics of an "ideal mark" more than any other marking system (see Table 1.1), it continues to expand in popularity and use because of its unique capabilities.

Biotelemetry includes two fundamentally different techniques—ultrasonic and radio tagging (see Box 7.1 for some terminology). *Ultrasonic tags* produce sound (acoustic) waves with frequencies between 20,000 and 300,000 cycles per second (20–300 kilohertz, kHz), beyond the range that humans hear. Electricity from the tag's battery vibrates a quartz or ceramic crystal (called a transducer) that generates the waves. The waves travel well through water, just as audible sound travels long distances under water with little loss of loudness or intensity. The vibrations are detected by other transducers mounted in a device called a hydrophone. The waves cause these transducers (sometimes called transponders) to vibrate, producing electric signals that are further transformed into audible or electronic signals.

Radio tags produce electromagnetic waves with frequencies between 27 and 300 million cycles per second (27–300 megahertz, MHz), which is within the range used by FM radio. In this case, electricity from the tag's battery creates very weak alternating electrical and magnetic currents in an antenna (Figure 7.2). The currents pass from the antenna into water or air. Radio waves travel poorly through water, losing energy rapidly as they radiate from the antenna. Waves that reach the water surface and escape, however, can travel through air for long distances with little additional loss of energy. The waves are detected by aerial antennas, in which the waves produce weak electric and magnetic currents. Like

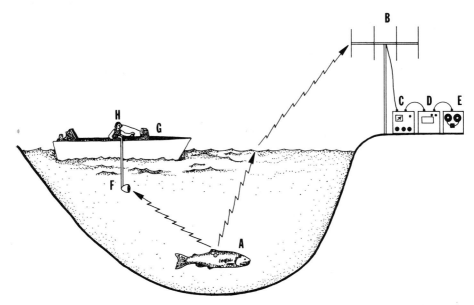

Figure 7.1 A typical biotelemetric tagging system, illustrated for radio or ultrasonic tagging. (**A**) Transmitter emitting ultrasonic or radio signals; (**B**) radio receiving antenna (Yagi); (**C**) radio receiver; (**D**) signal decoder; (**E**) data recorder; (**F**) ultrasonic receiver (hydrophone); (**G**) ultrasonic receiver; (**H**) headphones on a human listener. Reprinted from Winter (1983).

ultrasonic vibrations, these waves are then transformed into audible or electronic signals.

Both ultrasonic and radio tags are relatively bulky, and their attachment to animals is a major methodological choice. Today tags are attached one of three ways. External tags are attached like other external tags, stomach tags are force-fed to the animals, and body cavity tags are surgically implanted. Early tags were heavy and bulky, restricting their use to large, adult animals. Continuing technological advances have reduced the tag size so that small animals can be tagged. Japanese scientists have recently tagged dobsonfly larvae with radio tags only 17 mm long and weighing 0.2 g (Hayashi and Nakane 1989).

A biotelemetric study can generate enormous amounts of data about a few animals at one time. Because the tags broadcast continuously, researchers can monitor animals continuously, collecting more data points than anyone could ever use. Furthermore, the ability to collect data without ever recapturing the animal eliminates handling stress and greatly reduces the cost of each datum. Biotelemetric tags and receiving equipment are expensive, however, so most studies can afford to tag and monitor relatively few animals. The number of unique signals that can be distinguished is also relatively small, further restricting how many tagged animals can be individually recognized at any time (Stuehrenberg et al. 1990).

Biotelemetry can reveal several things about a tagged animal that other marking techniques cannot reveal. Pinpointing an animal's position without the disturbance of capture or direct observation shows habitat selection. Repeated location of an animal shows local movement patterns and defines territories and home

Box 7.1 Glossary of Biotelemetric Terms

Biotelemetry has a vocabulary of its own, drawn from the disciplines of electrical and mechanical engineering. Detailed understanding of the terms will require a reading of the appropriate chapters of a basic physics book, but this glossary can serve as a starting point.

Antenna	A long wire or set of wires through which radio waves are transmitted and received.
Drift	The variation in frequency of the waves produced by a radio transmitter or ultrasonic transducer. Low drift means that the wave frequency is very consistent over time.
Frequency	The rate at which waves are produced, usually expressed as cycles per second (hertz, Hz). Radio waves are expressed as megahertz (million cycles per second, MHz) and sound waves as kilohertz (thousand cycles per second, kHz).
Gain	The volume to which a received signal is amplified. A high gain refers to a loud volume, making the signal easier to hear, but also increasing the loudness of the background noise.
Hydrophone	One or more transducers through which ultrasonic waves are received. The transducers are attached to a pole and suspended below the water to receive the signals.
Null signal	The situation that occurs when a receiver (transducer or antenna) is oriented so that it receives no signal; consequently, no sound is heard.
Pulse length	The amount of time during each pulse that a signal is being transmitted. A pulse length less than the entire time per pulse produces a beeping sound that is easier to hear.
Pulse Rate	The number of pulses of a given wavelength per minute. Pulse rate and pulse length can be manipulated to produce a characteristic pattern (duration and interval) of beeps coming from a tag.
Transducer	A ceramic crystal through which ultrasonic waves are transmitted and received.
Transponder	A device that transmits a signal only when activated by another acoustic signal. In biotelemetry literature, transponder is sometimes used to specify a receiving transducer in the hydrophone.
Wavelength	The physical length of a wave, usually expressed in meters. Wavelength equals wave speed divided by frequency.

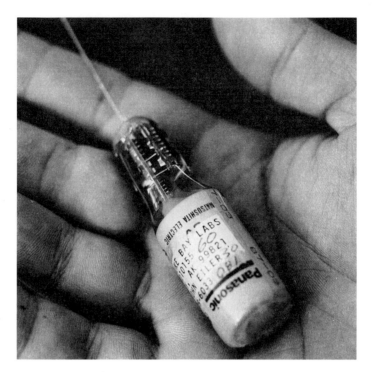

Figure 7.2 A basic radio tag, used on adult coho and sockeye salmon in Alaska. Reprinted from Eiler (1990).

ranges. Tags that broadcast different signals when animals are stationary, moving, or dead (i.e., not moving for a long time) allow study of daily activity patterns (Eiler 1990) that can be correlated with environmental conditions. These tags are particularly useful where or when animals cannot be seen or captured effectively, as in turbid water, in dangerous currents, or at night (Matthews et al. 1990).

Biotelemetric tagging can monitor large-scale movements. Broad search patterns with airplanes or earth satellites can locate tagged animals at great distances from their tagging locations. This can greatly increase efficiency in migration studies because only the tagged animals need be monitored; hundreds of animals do not have to be caught and examined to discover a tagged individual. The paths used by animals traveling around obstructions (dams, power plant intakes, bridge abutments) also can be mapped with biotelemetry (Stasko and Pincock 1977).

Biotelemetry is a major method for studying fish behavior and physiological condition in natural systems. Continuous monitoring can reveal highly specific activity patterns in both pristine and altered environments. Some tags change signals in response to different environmental and physiological conditions, allowing researchers to monitor the temperature and depth of the animal's location and certain physiological traits, such as body temperature, heart beat, and electrolyte balance.

Biotelemetric tags can also monitor inert objects efficiently. The movement of fish attraction devices, drifting at middepths in marine waters, can be tracked so the devices can be located for repairs and other modifications (Holland et al. 1985). In terrestrial experiments, radio tags have been used to tell whether remote

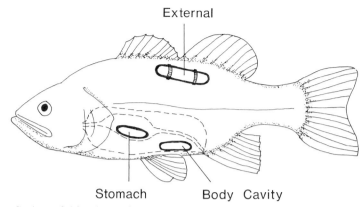

Figure 7.3 Styles of biotelemetric tag attachment, showing typical placement on a perciform fish.

animal traps have been triggered (Kenward 1987); similar uses in aquatic systems are possible.

7.2   ASSUMPTIONS FOR BIOTELEMETRY

The first assumption for using biotelemetric tags is that the tags do not change the physical condition or behavior of the tagged animals. This is a complicated question, because the two types of tags and three main types of tag attachment have different characteristics and consequences.

External tags are generally attached along the dorsal surface of an animal (Figure 7.3). The attachment site for fish is generally along one side, like transbody tags, posterior to the midpoint along the body. The site on crustaceans is variable, but generally centered on the carapace. Such tags produce the same effects as other external tags (see Chapter 3). Biotelemetric tags are large relative to basic external tags, however, so negative effects are presumably exaggerated. Recent studies, for example, have demonstrated that biotelemetric tags can increase the drag on swimming fish and shorten the time to exhaustion during continuous swimming (Lewis and Muntz 1984; Mellas and Haynes 1985). Thus, although external attachment may appear preferable because most professionals have experience with external tagging, the other attachment methods may be better in many cases.

Tags can be inserted into the stomachs of fish by pushing them past the esophagus with a plunger. Stomach insertion does not cause a wound and does not interfere with swimming. For fish that do not feed (e.g., salmon on spawning migrations), this technique is benign. For actively feeding fish, however, food intake may decline; Moser et al. (1990) found that 40% of coho salmon with tags in their stomachs did not feed. The presence of a stomach tag also may interfere with a fish's ability to inflate its air bladder (Stuehrenberg et al. 1990). For short-term studies, however, stomach tags may allow faster posttagging recovery time and may interfere less with normal behavior than biotelemetric tags attached in other ways.

Implanting tags within the body cavity is a favored attachment method,

especially for ultrasonic tags (Winter 1983). This technique has the same consequences as inserting internal anchor tags (see Chapter 3), but again the effects are
likely to be more extreme because of the size of the tag. Infections of the sutured
incision and the body cavity itself are possible, especially if the tag and incision
are not treated with antibiotics (Chisholm and Hubert 1985; Mellas and Haynes
1985). For longer-term studies, surgical implantation may be the most effective
because the tag does not interfere with feeding or movement, as do stomach and
external tags. The elaborate surgical process and relatively long posttagging
recovery, however, may make surgically implanted tags less efficient for short-
term studies.

The second major assumption is that all tagged animals remain tagged. For
externally mounted tags, the validity of this assumption is similar to that for other
external tags—some tags will fall off because the attachment devices fail or the
anchoring body tissue degenerates. Externally attached tags also fail occasionally
because water leaks into the tag where the attachment device joins the tag.

Stomach tags are lost through regurgitation or egestion. Regurgitation rates
vary greatly, depending on the fish species and the relative size of the tag. Recent
studies have documented regurgitation rates of 25% for sauger (Olson et al. 1990),
30% and 67% for coho salmon (Moser et al. 1990), and 80% for rainbow trout
(Mellas and Haynes 1985). Table 7.1 lists species known to retain or regurgitate
stomach tags. Regurgitation rates increase as relative tag size increases. Small
tags, in contrast, may be lost through egestion (Mortensen 1990). Like porridge
for Goldilocks, the tag meal must be "just right."

Loss of surgically implanted tags also may occur, as shown recently for channel
catfish (Marty and Summerfelt 1986) and rainbow trout (Chisholm and Hubert
1985). In these studies, individual fish reacted to the presence of the tag by
synthesizing muscle-like fibers around it. The fibers eventually surrounded the tag
and, through muscle-like contractions, forced it through softer adjacent tissues,
either the body wall or the intestine. Reactions like these cause the tag to be
expelled through the skin or via the alimentary tract. Rejection of the tag increases
with size; consequently, the tag generally should not exceed 2% of the tagged
animal's body weight.

The final assumption is that the tag's signals will be detected consistently and
identified accurately. In this regard, the success of a biotelemetric study depends
greatly on the quality of the tag, the characteristics of signal, and the capability of

Table 7.1 Fish species with high and low potential for retaining stomach tags. Adapted
from Staska and Pincock (1977) and others.

Regurgitation unlikely	Regurgitation likely
American shad	Coho salmon
Pink salmon	Rainbow trout
Chum salmon	Atlantic salmon
Sockeye salmon	Northern pike
Chinook salmon	White sucker
Lake trout	Atlantic cod
Brown bullhead	Yellow perch
American eel	Sauger
White bass	Skipjack tuna
Striped bass	
Bluefin tuna	

the receiver (Diana et al. 1990). The tag must broadcast throughout the life of the study, and its ability to do so depends on the type and size of battery and the current demanded by the tag. The frequencies, pulse rates, and pulse lengths (time on and off) of the signal must be easily heard and distinguished by a human listener. The signals often drift among nearby frequencies (Matthews et al. 1990), so the frequencies chosen for different tags must be far enough apart that a substantial margin for error can be accommodated. The tag must produce signals that are strong enough to be distinguishable from background noise (i.e., a signal-to-noise ratio greater than 0). The receiving station must be sensitive enough to detect signals from the farthest point in the study area, and the tuner must be sensitive enough to detect individual tags without interference.

These assumptions define the specifications for something close to an ideal tagging system. The ideal tag should weigh less than 2% of a tagged animal's body weight in water; some researchers have suggested using tags less than 1.5% of body weight (Mortensen 1990). The tag should be encased in a smooth, nonreactive coating; Marty and Summerfelt (1986) recommended a casing of medical grade silicone. The battery should be lithium–copper oxide, capable of delivering 600 milliampere-hours and a current drain of 0.2 milliamperes per day (Diana et al. 1990). The tag should broadcast signals with pulse rates of 50 or more pulses per minute and with pulse lengths of 30 or more milliseconds per cycle (Kenward 1987). If more than one pulse rate is used on the same frequency to identify different animals, pulse rates should differ by at least 20 pulses per minute (Eiler 1990). If more than one frequency is used to identify different animals within the same tracking area, the frequencies should differ by at least 10 kHz for radio tags (Kenward 1987); a corresponding difference of 10 MHz for ultrasonic tags is presumed appropriate as well.

These specifications, of course, do not assure the best operation under all conditions. Local knowledge and experience are always needed to select the most appropriate tagging system for each study. Furthermore, although early researchers often built their own tags, homemade tags are not recommended for most applications today. The exacting assumptions mentioned earlier require increasingly sophisticated tags, and commercial manufacturers have emerged to supply the necessary tags and expertise.

7.3 ULTRASONIC TAGGING

7.3.1 Advantages of Ultrasonic Tagging (Box 7.2)

Ultrasonic waves travel well through water. The signals remain strong as they radiate from the transducer, so tagged animals can be detected at great distances and depths. Detection distances up to 1 km are possible under ideal conditions. Consequently, ultrasonic tags work well for animals that travel far, live in deep water, or make extensive vertical migrations (Diana et al. 1990).

The loss of signal strength with distance is a direct function of increasing signal frequency (Stasko and Pincock 1977). At low frequencies (20 kHz), signals remain strong at great distances, but the transducer must be large to generate the signal. At high frequencies (300 kHz), signals weaken rapidly with distance, but the transducer can be small. Therefore, tags should be as large as possible (up to 2% of body weight), allowing the large transducer to transmit at the lowest frequency possible.

Box 7.2   Advantages and Disadvantages of Ultrasonic Biotelemetry

Advantages

- Remote sensing of tagged animals
- Suitable for all species
- Continuous monitoring possible
- Allows individual identification
- Long detection range in water
- Useful in fresh and salt water
- Highly directional signals
- Allows precise location of animals

Disadvantages

- Expensive and complicated system
- Few animals can be monitored at same time
- Effects on growth, survival, and behavior depend on specific conditions
- Not suitable for very small animals
- Not suitable for long-term studies
- Physical obstacles interfere with signals
- Signals must be received underwater
- Signal frequency can drift substantially

Ultrasonic waves travel equally well through both fresh and salt water. Because sound waves are mechanical phenomena, their transmission is not affected by the concentration of dissolved ions. In contrast, radio waves are strongly affected by conductivity; therefore, only ultrasonic tagging is useful for marine or estuarine telemetry.

Ultrasonic systems are highly directional. The hydrophone used to detect ultrasonic signals can be designed to receive signals only from a narrow beam, so that signals reflected from other surfaces are not received. Because all ultrasonic wavelengths are relatively short and transmission speeds are relatively slow, variations in the strength and pulse rate of signals are easy to detect. Consequently, studies that require very precise location of tagged animals often use ultrasonic tags (Stasko and Pincock 1977).

7.3.2   Disadvantages of Ultrasonic Tagging (Box 7.2)

Although dissolved solids do not affect ultrasonic waves, almost everything else does. Because the signals are physical, most physical obstacles reduce signal strength. Pressure and temperature variations can refract ultrasonic waves, so thermal stratification can deflect signals down into deep water rather than up to the surface (Winter 1983). Aquatic vegetation, turbidity, turbulence, and bottom irregularities all interfere with ultrasonic signals, reducing the range of reception. Matthews et al. (1990), for example, could hear ultrasonic signals over low-relief bottoms as far away as 1 km; the detection range declined to 50–500 m over high-relief rock reefs. The rough underside of ice also interferes with signals (Rusanowski et al. 1990). Because of this interference, ultrasonic tags are not

Table 7.2 Comparative characteristics of external, stomach, and body cavity locations for attaching biotelemetric tags to fish.

Characteristic	Attachment location		
	External	Stomach	Body cavity
Methodology			
Complexity	Medium	Low	High
Rate of attachment	Slow	High	Slow
Retention rate	Variable	Variable	Medium
Study length	Long	Short	Long
Animal suitability			
Invertebrate	Yes	No	No
Fish species	Most	Some	All
Small animals	Yes	Yes	No
Life history stage	All	Nonfeeding only	Nonspawning only
Effect on animal			
Growth	Medium	High	Low
Infection rate	Medium	Low	High
Survival	Medium	High	High
Behavior	Variable	High	Low

useful for studies in turbulent rivers, in waters with many obstructions (e.g., around power dams), and in turbid or heavily vegetated water (e.g., farm ponds).

Ultrasonic systems are also restricted by the need to detect signals with a receiver suspended under the water. Hydrophones are usually mounted on a pole that is submerged below the hull of the tracking boat. Consequently, the boat must travel at slow speeds to avoid damaging the hydrophone assembly. Slow speeds are also necessary because high speeds produce bubbles and turbulence around the receiving transducer, creating noise and distorting the arriving signals. The receiving heads of hydrophones must be expertly designed for streamlined passage through the water (Winter 1983; Holland et al. 1985).

Researchers have reported substantial drift in the frequency of signals produced by ultrasonic tags. This drift may require continuous tuning of the receiver, lowering the efficiency of scanning and tracking operations. It also necessitates rather large intervals between the frequencies for different animals tagged in the same water body, which reduces the number of tags that may be used at the same time.

7.3.3 Attaching and Localizing an Ultrasonic Tag

7.3.3.1 Tag Attachment

A fundamental decision in biotelemetry is the choice of tag attachment method. Each of the three methods has characteristics that make it advantageous or disadvantageous in different circumstances (Table 7.2). In general, external attachment is the most commonly used because it is adaptable for a wide variety of species and sizes of animals. Stomach insertion is appropriate in special circumstances only, and its success depends on species-specific reactions to a large swallowed object. Body cavity implants presumably are applicable for a wide range of species, but are restricted to larger animals and probably to long-term studies.

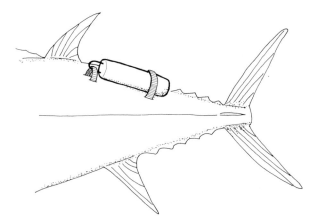

Figure 7.4 Attachment of an external ultrasonic tag. Adapted from Holland et al. (1985).

External Tag. In almost all cases, external tags are attached along the dorsal surface of a fish, similar to the location for transbody external tags (see Chapter 3). To be attached externally, ultrasonic transmitters usually must be fitted with a fastening device. Design of the fastening device should be customized for the species and size of tagged animals and the shape and size of the tag. The primary criterion should be securing the tag snugly so that it does not vibrate, causing abrasion or wound enlargement.

Holland et al. (1985) fashioned tags for tuna by incorporating a small wire loop into the tag and encasing all but the end of the loop with the other transmitter parts. They passed a plastic cinch through the loop and then through the fish's dorsal musculature, anchoring the anterior end of the tag. They placed an additional cinch around the body of the tag and through the dorsal musculature, anchoring the posterior end (Figure 7.4). Hurley et al. (1987) wrapped attachment wire around the tag several times and secured it by coating the tag and all but the ends of the wire with a plastic sealant (''tool-grip''); they used the two ends of the wire as they would for a Carlin tag, passing them through holes drilled in the dorsal scutes of shovelnose sturgeon and connecting them on the opposite side of the fish. Rusanowski et al. (1990) placed ultrasonic tags across the carapace of red king crabs like backpacks, held in place by threads bound to walking legs on opposite sides of the carapace.

Stomach Tag. Stomach insertion is a simple process. The fish should be anesthetized to reduce coughing reactions and immediate regurgitation of the tag. Insertion is easiest with a hollow tube fitted with a plunger (Figure 7.5). The tag is placed in the open end of the tube, flush with the end. The tube is inserted into the stomach, and the plunger is depressed as the tube is withdrawn, leaving the tag behind (Kenward 1987).

Each tagged fish should be monitored to assure its recovery from anesthesia and its retention of the tag. Fish must be held individually, so that the researcher can tell which fish regurgitated a tag. Although most regurgitation has been observed within a few hours of tagging (e.g., Moser et al. 1990), Stuehrenberg et al. (1990)

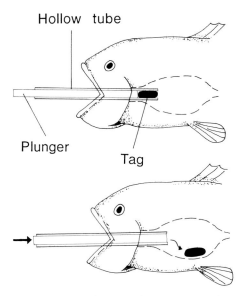

Figure 7.5 Equipment and procedure for inserting an ultrasonic tag into a fish stomach.

recommended holding fish for 24 hours. Given the substantial differences in regurgitation rates among species and among studies for the same species, a specific laboratory test of regurgitation rates with dummy transmitters should be performed as part of each project.

Body Cavity Tag. Placement of a tag in the body cavity is the most difficult attachment method because it requires surgery. It also requires caution in the selection of animals to be tagged. Fish preparing to spawn should not be tagged, both because the surgical procedure may rupture enlarged ovaries and testes and because the body cavity may have no space to accommodate the tag. To assure that the stomach and intestinal tract will be empty during implantation, fish should not be fed for 24 hours before surgery.

In all cases, the fish should be anesthetized, as described in Chapter 2. The fish should be placed in a tagging cradle for surgery, so most of the animal, including the gills, is submerged but the incision location is above the water line, thus avoiding contamination (Marty and Summerfelt 1986). The incision should parallel the ventral midline, but be made just off center and just anterior of the pelvic girdle (Winter 1983; Mortensen 1990). Because very few blood vessels feed this region, bleeding will be slight. The incision should be small—just long enough to insert the tag without tearing the tissue. It also should be shallow, just deep enough to cut the body wall without injuring the internal organs.

The tag should be disinfected before insertion into the body cavity. Summerfelt and Smith (1990) recommended a 1:1,000 benzalkonium chloride solution, followed by a rinse in sterile water before insertion. Marty and Summerfelt (1986) recommended injecting penicillin (5,000 International Units of Penicillin G per kilogram of fish, in their study) into the body cavity before suturing to inhibit internal infection. The incision should be closed with sutures or surgical staples placed at 4-mm intervals (Mortensen 1990). Suturing is the most time-consuming part of the process, and it involves several choices of techniques and materials, as detailed by Summerfelt and Smith (1990). The entire surgical process requires only a few minutes. Inexperienced workers should practice the surgical procedure, including incision, tag insertion, and suturing on several specimens before operating on study animals.

Tagged fish should be held individually until they are fully recovered. Because of the change in buoyancy caused by the tag, fish may float or swim abnormally for several hours (Mortensen 1990). In addition, because feeding can cause pressure on the tag and incision, fish should not be fed during the recovery period. During the recovery period, fish should be examined frequently for evidence of infection, rupture of the incision, and tag loss. Because the incision normally will heal rapidly and because fish held in captivity may change their behavior or become infected, fish generally should be released as soon as possible.

7.3.3.2   Tag Localization

Before beginning actual field locations, researchers should practice locating a stationary target at a known location (Kenward 1987). Researchers should first test their equipment and searching method so that the signal patterns become familiar. A tag can be attached to a fish carcass, which can then be anchored in the water at an appropriate depth and location. Trackers can practice approaching the tag from various directions, at various speeds, and with various receiver settings. This experience will greatly increase searching efficiency.

Several strategies are used to locate ultrasonically tagged animals, but the most common is tracking animals from a moving boat. Specifically designed vessels may be cost-effective for large-scale tagging operations (e.g., Holland et al. 1985), but most tracking boats are typical fisheries work boats outfitted with the necessary facilities. The basic need is a mounting device to hold the hydrophone below the water line and a stable, nonvibrating platform to hold the receiver.

Most studies use a directional hydrophone, which receives signals within a narrow angle (Figure 7.6). These hydrophones have either a single transducer surrounded by a cone that reflects signals into the center of the cone (like a satellite dish for television signals) or a line of transducers that amplifies signals received perpendicular to the line (Winter 1983).

An ultrasonic tag is located by traveling in the direction of a signal detected by the hydrophone. As the boat nears the tag, the signal will become stronger and less directional. As the signal strength increases in intensity, the volume and sensitivity (gain) of the receiver must be continuously lowered (Winter 1983). As the boat passes over the tag, the signal will become equally strong in all directions, then become strongest in the opposite direction. The boat can then be reversed and the equal-signal point approached again from the opposite direction. The tag is located where no difference in signal strength occurs in any direction.

Because the receiver qualities needed to detect the general direction of a distant tag (high volume and low sensitivity) are different from those needed to pinpoint a nearby tag (low volume and high sensitivity), a two-receiver system may be useful (Williams and White 1990). The first receiver is used to detect the tag initially and guide approach to it; this receiver is turned off as the boat nears the fish. The second receiver is then turned on and tuned to the same frequency; it allows precise definition of the tag location.

A second tracking strategy involves stationary receiving stations. The precise

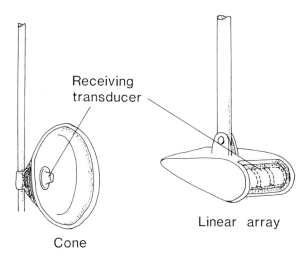

Figure 7.6 Stylized directional hydrophones for receiving ultrasonic signals. Redrawn from Stasko and Pincock (1977) and Winter (1983).

location of a tag can be determined by plotting the direction to the tag from two or more separated receiving stations. This process, called triangulation, requires accurate maps of the water body, upon which the receiving stations are accurately plotted. Highly directional hydrophones are aimed directly at the tag signal, compass bearings are taken for the directions indicated by the hydrophones, and corresponding lines are drawn on the map. The tag is located where the lines intersect (Figure 7.7). Because the accuracy of triangulation is greatest when the bearings are at 90° angles (Winter 1983), the receiving stations should be placed so that most of the probable tag locations will produce such angles. Although two receiving stations are sufficient in many cases, additional stations are often needed if the water body is large or has an irregular shape.

Stationary receiving stations also can detect the passage of animals past specific locations, such as a dam, stream mouth, or cove opening. In this case, the receiver should have a very narrow beam width, so that animals within only a narrow transect are detected. Omnidirectional receivers are also useful in special cases, such as detecting fish around fish attraction devices or water intake pipes.

If more than one animal is being tracked, the receiver must be tuned to different frequencies continuously. This is cumbersome if done by hand and can reduce the efficiency of tracking. Two options are available to reduce this problem. First, tags can transmit different pulse codes on the same frequency. As long as the codes have sufficiently different pulse rates and lengths, more than one tag can be tracked simultaneously. Second, receivers can be programmed to scan through a set of frequencies at a prescribed rate. The tracker can proceed along a standard route until she hears a signal on one of the scanned frequencies and then tune the receiver to that specific frequency for intensive tracking.

Most trackers use their own ears to detect signals. They generally wear headsets, which filter out the noise around them. Rusanowski et al. (1990), however, recommended not using headsets during cold weather because they are uncomfortable. Instead, they suggested amplifying the signal through a loud-speaker. Automatic signal processing also is available and is particularly desirable

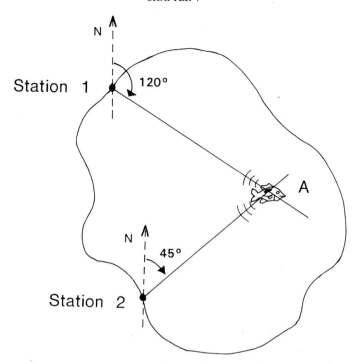

Figure 7.7 Example of a triangulation: the tag at point A is located by drawing lines along the compass bearings for simultaneous reception of the tag signal at stations 1 and 2.

for fixed receiving stations linked to computers. The automatic processors can record the direction of compass bearings or the simple presence or absence of a signal and store the records for subsequent analysis.

7.4 RADIO TAGGING

7.4.1 Advantages of Radio Tagging (Box 7.3)

The advantages and disadvantages of radio tags are essentially the opposites of those for ultrasonic tags—which is why both systems exist. Radio tagging also has the advantage of being widely used for tracking terrestrial animals. Consequently, radio-tagging equipment and techniques have developed rapidly and will continue to do so. For this reason alone, radio tagging may be preferable if the study conditions allow an otherwise equal choice between radio and ultrasonic tagging.

Radio signals are much less affected by physical obstacles in the water than are ultrasonic signals. Because they are electromagnetic waves, radio signals travel through many objects and reflect undistorted off many others. Consequently, radio tags are useful in water conditions in which ultrasonic tags will not work. They can be used effectively in turbulent water, such as high-velocity streams and rivers (Tyus 1982). Because they are less affected by surface or bottom irregularities, they can be used through ice and over high-relief bottoms (Diana et al. 1990).

Radio signals are detected in air, after they have radiated beyond the water. This makes detection of radio signals much more convenient than the detection of ultrasonic signals. Most of the signals that reach the water surface, however, are

---

Box 7.3 Advantages and Disadvantages of Radio Biotelemetry

Advantages

- Remote sensing of tagged animals
- Suitable for all species
- Continuous monitoring possible
- Allows individual identification
- Highly developed for wildlife uses
- Signals detected in air
- Not affected by physical obstacles
- Highly directional signals
- Long detection range in air
- Low drift among frequencies

Disadvantages

- Expensive and complicated system
- Effects on growth, survival, and behavior depend on specific conditions
- Signals lose energy rapidly in water
- Not suitable in saline water
- Tags usually carry protruding antennas
- Not suitable for very small animals
- Not suitable for long-term studies

---

reflected back into the water. Only the signals reaching the water surface at an angle of 6° or less from the vertical actually escape (Figure 7.8). Consequently, the signals leaving the water from a particular tag begin from a small-diameter circle, forming a clear focus at the water surface. Once in the air, radio waves travel at great speed with little loss of strength. Therefore, radio signals can be detected accurately at great distances by receivers on boats, airplanes, shoreline towers, or satellites. For all these reasons, large areas can be monitored efficiently with standardized listening stations or search patterns.

Radio tags transmit waves at very high frequencies and with considerable energy. Therefore, the drift of radio signals among frequencies is very low. Consequently, the difference in frequency among tags being tracked in the same area can be quite small, allowing a large number of animals to be followed simultaneously (Stasko and Pincock 1977).

7.4.2 Disadvantages of Radio Tagging (Box 7.3)

The strength of radio signals diminishes rapidly with distance in water. This loss is particularly severe in water with high conductivity. Hence, radio tagging is of little use in marine and estuarine waters (Winter 1983). Like ultrasonic signals, the loss of radio signal strength is more severe at higher frequencies. Therefore, lower frequencies should be used, especially if the tagged animals live deeper than a few meters below the surface (Eiler 1990). This assertion is currently under debate, and future developments in transmitter quality may improve the utility of higher frequencies. As with ultrasonic transducers, the size of a radio antenna must be

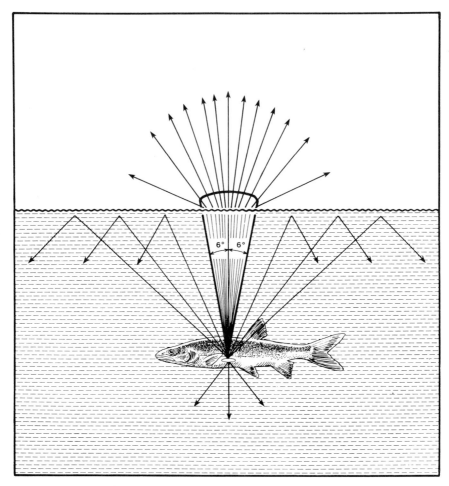

Figure 7.8 The path of radio waves leaving a submerged tag. Reprinted from Tyus (1982).

matched to the frequency of the signals being transmitted or received. Lower-frequency signals require longer antennas. Because of this relationship, frequencies lower than about 40 MHz are impractical for many studies (Kenward 1987).

A radio tag can broadcast signals only if an antenna is attached to the transmitter. The most common type of antenna protrudes from the tag as a thick wire, producing an additional trauma for the animal. This disadvantage is most problematic with stomach and body cavity tags. The alternative is a coiled antenna, called a tuned-loop antenna, which can be embedded within the tag (Kenward 1987). Coiled antennas generally have a shorter range, however, than straight antennas.

A general disadvantage—caution, actually—concerns the reliability of both ultrasonic and radio-tagging systems. Because each system uses sophisticated electronic components that must work together, the systems are more prone to malfunction than simple tagging techniques. Also, because of the profitable commercial market, many suppliers are available and product quality and service vary widely. Therefore, specifications for equipment should be carefully defined, and suppliers should be rigorously screened before decisions are made. As with most techniques, the advice of several acknowledged and independent experts is invaluable.

7.4.3   Attaching and Localizing a Radio Tag

7.4.3.1   Tag Attachment

The processes for attaching radio tags are the same as those for attaching ultrasonic tags (see section 7.3.3). The major difference is accommodating a transmitting antenna as part of the tag.

Transmitting antennas work best when they are straight and stout (Kenward 1987). The appropriate length of the antenna is a function of the wavelength, which in turn is a function of the signal frequency and the speed of wave transmission in water. The general formula for wavelength of radio signals in water (based on Kenward 1987, with modification for the dielectric constant of water given by Tyus 1982) is

$$\text{wavelength } (\lambda, \text{ in m}) = 33/\text{frequency (in MHz)}.$$

For a commonly used aquatic frequency of 50 MHz, for example, the signal wavelength in water is about 0.67 m.

Antenna lengths are selected as whole-number fractions of wavelength (i.e., λ, $\lambda/2$, $\lambda/4$, $\lambda/8$). For a 1/8-wavelength antenna transmitting 50-MHz signals, for example, the desired antenna length is about 8 cm.

For externally attached transmitters, the antenna should extend behind the tag, toward the tail of the fish. Antennas of surgically implanted tags also should extend towards the tail of the fish, passing through the body cavity wall into the musculature and out through the skin. Antennas of stomach tags generally must extend forward into the mouth of the fish; hence long antennas on smaller fish are likely to be bent, reducing their efficiency.

Tuned-loop antennas are the alternative to straight antennas. Tuned loops are placed on tags by winding the antenna into a coil. Tuned loops have shorter transmission ranges, but they avoid the risk of infection and behavioral change caused by straight, protruding antennas. Continuing improvements in tuned-loop transmitting antennas make them more useful as time passes.

7.4.3.2   Tag Localization

The general methods for tracking animals tagged with radios are the same as described for ultrasonic tags (section 7.3.3), except that radio signals are received in the air. As with ultrasonic tracking, practice is necessary to learn the capabilities and characteristics of each combination of tag, antenna, and environment.

The size and style of a receiving antenna are critical to the efficient detection of radio tags. As with transmitting antennas, the size of a receiving antenna is a function of wavelength, again related to the signal frequency. Because the signals are received in air, the relationship between wavelength and frequency differs from that in water:

$$\text{wavelength } (\lambda, \text{ in m}) = 300/\text{frequency (in MHz)}.$$

Thus, radio wavelengths for a given frequency are about nine times longer in air than in water. For the 50-MHz example described earlier, the wavelength in air is 6 m. Consequently, receiving antennas must be considerably longer than transmitting antennas; this often becomes the limiting factor for equipment and frequency choices.

Four styles of antennas are commonly used. The whip antenna (also called a dipole antenna) is the simplest type, consisting of a single straight element. Radio antennas for cars and portable radios are whip antennas. Whip antennas pick up signals from all directions, so they cannot indicate the direction from which the signal is coming. Whip antennas are generally made one-half the length of the wavelength being received; consequently, a frequency of 50 MHz would require a 3-m receiving whip antenna. Such long antennas can be used for airplane, satellite, or fixed-station tracking, but they are generally impractical for tracking in small boats or on foot. Because the receiving range of a whip antenna shrinks along with its length, shorter antennas ($\lambda/8$, for example) are limited to uses within a small area (e.g., a farm pond) or at a specific location (e.g., fish passing a fish ladder; Winter 1983).

The Yagi antenna is the most popular style. It consists of several (usually three) parallel elements attached to a perpendicular support which is in turn attached to a vertical pole (Figure 7.9). The rooftop television antenna is a Yagi. Each parallel element is slightly shorter than the previous element. Yagi antennas are popular because they are highly directional and are the most sensitive of common antennas (Tyus 1982). A Yagi antenna can detect signals from about twice as far away as a whip antenna of the same length. Because the signal strength is greatest when the shortest element is closest to the transmitter (Kenward 1987), Yagi antennas can detect both the path of the signal and the direction from which it is coming.

The longest element of a Yagi antenna is generally made equal to one-half the signal wavelength, just like a whip antenna. Therefore, Yagi antennas can be even more cumbersome than whip antennas because of their complex structure. This is most problematic when animals are tracked from land, such as along a stream-bank. Consequently, frequencies used with Yagi antennas may need to be higher than those used with whip antennas. For example, raising the signal frequency from 50 to 150 MHz allows the longest element of the Yagi to be only 1 m, a more manageable size.

A third antenna style is the H-antenna, composed of two equal-length parallel elements connected by a central rod. Through proper phasing of the signals received from the two elements, the antenna produces a very distinct null signal when the two elements are equally distant from the tag (Kenward 1987). This antenna is almost as sensitive as a Yagi and can be much smaller. It is bidirectional, however, indicating the path of the signal but not the direction from which it is coming.

The fourth antenna type is the tuned loop (Figure 7.10). For receivers, the tuned loop is basically a whip antenna bent into a circular or diamond shape, with both ends attached to the receiving unit. The circular antennas on portable televisions are tuned loops. For a tuned loop of the same length as a whip antenna, the receiving range is about 50% greater. Tuned-loop antennas are also directional, indicating the signal path, but cannot detect the direction of the signal in all cases (Kenward 1987). Tuned-loop antennas produce very strong signals when a tag is

Figure 7.9 A typical Yagi antenna being used in a small boat. Reprinted from Winter (1983).

near, especially when it is within the loop. Therefore, tuned-loop antennas are useful for locating animals precisely or for recovering tags that have been shed (Winter 1983). Also, because tuned-loop antennas are small and compact, they are useful for tracking in heavily obstructed locations, such as along streambanks or in dense marsh vegetation.

The procedure for locating an animal depends on the type of antenna. Regardless of the method, however, the antenna should be mounted as high as possible because signals increase in strength as they become more to the water surface (Kenward 1987).

Yagi antennas should be mounted at least one-half wavelength above obstacles in the boat to avoid reflective interference (Winter 1983). Because radio signals leaving water are generally polarized vertically (that is, the signals travel in a vertical plane), the elements of the Yagi antenna should be mounted so the plane of the elements is perpendicular to the water surface, as shown in Figure 7.9. The antenna should be mounted so that it can rotate freely in a 360° arc. The Yagi receives a peak signal when the plane of the elements is parallel to the bearing of the tag and receives null signals when rotated 90° from the tag in either direction. Winter (1983) recommended listening for the null signals rather than the peak signals, because the null signals are easier to distinguish. The antenna is rotated in a complete circle, and the bearing noted for the plane of the antenna at each

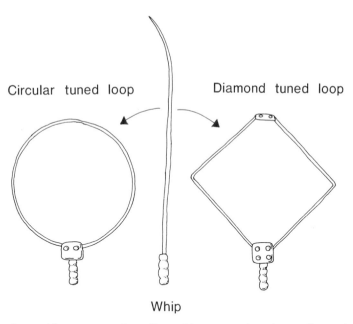

Circular tuned loop   Diamond tuned loop

Whip

Figure 7.10 A tuned-loop antenna is really a whip antenna bent into a diamond or circle.

of the two null points. The tag is located along the midline between these two nulls.

Kenward (1987), writing about wildlife tagging, recommended a different procedure. He suggested finding the strongest signal and then turning down the receiver volume (gain) until the signal becomes barely audible. Then the antenna is rotated away on one side and slowly moved back toward the target until the signal again becomes audible. Repeating the same operation from the other direction produces a second point where the signal again becomes audible. The bearing of the tag is the midline between these two bearings (Figure 7.11).

The procedure for using an H-antenna is similar. The plane of the two elements should be oriented vertically to receive the greatest amount of signal energy. Kenward (1987) suggested rotating the antenna until a sharp null occurs. The bearing to the tag is then 90° to either side of the plane of the antenna.

A tuned-loop antenna also works like a Yagi. It detects the peak signal when the plane of the antenna lies parallel to the tag bearing. The plane of the loop should be oriented vertically rather than horizontally for maximum signal reception. Either the Winter (1983) or Kenward (1987) method can be used for detecting the bearing. In addition, the direction of the tag along the bearing may be guessed by holding the loop against the chest of the tracker. In this orientation, the signal should be somewhat stronger when the tracker faces toward the tag (Kenward 1987).

7.5 NEW DEVELOPMENTS IN BIOTELEMETRY

Biotelemetry is developing rapidly because of its substantial promise for fisheries, wildlife, and general societal uses. Consequently, the capabilities of

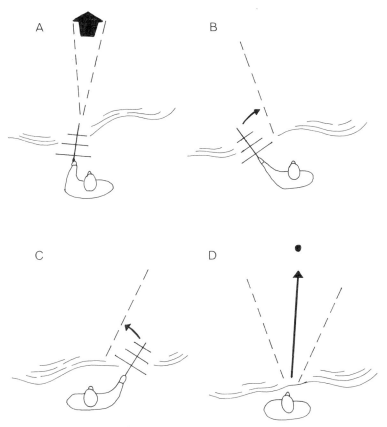

Figure 7.11 The Kenward (1987) procedure for finding a tag bearing: **(A)** the general direction of the peak signal is identified and the gain lowered; **(B)** the antenna is moved to one side and then moved slowly back toward the signal direction until the signal is heard; **(C)** the process is repeated from the other side; **(D)** the bisector of these two bearings is the tag bearing.

radio and ultrasonic tags will improve and the size of the tags will decrease consistently in the future. Undoubtedly, the disadvantages mentioned here will become less significant in the future, allowing biotelemetry to be used in a broader range of conditions and for a broader range of studies. Biotelemetry will also become more important as the kinds of studies undertaken become more detailed. Biotelemetry is almost the only technique that allows precise monitoring of animal behavior.

Tag manufacturers are constantly improving the technical performance of tags. An anticipated transmitter improvement is more consistent transmission frequency, reducing the drift problem (Kenward 1987). This will allow more tags to be used simultaneously, expanding the number of animals that can be effectively monitored in each study. Batteries are becoming smaller, more powerful, and more consistent in their delivery of power over extended periods, allowing longer studies and studies of smaller species and life stages.

As the quality increases, more control over signal characteristics will be possible. Hence, physiological and habitat data may be more reliably collected.

Pressure sensors, for example, have not been particularly useful in fisheries because the range in pressure needed to cause detectable changes in signal characteristics (e.g., pulse rate) is much greater than the pressure range experienced by animals in most aquatic ecosystems. In the future, however, better circuitry will probably allow the detection of smaller differences in depth and pressure.

More sophisticated signal characteristics may also allow individual identification of more animals. Different pulse codes on the same frequency are already in common use, increasing the number of animals that can be tracked, especially by automated monitoring systems. Rusanowski et al. (1990) have moved further, by developing tags that transmit two pulse rates at repeated intervals. This allows the assignment of a unique two-digit number to a tagged animal, making many animals identifiable on the same frequency.

7.6 REFERENCES

Chisholm, I. M., and W. A. Hubert. 1985. Expulsion of dummy transmitters by rainbow trout. Transactions of the American Fisheries Society 114:766–767.

Diana, J. S., D. F. Clapp, E. M. Hay-Chmielewski, G. Schnicke, D. Siler, W. Ziegler, and R. D. Clark, Jr. 1990. Relative success of telemetry studies in Michigan. American Fisheries Society Symposium 7:346–352.

Eiler, J. H. 1990. Radio transmitters used to study salmon in glacial rivers. American Fisheries Society Symposium 7:364–369.

Hayashi, F., and M. Nakane. 1989. Radio tracking and activity monitoring of the dobsonfly larva, *Protohermes grandis* (Megaloptera: Corydalidae). Oecologia (Berlin) 78:468–472.

Holland, K., R. Brill, S. Ferguson, R. Chang, and R. Yost. 1985. A small tracking vessel technique for tracking pelagic fish. U.S. National Marine Fisheries Service Marine Fisheries Review 47(4):26–32.

Hurley, S. T., W. A. Hubert, and J. G. Nickum. 1987. Habitats and movements of shovelnose sturgeons in the upper Mississippi River. Transactions of the American Fisheries Society 116:655–662.

Kenward, R. 1987. Wildlife radio tagging. Academic Press, London.

Lewis, A. E., and W. R. A. Muntz. 1984. The effects of external ultrasonic tagging on the swimming performance of rainbow trout, *Salmo gairdneri* Richardson. Journal of Fish Biology 25:577–585.

Marty, G. D., and R. C. Summerfelt. 1986. Pathways and mechanisms for expulsion of surgically implanted dummy transmitters from channel catfish. Transactions of the American Fisheries Society 115:577–589.

Matthews, K. R., T. P. Quinn, and B. S. Miller. 1990. Use of ultrasonic transmitters to track demersal rockfish movements on shallow rocky reefs. American Fisheries Society Symposium 7:375–379.

Mellas, E. J., and J. M. Haynes. 1985. Swimming performance and behavior of rainbow trout (*Salmo gairdneri*) and white perch (*Morone americana*): effects of attaching telemetry transmitters. Canadian Journal of Fisheries and Aquatic Sciences 42:488–493.

Mortensen, D. G. 1990. Use of staple sutures to close surgical incisions for transmitter implants. American Fisheries Society Symposium 7:380–383.

Moser, M. L., A. F. Olson, and T. P. Quinn. 1990. Effects of dummy ultrasonic transmitters on juvenile coho salmon. American Fisheries Society Symposium 7:353–356.

Olson, F. W., E. S. Kuehl, K. W. Burton, and J. S. Sigg. 1990. Use of radiotelemetry to estimate survival of saugers passed through turbines and spillbays at dams. American Fisheries Society Symposium 7:357–363.

Rusanowski, P. C., E. L. Smith, and M. Cochran. 1990. Monitoring the nearshore movement of red king crabs under sea ice with ultrasonic tags. American Fisheries Society Symposium 7:384–389.

Stasko, A. B., and D. G. Pincock. 1977. Review of underwater biotelemetry, with emphasis on ultrasonic techniques. Journal of the Fisheries Research Board of Canada 34:1261–1285.

Stuehrenberg, L., A. Giorgi, and C. Bartlett. 1990. Pulse-coded radio tags for fish identification. American Fisheries Society Symposium 7:370–374.

Summerfelt, R. C., and L. S. Smith. 1990. Anesthesia, surgery, and related techniques. Pages 213–272 in C. B. Schreck and P. B. Moyle, editors. Methods for fish biology. American Fisheries Society, Bethesda, Maryland.

Tyus, H. M. 1982. Fish biotelemetry: theory and application for high conductivity rivers. U.S. Fish and Wildlife Service FWS/OBS-82/83.

Williams, T. H., and R. G. White. 1990. Evaluation of pressure-sensitive radio transmitters used for monitoring depth selection by trout in lotic systems. American Fisheries Society Symposium 7:390–394.

Winter, J. D. 1983. Underwater biotelemetry. Pages 371–395 in L. A. Nielsen and D. L. Johnson, editors. Fisheries techniques. American Fisheries Society, Bethesda, Maryland.

Chapter 8

Genetic Identification and Marking

8.1 INTRODUCTION

Genetic identification, like biotelemetry, is quite different from traditional marking techniques. Whereas traditional techniques require altering an animal's body, genetic identification relies on recognizing inherent characteristics of the body—its genetic blueprint. As with biotelemetry, the utility of genetic information for identification is a product of modern science.

Genetic identification relies on our ability to detect differences in the structure of genes (Hallerman and Beckmann 1988) or gene products (Davis et al. 1990). Sometimes the genetically based differences are readily apparent (human eye color, for example) or easily detectable (human blood types). But subtle differences also exist, and their detection requires more sophisticated biochemical testing. This field has developed very rapidly in the past two decades, through the techniques of protein electrophoresis and mitochondrial DNA analysis, the two techniques described in this chapter. And developments are continuing, with growing emphasis on DNA fingerprinting, by which individual organisms can be uniquely identified.

Genetic-based identifiers are useful in fisheries when their distribution coincides with other important management differences. For example, if fish that spawn in separate rivers are genetically different and if the differences can be detected reliably, fish captured in a mixed fishery can be assigned to the appropriate spawning stocks. If fisheries managers suspect that organisms from a protected wild stock are being illegally caught and sold as cultured fish, genetic analysis may reveal the true origin of the marketed fish. Genetic characteristics also can be manipulated to create true genetic marks. Through selective breeding, the frequency of specific genetic traits can be increased or decreased, so that a population becomes identifiably different from others.

Research into biochemical genetic characterization of animals began about 30 years ago, as general interest in molecular biology and gene structure was beginning to expand (Shaklee and Phelps 1990). The earliest application of biochemical genetics to fisheries began in 1966 with Pacific salmon. Since then, genetic studies have been performed on more than 1,200 animal species, including some 200 fish species (Aebersold et al. 1987; Winans 1989).

Genetic identification is the most complex technique covered in this book. Aside from the need for in-depth understanding of genetics and biochemistry, the methodology requires exacting laboratory techniques. Interpretation of the results

155

is often indeterminate and may require multivariate statistical techniques. For these reasons, genetic identification projects always require the advice and assistance of expert geneticists.

Because of the complexities, this chapter presents an overview of genetic identification rather than detailed prescriptions. Even when specific procedures are described, they are intended primarily as examples. Persons planning to use genetic identification should review basic genetics and then read some of the several recent texts on biochemical genetics, such as Lewontin (1974), Nei (1975), Lewin (1987), Ryman and Utter (1987), Speiss (1989), Hillis and Montz (1990), and Kirby (1990). Subsequently, they should consult with fisheries geneticists to discuss their general and detailed plans.

8.1.1 A Primer on Basic Genetics

Some review of genetics is necessary as background for understanding genetic identification techniques and analysis. This is particularly important for protein synthesis, which is the basis for much genetic identification. Box 8.1 provides a brief glossary of technical terms, and the description of genetics that follows is adapted largely from Allendorf and Ferguson (1990).

The basic genetic material is the molecule deoxyribonucleic acid (DNA), arrayed with histone proteins to form chromosomes in the nuclei of cells. The DNA molecule can be imagined as a ladder, wrapped spirally around a hollow cylinder, producing the familiar double-helix shape. The ladder's supports are strands of alternating sugar and phosphate molecules, and the rungs are pairs of nucleotide bases. Each base is bound tightly to a sugar molecule on one side and loosely to its corresponding base on the other side.

The sequence of bases along the DNA molecule is the genetic information that determines an individual's inherited characteristics. Segments of each DNA molecule contain the codes for directing specific functions in a cell. Each of these segments is called a "locus." The loci that direct the synthesis of proteins (chains of amino acids that become muscle fibers, enzymes, and other chemically active compounds in the body) are of particular interest for genetic identification. Through a multistep transcription and translation process involving messenger (mRNA) and transfer (tRNA) ribonucleic acids, the DNA code at each locus directs the linking of amino acids together in the precise order to form a particular protein (Figure 8.1).

Mutation is the change in sequence of bases within a DNA locus. Mutations have four possible consequences, described here in terms of protein synthesis. First, a mutation may cause no change in the order of amino acid assembly; this happens if the code is redundant—that is, if more than one DNA base sequence represents the same amino acid. Second, a mutation may cause a change in amino acid order that is disadvantageous to the animal; if the disadvantage impairs an animal's survival or reproduction, the mutation will ultimately disappear. Third, a mutation may cause a change that is advantageous to the animal; if the advantage enhances survival or reproduction, the mutation may become widespread in the population, and the original sequence may disappear. Fourth, a mutation may cause a change in amino acid order that has no effect on the individual; such a mutation is called "neutral" with regard to selection, and it may remain in the population indefinitely, varying in frequency according to random events.

Box 8.1   Glossary of Fishery Genetics Terms

Allele	The specific DNA sequence at a locus that causes synthesis of a protein.
Allozyme	Slighty different forms of an enzyme that are synthesized by different alleles at a single locus and that are identifiable through electrophoresis.
Enzyme	A protein that is synthesized at a single locus and performs a specific catalytic function in an organism.
Gene	A sequence of DNA base pairs that performs a specific function, such as directing the synthesis of a protein.
Genome	The genetic information contained within and characterizing an individual organism; often refers to the sum of genes and alleles that we can list for an individual.
Genotype	The list of alleles for an individual at a particular locus or series of loci.
Isozyme	Slightly different forms of an enzyme that perform the same function but are synthesized at different loci and are identifiable through electrophoresis.
Locus	The location of a gene on a chromosome; used routinely as a synonym for "gene."
Monomer	A protein composed of only a single genetically synthesized subunit. (See multimer.)
Monomorphic	Designating a locus with only one allele in a population.
Multimer	A protein composed of two or more genetically synthesized subunits (two subunits make a dimer, three make a trimer, four make a tetramer, etc.).
Phenotype	The physical expression of a genotype.
Polymorphic	Designating a locus with two or more alleles in a population.

Neutral mutations are particularly important as a basis for genetic identification. The differences that occur in the DNA sequence at each particular locus are called alleles. If the DNA sequence at a locus is the same for every individual in a population, then the locus has only one allele and is called monomorphic. If two or more alleles at a locus occur in a population, the locus is called polymorphic.

Animals normally have two complete sets of chromosomes (i.e., they are diploid); thus, they also have two complete sets of complementary gene loci. A diploid organism inherits one set from each parent, through the normal process of sexual reproduction. The separation of the complementary genes of spawning

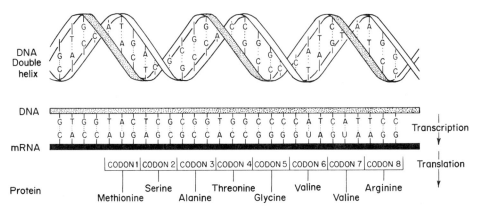

Figure 8.1   The process of synthesizing amino acid chains, from DNA to protein; A, C, G, and T are nucleic acid bases. Reprinted from Allendorf and Ferguson (1990).

animals to form gametes and their recombination as embryos produce a variety of possible combinations of alleles.

An animal may have the same allele at each of the complementary loci (homozygous) or different alleles (heterozygous). For example, if two alleles exist in the population (*A* and *a*), homozygous animals could have *AA* or *aa* genotypes at this locus, and heterozygous animals would have an *Aa* genotype. If three alleles were present (*A, a,* and *a'*), the homozygotes could have *AA, aa,* or *a'a'* genotypes, and the heterozygotes could have *Aa, Aa',* or *aa'* genotypes.

This story of genetic inheritance is greatly simplified for presentation but it is complicated in reality—and population genetics books must be consulted to understand how genetic variations may occur and how they may affect a particular genetic identification project.

One implicit complication in many studies does require definition here. The functions of some loci are unique; that is, only one complementary pair of loci performs a particular function. For example, a single locus may direct the synthesis of a particular enzyme. Some functions are not unique, however, but are encoded independently by more than one pair of loci. Thus, two loci may direct the synthesis of the same enzyme or its parts. Versions of the same enzyme coded by different loci are called isozymes.

8.1.2   Methods of Genetic Identification

8.1.2.1   Protein Electrophoresis

Protein electrophoresis identifies different genotypes by distinguishing slight physical differences in proteins (usually enzymes) produced by different alleles. The different forms of enzymes coded by a locus are called allozymes; consequently, the technique is sometimes called allozyme electrophoresis.

Tissue samples from individual animals are placed on a substrate (usually a starch-based gel slab), bathed in a current-carrying liquid, and exposed to an electrical current. Protein molecules migrate through the gel at different rates determined by their genetically based weight, net electrical charge, and three-dimensional structure. When the current is removed, the different molecules are

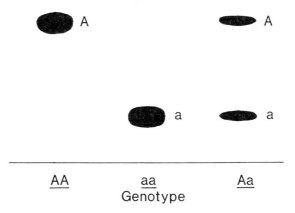

Figure 8.2   Example of a gel pattern of proteins produced by a polymorphic locus with alleles (*A, a*) for a fast-moving (A) and a slow-moving (a) monomeric protein.

arrayed across the gel at different distances from the origin of migration. The gel is treated with protein-specific stains, revealing the distribution of molecules as a banding pattern (Figure 8.2).

All homozygous individuals would have one band, representing all the identical protein molecules (either A or a in Figure 8.2) assembled under the direction of the single allele present (*A* or *a*; by convention, symbols referring to loci and alleles are italicized and symbols denoting proteins are not). Each heterozygous individual would have two bands (both A and a in Figure 8.2), representing the two protein molecules assembled under the direction of the two alleles.

A structural characteristic of proteins complicates this picture somewhat. Proteins are often composed of repeated subunits of smaller amino acid chains. A protein that is composed of a single subunit is called a monomer; one composed of two or more subunits is a multimer (also, a protein made of two subunits is a dimer, one composed of three subunits is a trimer, one composed of four subunits is a tetramer, etc.).

For homozygotes, the multimeric structure makes no difference for genetic identification. Because all the subunits in the multimer are identical proteins produced by the single allele present, all the multimers respond identically to electrophoresis. For example, a tetrameric protein synthesized by a homozygote with the *A* allele would have a protein composed of four identical A subunits (represented as AAAA). For heterozygotes, however, several different multimers could exist, depending on how the smaller subunit proteins were randomly assembled. A heterozygote with *A* and *a* alleles would have tetrameric enzymes composed of all combinations of A and a taken four at a time (represented as AAAA, AAAa, AAaa, Aaaa, and aaaa). If the different multimers have different weights and electric charges, they would produce more-complex, multiple-banded patterns (Figure 8.3). For the two-allele tetramer example, the pattern includes five bands, with densities proportional to their frequency (1 AAAA:4 AAAa:6 AAaa:4 Aaaa:1 aaaa). Interpretation of these more complex banding patterns is often difficult, requiring training, experience, and the advice of experts.

Electrophoretic patterns for a large sample of individual organisms reveal two important features of a population. First, patterns show the frequency distribution

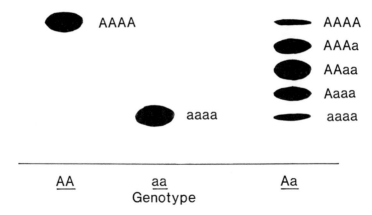

Figure 8.3 Example of a gel pattern of proteins produced by a polymorphic locus with alleles (*A, a*) for a fast-moving (A) and a slow-moving (a) subunit of a tetrameric protein.

of genotypes in the population. For the example in Figure 8.4, the population includes 50% *AA* homozygotes, 10% *aa* homozygotes, and 40% *Aa* heterozygotes. Second, patterns reveal the frequency distribution of alleles in the population. For the example in Figure 8.4, the population contains 70% allele *A* (two in each *AA* homozygote and one in each heterozygote) and 30% allele *a* (two in each *aa* homozygote and one in each heterozygote).

8.1.2.2 Mitochondrial DNA

The second method of genetic identification examines mitochondrial DNA (abbreviated as mtDNA). Although most DNA occurs in the nucleus of cells, mtDNA occurs in the mitochondria. Mitochondrial DNA is a circular molecule and is relatively small (about 15,000 to 18,000 base pairs long; Ferris and Berg 1987). Many copies of the mtDNA molecule occur in the mitochondria of each

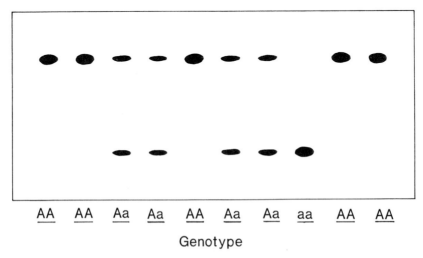

Figure 8.4 Example of a phenotypic pattern for a sample of 10 individuals with the same polymorphic locus for monomeric proteins shown in Figure 8.2.

cell, and they are usually identical among the cells of an individual organism (Billington and Hebert 1990).

Useful information for genetic identification is gathered by chemically digesting the mtDNA molecules. Specific enzymes, called restriction endonucleases or "probes," recognize specific sequences of bases in the mtDNA molecule (called recognition sites) and break the molecule apart wherever the recognition site occurs. If the recognition site occurs only once in the molecule, the mtDNA breaks from its circular form into a linear chain. If the recognition site occurs more than once, however, the molecule breaks into fragments of various lengths containing various numbers of genes. This mixture of fragments with differing lengths and, hence, differing weights, can be separated in an electrophoretic field much like that used for protein analysis. Many restriction endonucleases are available commercially, each operating at a different recognition site and producing a different pattern for an individual organism.

Just as with protein electrophoresis, the patterns of mtDNA fragments are inherited and the frequency distribution of fragment lengths for a specific restriction endonuclease may be characteristic of a population of animals. Unlike proteins, however, mtDNA is inherited only from the female parent, via egg tissue (Ferris and Berg 1987). Protein and mtDNA analyses, therefore, reveal somewhat different information, which can be used to advantage in some identification programs.

8.1.3 Uses of Genetic Identification

Genetic information has many uses in the biological analysis of individuals, populations, and species. As a form of identification, however, genetic information is generally used in fisheries to differentiate individuals and populations of different origins. Because genetic information is inherited, it reflects the long-term history of populations rather than short-term phenomena such as habitat use or local movements.

Genetic techniques have been used principally in fisheries to characterize mixed stocks of animals. Where animals from different spawning areas congregate together, the mixture can be apportioned to the respective reproductive stocks according to protein or mtDNA patterns (Utter and Seeb 1990). Such data can show which stocks of animals have migrated to a particular location and the migratory paths used by stocks from hatching to spawning. The ability to apportion a mixed group of animals to specific stocks can be used to allocate catch where competing groups claim rights to the harvest based on a stock's spawning location.

Genetic information also can help identify individuals that are not easily recognizable by standard taxonomic criteria. Fish eggs and larvae often can be separated into species on the basis of genetic information when they cannot be separated morphologically (Pella and Milner 1987). Outwardly similar species have been distinguished on the basis of genetic differences (Tsuyuki and Westrheim 1970), and Avise and Saunders (1984) used genetic information to classify hybrid sunfish, whose appearance varied widely among individuals.

The long-term stability of genetic information also can reveal the history of populations and species. Seeb et al. (1987) traced the probable pattern of northern pike recolonization in North American after the last ice age by comparing gene frequencies of various populations. Similar analyses can help determine if populations in particular locations are native or introduced, valuable information for identifying stocks eligible for protection or for use as brood fish for recolonization projects (Campton and Johnston 1985).

Finally, genetic information can document the effectiveness of stocking. If hatchery brood stock have a unique allele or lack an allele common among wild animals, their offspring may be distinguishable from wild animals after stocking. Genetic examinations of the enhanced stock in subsequent years will reveal what proportion of animals survived from the hatchery and from natural reproduction. If different genetic identifiers exist among the brood stocks at different hatcheries, even the relative effectiveness among hatcheries can be evaluated.

8.2 ASSUMPTIONS OF GENETIC IDENTIFICATION

The assumptions regarding the use of genetic information for stock identification relate mostly to the structure and function of the genetic material. Genetic materials are parts of complex reproductive and physiological systems, and their primary functions may affect their utility as genetic identifiers. As mentioned earlier, the consultation of expert geneticists is probably necessary to determine whether and how specific genetic characteristics affect a particular study. The assumptions described here, therefore, are only the more fundamental and obvious ones likely to be confronted in most studies.

One assumption for accurate stock identification by means of protein electrophoresis is that the chosen genetic features are inherited in simple Mendelian fashion (Utter and Seeb 1990). This assumption has at least two components. First, each locus must sort independently; that is, each locus must be on a separate chromosome. If two loci are linked (on the same chromosome) and assumed to be unlinked, then the information from the two loci will be systematically biased. Second, each allele must be expressed without dominance. That is, a heterozygote must form a pattern on the gel that is distinguishable from the corresponding homozygotes. This pattern may consist of the sum of the patterns of the two homozygotes or it may be a unique banding pattern. This assumption, as well as others relating to Mendelian inheritance, cannot be readily predicted, but must be tested in the preliminary stages of a genetics study. As described later, the search for suitable alleles may require screening as many as 50 different loci (Nei 1978). The substantial success of protein electrophoresis shows that a suitable set of alleles is likely to be available for most animal species.

Another assumption for accurate stock identification is that the allelic frequencies being monitored are stable—neither increasing nor decreasing naturally in abundance. This is particularly important if an allele's frequency is being purposefully changed to produce a genetic mark. This assumption is likely to be valid if a locus has many alleles (that is, if it is highly polymorphic) or if several alleles are relatively common (Utter and Seeb 1990). The assumption is less likely to be valid if similar alleles in other species have been shown to be deleterious or if the locus is linked to deleterious genes (Gharrett and Seeb 1990). The assumption is also less likely to be valid in populations under strong selective pressure, such as those experiencing genetic bottlenecks, founder effects, or rapid isolation. In particular, it will be invalid if a target allele itself is subject to strong positive or negative selection pressure.

The assumption of stability is readily tested by monitoring allelic frequencies through time. A suitable allele should not change in frequency over the life span of a cohort of individuals (Lane et al. 1990) or over several generations within a population (Utter and Seeb 1990).

Another assumption, common to all sampling techniques, is that the information provided by the sample is accurate for the population. Beyond routine guidelines about sample size, the sample of individuals examined genetically must be large enough to represent the frequencies of all alleles and genotypes. Rare alleles are likely to be underrepresented if the sample size is small because the probability of sampling homozygotes for a rare allele is very low. For example, a homozygote for an allele with a frequency of 5% will occur on average only once in a sample of 400 individuals.

An additional aspect of accuracy is whether or not genetic information will always detect stock differences when they occur. Stock differences may escape detection for several reasons. Different alleles may produce identical proteins, so that differences in allelic frequencies cannot be detected. Similarly, different alleles may produce proteins with molecular weights and charges that are so similar they cannot be distinguished electrophoretically. Most importantly, however, protein and mtDNA analyses examine only a small part of an individual's genetic material—never more than 1% (Utter et al. 1987). Therefore, although the observation of genetic variation generally signifies different stocks, the absence of observed variation does not mean that the stocks are the same.

8.3 ADVANTAGES OF GENETIC IDENTIFICATION (Box 8.2)

Both the advantages and disadvantages of protein electrophoresis and mtDNA analysis are similar for identifying stocks. Therefore, the two methods will be considered together in this and the following section.

A primary advantage of genetic methods for stock identification is that the methods are natural. No artificial tags or mutilation of body parts are needed because the identifier is a biochemical pattern revealed through genetic material or gene products. Even for genetic marking itself, in which allelic frequencies are purposefully changed, the marking process will not alter the growth, mortality, or behavior of the animals if the alleles are properly chosen to be selectively neutral.

Because the method is natural, each individual in the population carries information useful for the identification process. Artificial tags and mutilations must be applied to a captive population that will be released or to a small sample of a wild population that has been captured and will be released again; in both cases, few individuals in the larger population carry the mark. In contrast, if a genetic pattern is unique for a population, every individual can be positively identified as a member of that population. Even if identification is based on proportional allelic frequencies, every individual contributes to the creation of the frequency distribution (Pella and Milner 1987). Therefore, the number of individuals generally needed for genetic identification is in the hundreds, rather than the thousands usually needed for a conventionally marked population.

Box 8.2   Advantages and Disadvantages of Genetic Identification

Advantages

- Natural method, requiring no artifical marks
- All individuals carry information
- All life stages carry information
- Information lasts throughout life span of individual
- Information passes between generations
- Sufficient polymorphism available in most species
- Experience available from medical and biological fields
- Inexpensive per sample

Disadvantages

- Often requires sacrificing animals
- Technically complex
- Interpretation of results is difficult
- Information usually about groups, not individuals
- Experts needed for successful use

Genetic information also lasts a lifetime. Every individual inherits its identification when egg and sperm fuse, allowing continuous identification throughout the life span. Usually, geneticists can analyze genetic information regardless of an individual's size or life stage because only a minute tissue sample is needed. Thus, great detail can be revealed about a population, from egg to spawning adult (Milner et al. 1985).

A related advantage, unique to genetic identification, is that genetic information transfers from one generation to the next (Utter and Seeb 1990). Although an individual's genetic makeup may differ from its parents' because of reproductive recombination, allelic frequencies for a stock are typically stable through generations (Pella and Milner 1987). Mitochondrial DNA shows even more fidelity between generations, because it is inherited via the egg tissue from the female parent.

A technical advantage is that many possible genetic identifiers are available. Many aquatic species exhibit substantial polymorphism (about 5% of loci are polymorphic for the average fish species; Winans 1989), providing the heterogeneity needed to differentiate stocks. Polymorphism varies widely among species, however, in both quantity and locus. Generally, polymorphism is greater in freshwater species than in marine species (Wirgin et al. 1990). Polymorphism is also more common in mtDNA than in proteins, partly because mtDNA mutates more rapidly than nuclear DNA (Ferris and Berg 1987). For all these reasons, an expansive baseline survey of possible heterogeneity is necessary for every species under study. Krueger et al. (1989), for example, examined 102 loci of lake trout in Lake Ontario to determine the extent and locations of polymorphism.

Another methodological advantage is that genetic identification is widely practiced in biological and medical disciplines. Geneticists from these disciplines share similar experiences because genetic materials and proteins have similar biochemical properties throughout the animal kingdom. Although communication is sometimes impaired by lack of standardization, the popularity of genetic investigations greatly stimulates the development of techniques and applications and makes specialized equipment and materials more available.

Lastly, genetic identification is relatively inexpensive. Provided that adequate polymorphism exists in a species, the process of conducting protein electrophoresis for one individual is approximately one-tenth as expensive as physical tagging, release, and recovery methods (Milner et al. 1985). As with other modern identification methods, genetic techniques will surely become less expensive and more widely applicable in the future.

8.4 DISADVANTAGES OF GENETIC IDENTIFICATION (Box 8.2)

A principal disadvantage of genetic information gathering is that sampling usually requires sacrificing the individual animal. Genetic information is revealed best in the soft tissues of internal organs; collecting enough tissue generally requires killing the animal. Improvements in technique occur regularly, however, and many tests now can be done with very small samples of blood, fin, skin, or muscle tissue, for both protein and DNA analyses (Carmichael et al. 1986; Billington and Hebert 1990). Also, because genetic materials are passed from a spawning animal directly to its offspring, egg and sperm tissue can sometimes be used to identify a highly valuable adult.

Extracting genetic information from animal tissue is technically complex. After tissues are collected, they must be handled expertly because even short periods of improper handling or storage can lead to degradation of protein and DNA molecules (Seeb et al. 1990). Most work requires specially equipped laboratories dedicated principally to genetic analysis. Within the laboratory, storage, handling, and processing of samples must meet exacting standards. For these reasons, all aspects of genetic analysis must be fully documented, and all procedural modifications should be reviewed by peers, tested for repeatability, and formally documented (Shaklee and Phelps 1990).

The interpretation of genetic information can be difficult. The examples in this chapter are purposefully simple, to serve as basic illustrations. In reality, stained electrophoretic gels often reveal patterns whose interpretation requires considerable expertise and experience. With multiple loci, alleles, and multimers, the complexity can be intimidating, especially when the species, geographic areas, or genetic loci have not been previously studied.

Genetic stock identification usually produces statistical information about groups rather than absolute information about individuals. Individual animals can be positively assigned to a stock only when an allele or allelic pattern is fixed (that is, it occurs uniquely in a single stock). Fixed patterns occur rarely; in most cases, the same alleles exist in many stocks, but at different frequencies. The process of apportioning a mixed group of animals to their original stocks, therefore, is a statistical question of deciding the most likely proportions of separate stocks (each with known allelic frequencies) that produced the observed allelic frequencies (Shaklee and Phelps 1990).

These statistical processes create classification errors. Rare alleles may not be well represented in baseline data, impairing the classification of individuals containing rare alleles to the correct stock. Similarly, some electrophoretic patterns may not be interpretable because of their novelty or complexity. Such patterns are usually eliminated from the analysis as "unknowns" and later assigned to the known stocks according to the ratios determined from the remaining sample. Unusual patterns, however, may represent one or more additional stocks that cannot be distinguished with current techniques (Shaklee and Phelps 1990). Strict and explicit statistical protocols are necessary to control these possible errors.

The compelling conclusion from these disadvantages must be the same as given earlier—genetic identification should be conducted by experts. From conception to interpretation, the rigors of this approach defy its use by the typical fisheries manager or researcher. Agencies are most likely to develop successful genetic identification programs, therefore, if they can employ a genetics staff and operate a dedicated genetics facility. Other agencies should contract genetic expertise from regional genetics programs that can serve many clients centrally.

8.5   PROTEIN AND mtDNA ELECTROPHORESIS

Because experts are needed for genetic identification, electrophoretic techniques are presented here in general rather than in detail. This section describes the steps in a genetic identification project, indicating the decisions that must be made and the choices possible. Recent references with step-by-step details include Aebersold et al. (1987) and Leary and Booke (1990) for protein electrophoresis; Ferris and Berg (1987) for mtDNA analysis; Whitmore (1990) for protein, mtDNA, and genomic DNA analyses; and Shaklee and Phelps (1990) for overall program operation.

8.5.1   Collecting Sample Organisms

The first step in electrophoresis is collecting animals from the study population. The need to define the sampling process is just as important for electrophoresis as it is for any sampling, because representative and random sampling are required to avoid bias in the results. Because the objectives of genetics studies and the corresponding laboratory techniques may vary greatly among studies, explicit decisions are needed regarding the time of collection, the collection locations, and the sizes, sexes, and life stages of the collected animals.

Genetic studies (especially those for stock identification) usually involve two separate collecting periods—one for a baseline survey and another for the experimental survey. A baseline survey describes the polymorphism of a known stock. Animals are collected at a time and place where the stock is isolated from other stocks (e.g., on a single-stock spawning ground). Genetic information from this sample will reveal the frequencies of alleles in the stock for various loci. Comparisons of baseline data among stocks will show which loci are useful for distinguishing stocks in mixed groups. In general, 50 to 100 individuals, examined at 20 or more loci, are recommended for stock characterization (Ihssen et al. 1981; Utter and Seeb 1990). For example, Krueger et al. (1989) collected 40–94 lake trout from each of 16 locations in the Lake Ontario basin as the baseline for comparing polymorphisms.

A second collection is needed to assign individuals of unknown origin to their respective stocks. This is the experimental sample, collected at a time and place where information about the identity of unknown animals is desired (e.g., on the fishing grounds). The number of individuals needed depends on several factors. Larger sample sizes are needed if the species exhibits relatively little polymorphism or if the original stocks differ relatively little in allelic frequencies. Ihssen et al. (1981) recommended collecting a sample of 200 individuals for examination at 9 or more loci.

Animals should be collected alive for tissue sampling. Proteins (and especially enzymes) begin to decompose immediately after death, causing changes in structure, biochemical responsiveness, and total concentration; all these changes can reduce the effectiveness of electrophoretic procedures. Therefore, animals that have been dead for any period of time without proper handling are unlikely to provide useful tissues for electrophoresis. Enzyme concentrations in living animals also change under stress, so animals should be maintained in favorable environmental conditions and handled gently and sparingly.

Many electrophoretic studies require sacrificing animals. This is especially likely early in a study, when baseline data are being collected for many loci, requiring large tissue samples from several organs. If animals must be sacrificed for tissue sampling, two strategies have been recommended. Ferris and Berg (1987) recommended collecting tissue samples immediately after sacrificing the animals, to stop biochemical reactions that may continue after death. Leary and Booke (1990), however, recommended retaining whole specimens because small tissue samples can dehydrate in cold storage, also causing loss of enzyme activity.

8.5.2 Collecting and Storing Tissue Samples

Because different proteins are more readily identified from different tissues, several tissues types are usually collected for general studies (Shaklee and Phelps 1990). Protein studies typically require heart, liver, eye, and muscle tissues, and mtDNA studies require kidney, liver, and spleen tissues (Ferris and Berg 1987); egg tissue and blood are also sampled frequently. As new techniques are developed, allowing additional loci to be examined, the list of sampled tissues will surely change.

The quantity of tissue needed varies greatly. Newer techniques, used mostly in research, sometimes require only minute amounts of tissue, which can be extracted without sacrificing the animal. However, several grams of each tissue are generally needed for routine analysis and for examination of a broad range of loci (Aebersold et al. 1987; Leary and Booke 1990). Mitochondrial DNA analysis requires 50–100 g of tissue.

Dissected tissues should be placed directly into clean plastic or glass tubes that will serve later as preparation vessels. This eliminates possible contamination and mislabelling during transfers. Each tissue should be divided among several tubes, one each for the various analyses that will be conducted and several others for replication and long-term storage. Because new techniques are being developed regularly, keeping samples in long-term storage will allow future evaluation of genetic information without the need for collecting additional animals (Wirgin et al. 1990).

If analysis will occur within 2 days of collection, Leary and Booke (1990) advised that either whole specimens or tissue samples can be kept refrigerated or on wet ice. For longer periods, however, whole specimens or dissected tissues must be frozen. Dry ice should be used in the field, providing a temperature as low as −80°C. Proper icing (with wet or dry ice) requires placing an ice layer on the bottom of the container, covered by alternating single layers of tissue samples or whole animals and ice (Aebersold et al. 1987). For samples that will be analyzed within 2 months, a storage temperature of −20°C is sufficient, but longer storage requires temperatures of at least −40°C and preferably −80°C (Leary and Booke 1990).

Temperature requirements for mtDNA analysis are generally less extreme. Grewe and Hebert (1988), for example, noted that mtDNA samples can be kept on wet ice for 10 days without loss of yield. Keeping samples on wet ice in the field and later storing them at −20°C may be sufficient (Ferris and Berg 1987; Schweigert and Withler 1990). However, colder storage is always desirable and should be used if available.

Some tissues for mtDNA analysis can be freeze-dried or preserved in formalin or other media. Consult current literature for developments in alternative modes of preservation.

8.5.3 Preparing Tissues

Protein electrophoresis requires little tissue preparation. The frozen tissues must be cut into smaller pieces and placed into separate tubes as needed. The quantity of tissue required must be determined for each analysis, but Aebersold et al. (1987) suggested that 0.75 g is required for most routine analyses. Only a few tissue samples (10 or fewer) should be prepared at one time, and all samples should be kept in an ice-water bath during processing.

Cell membranes must be ruptured to release proteins, so the tissue has to be homogenized. The tissue is suspended in a small amount of solution and then ground mechanically with a glass rod or ruptured ultrasonically (Leary and Booke 1990). The grinding solution can be distilled water, a special grinding solution, or the buffer solution that will be used subsequently in the electrophoresis process itself (Box 8.3). As with all chemical procedures, the precise recipes and performances of various grinding solutions should be carefully recorded and willingly shared with colleagues (Aebersold et al. 1987; Shaklee and Phelps 1990). After grinding, the resulting mixture can be centrifuged to separate remaining tissue fragments from the homogenate (Leary and Booke 1990).

The preparation of tissues for mtDNA analysis is much more involved. The mtDNA must first be isolated from other cellular components, including nuclear DNA. This requires ultracentrifugation in a cesium chloride medium, sometimes more than once (Ferris and Berg 1987). Although this is an exacting laboratory process, it is now routine for experienced geneticists. Because several different analyses are usually conducted, the homogenate should be separated into the required number of tubes.

The resulting mtDNA homogenate must then be treated with restriction endonucleases to cleave the molecule. Each restriction endonuclease recognizes a specific sequence of bases, either 4, 5, or 6 bases long (called recognition sites). The utility of each restriction endonuclease depends on study objectives and the amount of polymorphism in the species being examined. Generally, restriction

Box 8.3 Recipes for Electrophoresis Buffers

Electrophoresis uses a variety of solutions to homogenize tissues, dissolve starch, carry electrical current, and stain gels. The best recipe for each depends on many factors, including the individual preferences of scientists. The following three recipes for gel and tray buffers were offered by Leary and Booke (1990) to fit most needs in electrophoresis.

Amine–Citric Acid Buffer

Gel buffer	Citric acid at 0.42 g/L
	Adjust pH to 6.1 with N-(3-aminopropyl)-morpholine
Tray buffer	Citric acid at 8.40 g/L
	Adjust pH to 6.1 with N-(3-aminopropyl)-morpholine
	Run at 50 milliamperes and 125–150 volts for 3 hours (thin gel) or 150–175 volts for 5 hours (thick gel)

Tris–Boric Acid–EDTA Buffer

Gel buffer	Boric acid at 1.55 g/L
	EDTA at 0.34 g/L
	Tris at 5.45 g/L
	Self-adjusts to pH 8.4
Tray buffer	Boric acid at 5.2 g/L
	EDTA at 1.1 g/L
	Tris at 18.2 g/L
	Self-adjusts to pH 8.4
	Run at 50 milliamperes and 200–250 volts for 3–4 hours (thin gel) or 250–300 volts for 5–6 hours (thick gel)

Tris–Citric Acid Buffer

Gel buffer	Citric acid at 10.5 g/L
	Tris at 36.3 g/L
	Add above to 900 mL distilled water
	Add 100 mL of tray buffer
	Self-adjusts to pH 8.5
Tray buffer	Boric acid at 18.54 g/L
	Lithium hydroxide at 2.5 g/L
	Self-adjusts to pH 8.1
	Run at 50 milliamperes and 150 volts, increasing to 200 volts as current drops, for 4 hours (thin gel) or 6 hours (thick gel)

endonucleases that recognize 6-base sequences reveal less polymorphism than do those that recognize 4-base or 5-base sequences (Wirgin et al. 1990). Biochemical supply companies sell many restriction endonucleases and provide detailed instructions for their use.

8.5.4 Producing Starch Gels

Electrophoresis occurs in a solid physical medium—a gel—that provides the substrate through which protein molecules or DNA fragments move. The electrophoretic gel is analogous to the paper used in paper chromatography. It is the medium for separating molecules, and different media may be needed for different types of molecules.

Analyses of mtDNA fragments typically are performed on 0.7–1.0% agarose gels (for 5-base or 6-base restriction endonucleases) or on 3–5% acrylamide gels (for 4-base restriction endonucleases; Ferris and Berg 1987). Both agarose and acrylamide gels are available from biochemical supply companies.

Protein electrophoresis, however, uses starch gels that must be homemade. Because starch gels are useful for only one or two days after preparation, their production is necessary just before each electrophoretic analysis. The process is routine, but, like all aspects of this work, must be completed with sufficient skill to assure consistently uniform results. Although the specific steps used in various laboratories differ, the following general procedure, adapted from Aebersold et al. (1987) and Leary and Booke (1990), illustrates the basic approach.

(1) The procedure requires a supply of hydrolyzed powdered starch and a quantity of gel buffer solution. Generally, 12 g of starch are used for every 100 mL of gel buffer, producing a 12% starch gel.

(2) The starch is added to about one-third of the gel buffer in a large Erlenmeyer flask and swirled vigorously to suspend the starch.

(3) The remaining gel buffer is heated to boiling in a separate flask and then added to the starch suspension. The starch suspension must be swirled just before the heated buffer is added, to assure complete dissolution of the starch.

(4) The resulting viscous gel mix is heated again to boiling, until numerous small bubbles begin rising to the surface.

(5) The mix is degassed with an aspirator or vacuum line for 30–60 seconds, until only large bubbles remain.

(6) The starch mix is poured rapidly into the gel mold, and remaining bubbles, lumps, or contaminants are removed with a pipet.

(7) The gel is allowed to cool to room temperature, which occurs rapidly, and then can be used. Gels should be covered with plastic wrap after cooling to prevent them from drying out before use.

Many recipes for gel buffer solutions are used, providing the proper pH and other conditions for specific proteins. Three buffer solutions are most common, however, and have proven suitable for most routine analyses and most species (Box 8.3).

Although commercial molds are available, many geneticists make their own, customized in size and thickness to their specific needs (Aebersold et al. 1987; Leary and Booke 1990). Supplies for a mold include a stand (an inverted porcelain pan or polystyrene cups); a glass plate that provides the base for the gel; long,

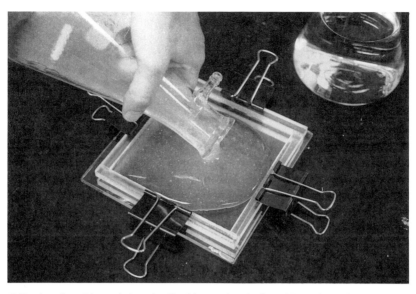

Figure 8.5 A gel mold receiving the liquid starch solution. Photo by Eric Hallerman and the author.

narrow (15–20 mm) plexiglas strips that form the sides of the mold; and clamps to attach the plexiglas strips to the base (Figure 8.5). Molds are usually rectangular; typically the inside dimensions are about 21.5 cm long, 1.5 cm wide, and 0.6–1.2 cm deep (Leary and Booke 1990).

8.5.5 Loading the Gel

The process of placing the homogenized tissues on the gel (loading) involves two major steps. First, the gel is cut into two pieces to receive the tissue samples. The cut is along the gel's long dimension, about 2.5–3.0 cm from one edge. The larger piece is called the anodal strip, and the cut edge of that strip is called the origin; the smaller piece is called the cathodal strip (Leary and Booke 1990). Later, when current is applied to the gel, the positive pole will be at the far end of the anodal strip and the negative pole at the far end of the cathodal strip. The cathodal strip is pushed carefully away from the anodal strip, exposing the origin to receive the samples.

The second step is preparation of the sample-containing wicks and their placement along the origin. The wicks are made by cutting heavy filter paper into squares or rectangles approximately 3–4 mm wide. Each wick holds the tissue homogenate for one individual. Two protocols for wetting wicks include dipping a rectangular wick into tissue homogenate until it is about three-fourths soaked (Aebersold et al. 1987) or completely soaking a square wick and then blotting it to absorb excess homogenate (Leary and Booke 1990). In either protocol, removal of excess homogenate is necessary to avoid mixing of samples through leaking onto the gel surface or the underlying glass plate.

Each wick is placed on the origin of the anodal strip (Figure 8.6). Gels typically hold 20 to 50 wicks, depending on the gel's dimensions. The first wick should be placed about 5 mm from one end of the origin, and additional wicks are placed

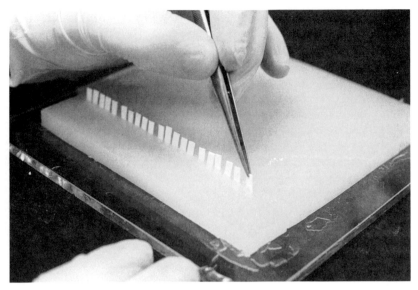

Figure 8.6 Soaked wicks in place on a starch gel. Note that a wide space is left between adjacent wicks to prevent contamination. Photo by Eric Hallerman and the author.

along the origin, leaving approximately 1 mm between adjacent wicks to avoid mixture of samples (Leary and Booke 1990). Tracer wicks, soaked in diluted red food coloring, should be placed at both ends of the origin and after every tenth sample wick. Standard wicks, soaked in known solutions of the particular proteins being analyzed, also should be placed at intervals along the gel.

The cathodal strip is then pushed carefully back against the origin, squeezing the wicks between the two gel strips. Complete contact is necessary between the two strips, without air bubbles or gaps, because movement of the proteins requires an uninterrupted electrical field along the gel (Aebersold et al. 1987).

8.5.6 Running the Starch Gel

The gel must be kept cold, either in a refrigerator or on a cold plate, during the electrophoretic run, because the heat generated by the current can denature the proteins. Most of the gel, except for the outside edges, should be kept covered with plastic wrap, to prevent it from drying during the run (Leary and Booke 1990).

The gel is incorporated into an electrical circuit that will provide direct current for the electrophoretic run (Figure 8.7). Trays of electrolyte solution are placed along the two opposite sides of the gel parallel to the origin. The tray solution must be matched to the buffer solution used to create the gel (Box 8.3). Absorbent cloths (e.g., disposable dishcloths) are soaked in each tray; one end of each cloth is left in the tray and the other end is placed in contact with the adjacent side of the gel, making a continuous connection along the exposed edge of both the anodal and cathodal strips. Capillary action keeps the absorbent cloths wet, maintaining the electrical circuit during electrophoresis (Leary and Booke 1990). Electrodes from the power source are immersed in the tray solutions, with the positive electrode (anode) connected to the tray of the anodal strip and the

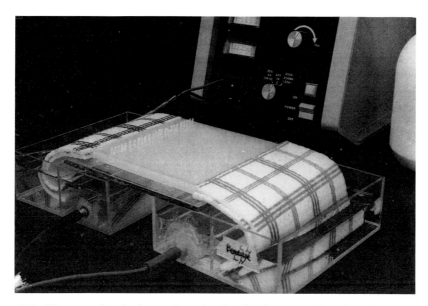

Figure 8.7 The completed electrophoretic circuit, demonstrating the placement and connections of electrolyte trays. For an actual run, the gel and tray assembly would be refrigerated or otherwise cooled. Photo by Eric Hallerman and the author.

negative electrode (cathode) connected to the tray of the cathodal strip. Electrodes must be made of an inert metal (usually platinum), so they do not electrolyze while passing current (Leary and Booke 1990).

An electrical charge of 125–350 volts is applied to the gel, with a current no higher than 70 milliamperes (Aebersold et al. 1987; Leary and Booke 1990). After 10–15 minutes, the current is turned off and the wicks are removed (if left in the gel, the wicks become dry and inhibit current flow). The origin between the anodal and cathodal strips should be cleaned carefully to remove pieces of sample wicks. The cathodal strip is again pushed against the anodal strip, assuring that no gaps or air bubbles occur, because any disruptions will cause uneven current flow and inconclusive results (Aebersold et al. 1987). Current is then started again, and the gel is run until the marker dye reaches the end of the anodal strip. Run time is usually from 3 to 5 hours (but may be much greater), depending on the gel, buffer, and current used. As with other aspects of biochemical techniques, the precise conditions of every run should be recorded in detail.

8.5.7 Staining the Starch Gel

After the gel has been run, it can be sliced into thin horizontal slabs for staining. Gels can be sliced into as many as 6–7 slabs, each about 1 mm thick. Commercial slicers are available, but many geneticists slice gels by hand, using thin nylon or monofilament thread held taut on opposite sides of the gel and drawn through the gel like a cheese slicer (Aebersold et al. 1987; Leary and Booke 1990). The gel is sliced from the bottom up, with the proper depth of each cut guided by plexiglas strips stacked as spacers along the long ends of the gel. After each cut is made, another spacer is added, guiding the thread along a higher pass through the gel. The top slice is typically rubbery and uneven in thickness; it is generally

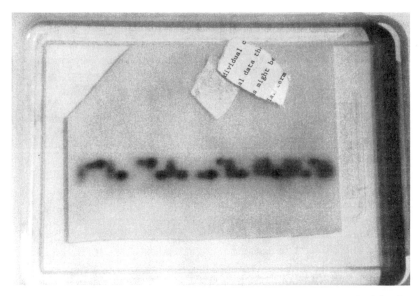

Figure 8.8   A stained gel. The scrap paper is placed on the gel as a standard for focusing the camera. Because the stained bands are somewhat diffuse, they always appear blurry on the gel. Photo by Randy Hoover.

discarded. Both anodal and cathodal pieces of the gel should be sliced, because some proteins may migrate toward the cathode rather than toward the anode.

The gel slices are peeled apart carefully and placed in separate dishes for staining. Even if a slice breaks, it can be used for analysis. Because gel slices can be misoriented during staining, one corner of each slice must be marked to designate the original location of the first sample (Leary and Booke 1990).

Specific stains are needed for each protein. Most are histochemical stains, which include an enzyme that reacts with the protein on the gel and a stain that recognizes the reaction products (this is why retaining protein integrity is so important during electrophoresis; Leary and Booke 1990). Aebersold et al. (1987) listed recipes and buffer conditions for more than 45 common stains. The appropriate stain is poured over the gel slice, sometimes suspended in a warm liquid agar solution. About 25 mL of stain is needed to cover a typical gel slice (Aebersold et al. 1987). Most stains must be incubated in the dark, at 37°C for 0.5–3 hours, to increase the reaction rate. The location and density of the proteins will become visible, either in normal ultraviolet light, as colored bands (Figure 8.8).

Band locations and sizes can be measured directly from the stained gel slice. Alternatively, the gel can be photographed in a standardized way and measurements can be made from the photograph. Instant photography should be used so that the quality of the photograph can be determined immediately. Photographs also serve as useful archives for the data, allowing subsequent reanalysis if needed (Beacham et al. 1985). Gels also can be preserved for later analysis; Leary and Booke (1990) recommended fixing gels stained with alcohol-insoluble stains by soaking them for 1–2 days in a methanol–acetic acid solution.

8.5.8   Processing mtDNA Gels

The process for reading mtDNA gels is identical in concept to protein staining, but is much different in practice. Three techniques are used, as described in more detail by Ferris and Berg (1987) and Wirgin et al. (1990). The first technique is staining with an ethidium bromide solution, which reacts with the DNA and is visible under ultraviolet light.

The other two techniques are used when only small quantities of mtDNA are available. In each case, the mtDNA is labelled with radioactive phosphorus (^{32}P). One technique involves attaching radioactive nucleotides to the end of each mtDNA fragment (called end-labeling); the other transfers mtDNA fragments to a different solid substrate and labels them with complementary radiolabeled DNA (called Southern blotting). In both cases, the final step is incubating the materials in the presence of X-ray film, which reveals the locations of the labeled DNA fragments.

8.5.9   Nomenclature for Protein-Coding Loci and Alleles

Protocol for naming loci and alleles involved in protein electrophoresis has recently been standardized through a committee of the American Fisheries Society (Shaklee et al. 1990). This protocol should be followed in all cases, so that the results of any study can be readily interpreted by others and can be compared to similar studies in other locations.

Loci are designated by two- to five-letter abbreviations of their encoded protein, in uppercase italics. If more than one locus encodes for the same protein, the loci are further designated by adding a dash followed by an Arabic number. The order of numbering is based on the relative distance moved by the most common allele of each locus in the same electrophoretic field; the locus whose allele travels the least distance is given the number 1. The end of each locus abbreviation is indicated with an asterisk. For example, the enzyme aspartate aminotransferase is encoded by two loci; they are designated as *AAT-1** and *AAT-2**, with *AAT-1** designating the slower of the two (Leary and Booke 1990).

Alleles at a particular locus are designated by an initial asterisk followed by an italicized number or lowercase letter. Most frequently, the most common allele for a population at a locus is designated as the standard and given the number **100*. Other alleles at that locus are numbered according to the percentage distance they migrate during electrophoresis, relative to the standard. Thus, an allele that migrated only half as far as the standard would be designated **50*; one that traveled twice as far as the standard would be **200*. If these were three alleles for the first locus encoding for aspartate aminotransferase, their complete designations would read *AAT-1*50, AAT-1*100*, and *AAT-1*200* (Leary and Booke 1990).

Additional rules of nomenclature are described in more detail by Leary and Booke (1990) and Shaklee et al. (1990).

8.5.10   Maintaining Standardization

The recent standardization of locus and allele names underscores the general need for standardization throughout these techniques. Genetic stock identification (and other genetic information) is most useful when it can be compared across populations and even species. For this to occur, data must be comparable from laboratory to laboratory, year to year, and population to population. For this reason, Shaklee and Phelps (1990) have repeatedly stressed the essential need for standardization and trading of laboratory techniques. Recipes for all reagents, including starch gel solutions, buffers, stains, and other carriers, must be explicitly maintained and reported. Any changes in technique, equipment, or conditions of analysis also must be recorded, with attendant descriptions of the effect on the procedure.

Laboratories also should maintain and trade allele mobility standards. These standards can be run in different laboratories as a basis for comparing the distance traveled by known enzymes (Shaklee and Phelps 1990), providing the means for translating results among studies. Geneticists also should conduct blind tests of their techniques by randomly processing animals of known allelic profile through their entire process, from tissue sampling through interpretation.

8.6 PRODUCING GENETIC MARKS

The utility of genetic stock identification can be greatly enhanced if a population can be purposefully marked with a unique genetic feature. In the strictest sense, this is the only true ''mark'' analogous to other marking techniques described in this book.

The ideal goal of genetic marking is to fix one or more alleles in a population (that is, to cause it to be present in every individual). In most cases, however, the practical goal must be to increase the allelic frequency in the population so that it differs substantially from frequencies of the same allele(s) in other populations. Because the genetic feature used is almost always a naturally occurring allele, this technique is basically a screening process.

Currently, most genetic marks are developed in animal populations by manipulating the reproduction of individuals, allowing those with the desired allele to reproduce and preventing those without it from reproducing. Genetic marking by this means is possible only if reproduction can be controlled, such as in hatcheries or in natural settings where wild spawners can be intercepted, examined for alleles, and then sorted. Genetic engineering techniques now allow insertion of a marker directly into the genome of an individual, which, in turn, can introduce the marker into a population by normal reproduction. This approach may become important to fisheries in the future, but release of genetically engineered animals into the wild is controversial, and the subject is not treated in this book.

The first step in producing a genetic mark is choosing appropriate loci and alleles. Baseline genetic profiles are needed for the populations of concern. These data reveal which loci have alleles that are rare enough in most populations to be distinctive and abundant enough in one population to allow rapid spread as a mark (Utter and Seeb 1990). As described earlier, at least 50–100 individuals should be examined at 20 or more loci for a baseline study (Ihssen et al. 1981; Gharrett and Seeb 1990).

After the marker alleles have been selected, individuals with those alleles must be identified. Because the animals must be kept alive to allow their reproduction, the tissue sampling process must be benign, usually consisting of muscle, blood, or eye tissue (Carmichael et al. 1986). For a captive population, the brood stock must be individually tagged and sampled for electrophoresis. For a wild stock, spawning fish must be collected in the most appropriate way, usually via traps or weirs on the migratory path to the spawning grounds. Each spawning animal must be individually tagged and sampled for electrophoresis. During electrophoresis, the animals must be held in captivity. Therefore, the electrophoretic analysis must occur quickly, both to prevent mortality and to assure that the fertility of the captive animals' gametes is maintained (Utter and Seeb 1990).

Desired spawners are chosen based on the electrophoretic results. Homozygotes for the marker allele are the most desirable, but are also likely to be rare. Heterozygotes with the marker allele are somewhat desirable, but homozygotes for other alleles are clearly undesirable. In practice, the need to retain a relatively large spawning population will require a selection strategy that eliminates undesired spawners rather than a strategy that allows only desired spawners to spawn. With such a strategy, homozygotes without the marker alleles are removed from the spawning population, along with heterozygotes to the extent possible (Gharrett and Seeb 1990). Because one male can fertilize many females, the selection process is sometimes performed on males only. This reduces the speed with which the marker increases in abundance, but it also reduces the cost and risk of the selection process (Seeb et al. 1986). After selection, the remaining individuals are released to spawn naturally or are retained for hatchery spawning.

The selection process must be managed carefully to avoid various unintended genetic problems. Inbreeding, genetic bottlenecks, introduction of deleterious genes, and small effective population size all may impair the adaptiveness of the marked population (e.g., Edds and Echelle 1989). To avoid small effective population size, Utter and Seeb (1990) recommended using at least 25 males and 25 females to establish a marked population. Going slowly, therefore, is probably a good strategy, even though several generations of selective breeding may be needed to establish a genetic mark. During that time, the population should be monitored regularly to assure that the mark is continuing to increase in abundance and is inherited as anticipated (Gharrett and Seeb 1990; Shaklee and Phelps 1990).

8.7 ANALYSIS OF GENETIC INFORMATION

Genetic analyses can generate large quantities of data. The information from one individual may involve many tissues and loci. When combined for many individuals, the data produce frequency distributions for the surveyed loci; each distribution is an independent glimpse at the group's genetic composition. In some cases, data analysis is readily completed by hand, but in cases involving many loci and many populations, the data will usually required computerized storage, manipulation, and analysis (Shaklee and Phelps 1990).

The basic identification question asked of genetic information is how the mixed groups of individuals can be separated into proportions that can be assigned to original stocks. In the simplest case of two original stocks contributing to a mixture, the analysis is equivalent to calculating a weighted average (Pella and Milner 1987).

If two populations, A and B, each have a different frequency of an allele (C_A and C_B), and the frequency of the allele in a mixed sample of the two populations is known (C_M), then the proportion of the two populations is estimated as

$$XC_A + (1 - X)C_B = C_M,$$

X being the proportion of A and $(1 - X)$ the proportion of B. For example, if an allele is present in population A at a frequency of 0.1, in population B at 0.7, and in a mixed group at 0.3, then the mixed group's composition most likely is 0.67 population A and 0.33 population B.

If the mixed group contains individuals from more than two stocks, the computations become indefinite. The weighted average computation must be replaced by a maximum-likelihood estimator, which is an iterative computation (Millar 1987). And when several loci are analyzed at the same time, multivariate statistics are generally needed.

A valuable aspect of genetic information is that the same data used for stock identification also can be used for a variety of other purposes. These purposes, which involve studying the degree of genetic variation within and among individuals, populations and species, are highly important matters in fisheries management, especially as conserving genetic diversity becomes a more active goal of fisheries agencies. Leary and Booke (1990) provided a general description of these uses, as did Nei (1987) for genetic distance and Waples and Smouse (1990) for gametic disequilibrium.

8.8   NEW DEVELOPMENTS

Genetic techniques continue to evolve rapidly. New developments occur regularly, improving some current techniques and making others obsolete. The methodological journey from protein electrophoresis to mtDNA analysis and then to DNA fingerprinting has been very rapid, leaving many fisheries workers confused regarding the place and value of protein electrophoresis. Although geneticists working in basic sciences have largely abandoned protein electrophoresis, the technique is still highly valuable in fisheries because the information it provides is often sufficient to answer—inexpensively—fundamental stock identification questions. Therefore, protein electrophoresis is likely to hold a dominant position in applied fisheries genetics for some time.

At the same time, however, DNA fingerprinting is becoming more accessible for fisheries use. DNA fingerprinting is the process of analyzing nuclear DNA, which exists as billions of bases organized into approximately 100,000 genes in fishes (Hallerman and Beckmann 1988). The techniques for analyzing nuclear DNA are similar to those for analyzing mtDNA. When treated with a restriction endonuclease, however, nuclear DNA forms hundred of thousands of DNA fragments. During electrophoresis, these fragments migrate across the gel, but their variety and number cause a continuous smear.

To separate some of the fragments, the DNA is transferred to filter paper and subjected to the Southern blot technique mentioned for mtDNA. The transferred DNA is treated with specific radioactive probes that recognize and hybridize with unique DNA sequences. Autoradiography is then used to depict the pattern of DNA bands for a particular individual. By using radioactive probes that react with recurring DNA sequences (those sites are most likely to have polymorphisms), the resulting patterns will be different for every individual—producing DNA fingerprints (Castelli et al. 1990).

As DNA fingerprinting finds wider uses in human medicine and law, access to public and commercial laboratories for DNA analysis will increase for fisheries.

DNA fingerprinting has already been used in some fisheries law enforcement to indicate the precise genetic history of disputed catches.

Improved techniques are also making older genetic methods more useful. Phillips and Ihssen (1990) and Phillips et al. (1989) recently used chromosome numbers, fragments, and visible markers on chromosomes to identify organisms. Immunogeneticists are also exploring the genetic differences expressed in antibodies, using traditional serological techniques to characterize differences in protein structure (Davis et al. 1990; Utter and Seeb 1990). Without question, the utility of genetic techniques will continue to expand in fisheries. As fisheries workers strive to understand the mechanisms that govern the lives of individual animals and populations, their discoveries will move closer to the genetic basis of performance—allowing the greater use of those genetic differences as marks of identification.

8.9 REFERENCES

Aebersold, P. B., G. A. Winans, D. J. Teel, G. B. Milner, and F. M. Utter. 1987. Manual for starch gel electrophoresis: a method for the detection of genetic variation. NOAA (National Oceanographic and Atmospheric Administration) Technical Report NMFS (National Marine Fisheries Service) 61.

Allendorf, F. W., and M. M. Ferguson. 1990. Genetics. Pages 35–63 in C. B. Schreck and P. B. Moyle, editors. Methods for fish biology. American Fisheries Society, Bethesda, Maryland.

Avise, J. C., and N. C. Saunders. 1984. Hybridization and introgression among species of sunfish (*Lepomis*): analysis by mitochondrial DNA and allozyme markers. Genetics 108:237–255.

Beacham, T. D., R. E. Withler, and A. P. Gould. 1985. Biochemical genetic stock identification of chum salmon (*Oncorhynchus keta*) in southern British Columbia. Canadian Journal of Fisheries and Aquatic Sciences 42:437–448.

Billington, N., and P. D. N. Hebert. 1990. Technique for determining mitochondrial DNA markers in blood samples from walleyes. American Fisheries Society Symposium 7:492–498.

Campton, D. E., and J. M. Johnston. 1985. Electrophoretic evidence for a genetic admixture of native and nonnative rainbow trout in the Yakima River, Washington. Transactions of the American Fisheries Society 114:782–793.

Carmichael, G. J., J. H. Williamson, M. E. Schmidt, and D. C. Morizot. 1986. Genetic marker identification in largemouth bass with electrophoresis of low-risk tissues. Transactions of the American Fisheries Society 115:455–459.

Castelli, M., J-C. Philippart, G. Vassart, and M. Georges. 1990. DNA fingerprinting in fish: a new generation of genetic markers. American Fisheries Society Symposium 7:514–520.

Davis, W. C., R. A. Larsen, and M. L. Monaghan. 1990. Genetic markers identified by immunogenetic methods. American Fisheries Society Symposium 7:521–540.

Edds, D. R., and A. A. Echelle. 1989. Genetic comparisons of hatchery and natural stocks of small endangered fishes: Leon Springs pupfish, Comanche Springs pupfish, and Pecos gambusia. Transactions of the American Fisheries Society 118:441–446.

Ferris, S. D., and W. J. Berg. 1987. The utility of mitochondrial DNA in fish genetics and fishery management. Pages 277–300 in Ryman and Utter (1987).

Gharrett, A. J., and J. E. Seeb. 1990. Practical and theoretical guidelines for genetically marking fish populations. American Fisheries Society Symposium 7:407–417.

Grewe, P. M., and P. D. N. Hebert. 1988. Mitochondrial DNA diversity among broodstocks of the lake trout, *Salvelinus namaycush*. Canadian Journal of Fisheries and Aquatic Sciences 45:2114–2122.

Hallerman, E. M., and J. S. Beckmann. 1988. DNA-level polymorphism as a tool in fisheries science. Canadian Journal of Fisheries and Aquatic Sciences 45:1075–1087.

Hillis, D. M., and C. Montz. 1990. Molecular genetics. Sinauer Associates, Sunderland, Massachusetts.

Ihssen, P. E., H. E. Booke, J. M. Casselman, J. M. McGlade, N. R. Payne, and F. M. Utter. 1981. Stock identification: materials and methods. Canadian Journal of Fisheries and Aquatic Sciences 38:1838–1855.

Kirby, L. T. 1990. DNA fingerprinting: an introduction. Stockton Press, New York.

Krueger, C. C., J. E. Marsden, H. L. Kincaid, and B. May. 1989. Genetic differentiation among lake trout strains stocked into Lake Ontario. Transactions of the American Fisheries Society 118:317–330.

Lane, S., A. J. McGregor, S. G. Taylor, and A. J. Gharrett. 1990. Genetic marking of an Alaskan pink salmon population, with an evaluation of the mark and the marking process. American Fisheries Society Symposium 7:395–406.

Leary, R. F., and H. E. Booke. 1990. Starch gel electrophoresis and species distinctions. Pages 141–170 in C. B. Schreck and P. B. Moyle, editors. Methods for fish biology. American Fisheries Society, Bethesda, Maryland.

Lewin, G. 1987. Genes III. Wiley, New York.

Lewontin, R. C. 1974. The genetic basis of evolutionary change. Columbia University Press, New York.

Millar, R. B. 1987. Maximum likelihood estimation of mixed stock fishery composition. Canadian Journal of Fisheries and Aquatic Sciences 44:583–590.

Milner, G. B., D. J. Teel, F. M. Utter, and G. A. Winans. 1985. A genetic method of stock identification in mixed populations of Pacific salmon, Oncorhynchus spp. U.S. National Marine Fisheries Service Marine Fisheries Review 47(1):1–8.

Nei, M. 1975. Molecular population genetics and evolution. Elsevier, New York.

Nei, M. 1978. Estimation of average heterozygosity and genetic distance from a small number of individuals. Genetics 89:583–590.

Nei, M. 1987. Genetic distance and molecular phylogeny. Pages 193–224 in Ryman and Utter (1987).

Pella, J. J., and G. B. Milner. 1987. Use of genetic marks in stock composition analysis. Pages 247–276 in Ryman and Utter (1987).

Phillips, R. B., and P. E. Ihssen. 1990. Genetic marking of fish by use of variability in chromosomes and nuclear DNA. American Fisheries Society Symposium 7:499–513.

Phillips, R. B., K. D. Zajicek, and P. E. Ihssen. 1989. Population differences in chromosome-banding polymorphisms in lake trout. Transactions of the American Fisheries Society 118:64–73.

Ryman, N., and F. Utter, editors. 1987. Population genetics and fishery management. University of Washington Press, Seattle.

Schweigert, J. F., and R. E. Withler. 1990. Genetic differentiation of Pacific herring based on enzyme electrophoresis and mitochondrial DNA analysis. American Fisheries Society Symposium 7:459–469.

Seeb, J. E., L. W. Seeb, D. W. Oates, and F. M. Utter. 1987. Genetic variation and postglacial dispersal of populations of northern pike (Esox lucius) in North America. Canadian Journal of Fisheries and Aquatic Sciences 44:556–561.

Seeb, J. E., L. W. Seeb, and F. M. Utter. 1986. Use of genetic marks to asses stock dynamics and management programs for chum salmon. Transactions of the American Fisheries Society 115:448–454.

Seeb, L. W., J. E. Seeb, R. L. Allen, and W. K. Hershberger. 1990. Evaluation of adult returns of genetically marked chum salmon, with suggested future applications. American Fisheries Society Symposium 7:418–425.

Shaklee, J. B., F. W. Allendorf, D. C. Morizot, and G. S. Whitt. 1990. Gene nomenclature for protein-coding loci in fish. Transactions of the American Fisheries Society 119:2–15.

Shaklee, J. B., and S. R. Phelps. 1990. Operation of a large-scale, multiagency program for genetic stock identification. American Fisheries Society Symposium 7:817–830.

Speiss, E. B. 1989. Genes in populations. Wiley, New York.

Tsuyuki, H., and S. J. Westrheim. 1970. Analyses of the *Sebastes aleutianus–S. melanostomus* complex, and description of a new scorpaenid species, *Sebastes caenaematicus,* in the northeast Pacific Ocean. Journal of the Fisheries Research Board of Canada 27:2233–2254.

Utter, F., P. Aebersold, and G. Winans. 1987. Interpreting genetic variation detected by electrophoresis. Pages 21–46 *in* Ryman and Utter (1987).

Utter, F. M., and J. E. Seeb. 1990. Genetic marking of fishes: overview focusing on protein variation. American Fisheries Society Symposium 7:426–438.

Waples, R. S., and P. E. Smouse. 1990. Gametic disequilibrium analysis as a means of identifying mixtures of salmon populations. American Fisheries Society Symposium 7:439–458.

Whitmore, D. H., editor. 1990. Electrophoretic and isoelectric focusing techniques in fisheries management. CRC Press, Boca Raton, Florida.

Winans, G. A. 1989. Genetic variability in chinook salmon stocks from the Columbia River basin. North American Journal of Fisheries Management 9:47–52.

Wirgin, I. I., P. Silverstein, and J. Grossfield. 1990. Restriction endonuclease analysis of striped bass mitochondrial DNA: the Atlantic coastal migratory stock. American Fisheries Society Symposium 7:475–491.

Chapter 9

Chemical Marks

9.1 INTRODUCTION

Chemical marks are consistent differences in the chemical composition of animals' body tissues that can be recognized by humans. The differences may occur naturally, caused by chemical differences in water and food or by genetic variation. For example, striped bass from freshwater, marine, and estuarine areas contain different concentrations of calcium and other elements in their scales (Belanger et al. 1987). The differences may also be induced, as when hatchery workers add a detectable chemical to the feed of hatchery-raised fish.

No doubt all animals, like snowflakes, differ in some way. The important condition for chemical marking, however, is that the differences can be detected consistently. Thus, chemical marking depends on the skill of analytic chemists and the development of rapid and inexpensive methods for indicating the presence and concentration of chemicals in living tissue. Currently, almost all chemical marks are recognized through radiation measurements of some kind, the series of techniques that are known as instrumental analysis (Behrens Yamada and Mulligan 1990).

The chemical characterization of organisms is a common scientific procedure. It is a basic tool of paleoscientists for dating and categorizing ancient materials (Coutant 1990), and forensic experts use chemistry to analyze crime clues (Lasswell 1990). In fisheries, however, chemical marks have played only a minor role. Much has been written about chemical marks, but virtually all uses have been experimental tests of the techniques. Chemical marks may become more important in the future, however, if suitable analytic techniques become less expensive and more accessible to fisheries workers.

Chemical marking includes two techniques—elemental marking and fluorescent marking. *Elemental marks* depend on detecting the presence and concentration of various metallic elements. Any body tissue and body chemical can be analyzed, but most researchers have focused on bones and scales (Lapi and Mulligan 1981). Such hard tissues are especially useful because the chemicals are bound permanently. Most elemental analysis is of alkaline or rare earth elements (the ones in the middle of the periodic table) that exist in tissues naturally or are incorporated as analogues for common elements. The elements can be detected by a variety of techniques for measuring radiation, such as atomic absorption spectroscopy or X-ray-excited optical luminescence (Muncy and D'Silva 1981).

The second method introduces *fluorescent compounds* into the animal's body. Various types of tetracycline (including oxytetracycline) and calcein have been used almost exclusively. Both are attractive because they fuse with calcium, becoming permanently deposited in bones and scales (Wilson et al. 1987). These compounds are detected by viewing the appropriate tissue under ultraviolet light, in which the compounds produce a green or yellow light.

Chemical marks are useful in a variety of circumstances. As with genetic identifiers, chemical marks are appropriate for stock identification and separation. The natural chemical composition of animals can be used to distinguish among spawning and rearing locations. Grahl-Nielsen and Ulvund (1990), for example, used differences in fatty acid profiles to distinguish among stocks in studies of herring, seals, and fish parasites. Similarly, Knutsen et al. (1985) used fatty-acid composition to identify Atlantic cod and haddock eggs, normally indistinguishable based on appearance. Such analysis is especially useful for anadromous animals, which begin life in fresh waters with highly different chemical characteristics (Lapi and Mulligan 1981).

Chemical marks can be applied to hatchery fish, for evaluation of fry-stocking programs (Lorson and Mudrak 1987) and hatchery techniques (Behrens Yamada and Mulligan 1987). Marking hatchery fish with chemicals is likely to become more important in the future, as the need to distinguish between illegally caught wild fish and legally purchased hatchery fish becomes necessary (Guillou and de la Noüe 1987; Muncy et al. 1990).

Chemical marks also can be used to collect or verify time-dependent data. For example, fluorescent chemicals can be fed to animals at known intervals. The location of fluorescent rings in the otoliths or other hard tissues of these animals can then be compared to the pattern of other rings to verify that the tissues accurately record age; Myrick et al. (1984) used this technique to analyze growth patterns on spinner dolphin teeth. Hard tissues can also reflect the environmental history of an animal because the tissues produced at each time and place will bear the chemical composition of the water in which the animal was living (Coutant 1990). The elemental composition of a salmon's scales, for example, will differ between the center, which formed while the fish was in fresh water, and the marginal areas, most of which formed in salt water.

9.2   ASSUMPTIONS FOR CHEMICAL MARKS

The fundamental assumption of chemical marking is that neither the marking process nor the introduced chemical changes the life of the animal. If the chemicals themselves are not harmful, chemical marking is a gentle process. As with genetic marking, stress on the marked animals is low because no extra handling is needed and no foreign objects are attached (Muncy et al. 1990). Consequently, behavior is not affected and predation risk is not increased (Behrens Yamada et al. 1979).

The chemicals must be nontoxic. This is such an obvious concern that most researchers have used natural or therapeutic materials, reducing the likelihood of biological harm (Behrens Yamada and Mulligan 1990). Nevertheless, high concentrations or long exposures to any chemical can be harmful (Tsukamoto 1985), so every proposed chemical mark and marking process should be carefully evaluated.

The second assumption is that chemical marks remain identifiable on the marked animals throughout the desired interval. The validity of this assumption is tenuous because the longevity and detectability of chemicals depend on many

Box 9.1   Advantages and Disadvantages of Chemical Marking

Advantages

- Chemicals used are natural, nontoxic to animals or humans
- Applicable to all sizes and life stages, including eggs
- Many animals marked simultaneously
- Useful on many taxa (presumably)
- Long-lasting marks
- Nonstressful, nonintrusive marking process

Disadvantages

- Often requires sacrificing animal
- Detection becomes harder as animal grows
- Individual marks not available
- Elemental marks require analytic chemistry
- Environment and genetics can affect concentration of chemicals
- Interpretation is statistical rather than absolute
- Detailed pretesting needed for each taxon

variables. Induced marks, both elemental and fluorescent, often become less detectable through time, because the increasing size of the animal lowers the chemical's concentration in the tissue or because more chemical may be absorbed from the environment (Behrens Yamada et al. 1979). Chemical retention also varies depending on the tissues in which it is originally deposited (Koenings et al. 1986) and on the species being marked (Beckman et al. 1990).

The variability of individual animals also complicates this assumption. Ulvund and Grahl-Nielsen (1988) recorded varying fatty-acid profiles of Atlantic cod eggs from different females and from different spawnings by the same female. Similarly, Belanger et al. (1987) detected differences in scale composition as a function of size, age, and sex of striped bass. Obviously, a comprehensive baseline study is needed before the accuracy of either a natural or an induced chemical mark can be accepted.

9.3   ADVANTAGES OF CHEMICAL MARKS
(Box 9.1)

Chemical marks can be placed on animals of any size. Because the techniques rely on the incorporation of the chemicals into the body from water or food, all life stages can be marked (Behrens Yamada and Mulligan 1987). Chemical marks can be induced before the animals start feeding, even at the egg stage. Walleye eggs, for example, have been chemically tagged during the water-hardening stage (Muncy and D'Silva 1981). When marking is based on the natural chemical profile of the animal, then every animal grows its own mark.

Because of the marking procedures, many animals can be marked simultaneously. If the chemical is introduced through the feed at a hatchery, for example, every animal can be marked. Similar efficiencies can be produced by immersing animals in water containing the chemical. When such a large proportion of a population is marked, the recovery process becomes less expensive and more useful.

Chemical marks can be applied to all kinds of animals. Although this chapter concentrates on fish, chemical marks should be equally useful on invertebrates, mammals, and reptiles. Chemical marking of crustaceans would only be useful for studies covering one molt cycle, however, if the chemical is deposited in the exoskeleton. Chemical marking of molluscs might be especially useful if the chemicals were permanently incorporated into the shell.

Applying chemical marks is generally inexpensive. Chemicals are introduced into animals through immersion in water, consumption of hatchery food, or injection. In all cases, the chemical is used in low concentrations, and the desired chemicals are abundant and relatively inexpensive (Behrens Yamada et al. 1979; Grahl-Nielsen and Ulvund 1990). Detection of chemical marks and characterization of chemical composition are more expensive than external marking because of the need for dissection (except for scales) and chemical analysis. Proponents of chemical marking argue, however, that although the analysis of each specimen may be more costly (in time and money), the recapture process will be very inexpensive if every individual is marked—thus, the overall operation is likely to be cost effective in many situations.

Chemical marks vary in longevity, but many last for a long time. In tests of marks incorporated into hard tissues, marks were detectable to the end of tests ranging from 5 months to 2 years (Tsukamoto 1985; Bilton 1986; Behrens Yamada and Mulligan 1987; Lorson and Mudrak 1987). Moreover, marked tissues retain their marks in storage for long periods after dissection. Fluorescent compounds have been successfully read on hard tissues up to 24 months after dissection (Babaluk and Campbell 1987; Wilson et al. 1987).

9.4   DISADVANTAGES OF CHEMICAL MARKS (Box 9.1)

Detecting chemical marks often requires sacrificing the animal in order to collect the necessary tissue. Although scales, fin rays, spines, or a small soft-tissue sample may be sufficient in some cases, most techniques use hard tissues such as otoliths or vertebrae (Tsukamoto 1985). Consequently, chemical marks are usually inappropriate for rare or precious animals.

Chemical marks become less detectable as an animal ages, for two reasons. First, the chemical in living tissue is gradually removed from the marked tissue by natural cell turnover. The rates of tissue turnover vary; soft tissues purge chemicals quickly and hard tissues purge them more slowly. Terbium chloride deposited in walleye eggs, for example, disappeared in 3 weeks (Muncy and D'Silva 1986). Among hard tissues, Muncy and D'Silva (1986) concluded that otoliths retained chemicals best, then bones, and scales least.

Second, the chemical declines in total concentration over time as new tissue accumulates (Behrens Yamada et al. 1979; Muncy et al. 1988). This is particularly true for induced chemical marks, because the chemical is introduced during a brief interval, usually early in the life span. This difficulty can be offset by analyzing only the portion of the tissue that is likely to contain the chemical. For example, if strontium were introduced into larval fish via the diet, then only the central core of an otolith, vertebra, or scale need be dissected, ground, and analyzed (Behrens Yamada and Mulligan 1982).

The analytic procedures for detecting chemical marks can be difficult and time-consuming. For all elemental marking, detection will require the services of an analytic chemist, and all detection will require specialized and sensitive equipment. Muncy et al. (1988, 1990) considered the absence of inexpensive, effective field and laboratory detection techniques to be the largest single hindrance to chemical marking.

Chemical marks can identify animals only as members of groups. When the marks are natural, their limitations resemble those of genetic marks (Chapter 8); when induced, their limitations resemble those of external marks like fin clips and brands (Chapter 4). Because only a few chemicals are suitable, relatively few marks are possible. As detection capabilities improve, more chemicals may become useful, allowing the simultaneous use of several chemicals (Behrens Yamada and Mulligan 1990). For the present, however, chemical marks can basically differentiate two groups—marked and unmarked—in any water body (e.g., hatchery and naturally produced fish).

Both the natural and induced chemical composition of animals are affected by environmental and genetic conditions, complicating the interpretation of a mark. As described above, animals within a population vary in chemical content, and the same animal's chemistry may vary over time. In field trials, for example, Behrens Yamada et al. (1979) detected increasing strontium concentrations in coho salmon vertebrae over a 1.5-year period. Similarly, some genetic control of chemical composition is likely, as shown for salmon (Behrens Yamada et al. 1987). The uptake of chemicals is also affected by water chemistry; for example, in salt water, oxytetracycline chelates with calcium, preventing its movement across membranes (Hettler 1984). For all these reasons, the success of a chemical marking and detection program depends greatly on a thoroughly understood and carefully controlled environment.

In practice, the characterization of animal populations based on chemical composition is analogous to that based on genetic profiles: it is a statistical process, not an absolute one. As with genetic identifiers, the procedure is to estimate the probability that an animal belongs to one group or another based on group average (Mulligan et al. 1983). Baseline profiles for every population are needed as reference data for comparison with the animals to be identified and classified.

9.5 CHEMICAL MARKING METHODS

9.5.1 Choosing a Chemical

The chemicals used to mark animals are generally those with electronic configurations similar to chemicals abundant in animal tissues. Many chemicals have been tried, but only a few are commonly used (Table 9.1).

Because of the desire to mark animals permanently, most scientists have used chemicals that act like calcium, the main component of bones, otoliths, and scales. These are generally alkaline earth or rare earth elements, all of which have the same number of outer shell electrons as calcium. Many of these elements are

Table 9.1 Chemicals tested or used as marks (adapted from Behrens Yamada and Mulligan 1990).

Element or compound type	Name	Primary body tissue analyzed	Utility
Alkali metals	Rubidium	Whole body	Medium
	Cesium	Whole body	Uncertain
Alkaline earths	Strontium	Bones, scales	High
	Barium	Bones, scales	Uncertain
Transition metals	Manganese	Bones, scales	Medium
Rare earths	Samarium		Uncertain
(Lanthanide series)	Europium		Uncertain
	Terbium	Scales	Low
Fatty acids		Heart, jaw bone, eggs	Medium
Antibiotics	Tetracycline	Bones, scales	High
Calcein		Bones, scales	Uncertain

quite common, especially strontium (we are most familiar with radioactive strontium, as an environmental pollutant, but nonradioactive strontium is a common, nontoxic element). Strontium has been used most frequently because it is readily absorbed into hard tissues. It is a good choice in fresh waters, but not in salt water because it is too common naturally (Behrens Yamada and Mulligan 1987). The rare earth element terbium also has been tested and may deserve additional examination because it is absorbed well at low concentrations (Muncy et al. 1990).

Rubidium and cesium, which are alkali metals, have been tested as marks because they can substitute for potassium, also an alkali metal, in intracellular fluid (Behrens Yamada and Mulligan 1990). These chemicals are not retained permanently, however, and are appropriate only for short-term projects.

The second group of chemicals used to mark animals are fluorescent compounds. These chemicals also are most successful when incorporated into hard tissue. The two most common compounds are tetracyclines (including oxytetracycline), which are broad-spectrum antibiotics widely used in human medicine, and calcein, a calcium-containing compound. Tetracycline is by far the most popular, useful on all types of animals in all waters. Tetracycline is particularly useful when complex chemical analysis is not possible and when the study period is shorter than 2 years.

In all cases, the chemical's performance should be tested in all aspects of a project. These tests must assure that the chemical does not harm the animal, that it produces readable marks, that the marks remain while the animals are swimming at large in the environment, and that the detection procedure works. Before any chemical is used on an animal, the project director must have a thorough understanding of the chemical's physiological mode of action, of restrictions on the chemical's use (as listed on the manufacturer's label, on "material safety data sheets," and in pertinent testing documents), and of necessary safety precautions. Consultation with public health and safety officials should be part of the planning of chemical marking projects.

9.5.2   Creating the Chemical Mark

Chemical marks are applied by immersing an animal in a solution of the chemical, by feeding it a diet containing the chemical, or by injecting the chemical directly into its body. Each technique is appropriate for different situations.

Immersion is the most common technique. It can be used for all life stages, including eggs and nonfeeding larvae. Immersion is also advantageous because many animals can be marked simultaneously and exposure to the chemical is uniform among all animals. Immersion should be timed for the period when the body membrane is most permeable, allowing the largest chemical flux into the body. Thus, eggs should be immersed during water hardening (Muncy and D'Silva 1981), and larval immersion should begin at hatching (Behrens Yamada and Mulligan 1987).

Table 9.2 lists reported or recommended immersion concentrations and times for the most common chemicals. In general, fish should be held in relatively low concentrations of strontium for relatively long periods because this enhances the uptake of large amounts of the element into the body. Behrens Yamada and Mulligan (1990) recommended holding fish in a strontium concentration of 1 mg/L for 40 to 60 days. Immersions in fluorescent compounds have been for much shorter times and at higher concentrations, in order to produce a dense narrow band of fluorescence into hard tissues. Published recommendations have ranged up to 500 mg/L for only 1–2 hours for tetracycline (Hettler 1984) and to 100–200 mg/L for 2–4 hours for calcein (Beckman et al. 1990). With these recommendations as guidelines, the optimum exposure should be determined in preliminary tests for each species and life stage to be marked. Because fish must be crowded together during short immersions at high concentrations, water quality must be monitored and continuously maintained at high levels. Chemical concentration also should be monitored so that any decrease due to dilution or absorption on tank walls can be corrected.

The second technique incorporates the chemical in the animal's food. Obviously, this technique is only useful if the animals will be fed in a hatchery or other confined environment (e.g., a farm pond) for extended periods. Feeding may be less expensive than immersion because the chemical is concentrated in the food rather than dispersed in the water (Behrens Yamada and Mulligan 1990). Feeding may be disadvantageous, however, because the feed must be customized to include the chemical (either at the mill or in the laboratory), the chemical may make the feed unpalatable, and the chemical may be unevenly consumed among heavily and lightly feeding fish.

Feeding rates are expressed either in mass per kilogram of fish being fed or in mass per kilogram of food being fed (Table 9.2). As with immersion, elemental chemicals generally should be fed for longer periods. Behrens Yamada and Mulligan (1990), for example, recommended 10 g strontium/kg food, fed for 40 to 60 days, and 5 g rubidium/kg food, fed for 40 days. Shorter feeding periods and higher concentrations are generally desired for fluorescent marks. Bilton (1986) recommended feeding oxytetracycline at a rate of 500 mg/kg food for 4–13 days.

If the chemicals are destined for hard tissues, feeding should be delayed until hard tissues, specifically scales and otoliths, begin to form (Koenings et al. 1986). This timing will vary among species, and thus should be chosen for each study from detailed life history information. The only exception to delayed feeding

Table 9.2 Reported or recommended concentrations and exposure times for marking aquatic animals with strontium and tetracycline by immersion, feeding, or injection.

Chemical	Concentration and exposure	Taxon	Reference
Immersion			
Strontium	1 mg/L, 40 days	Sockeye salmon (fry)	Behrens Yamada and Mulligan (1990)
	1 mg/L, 49 days	Sockeye salmon (larvae)	Behrens Yamada et al. (1987)
	1 mg/L, 60 days	Sockeye salmon (fry)	Behrens Yamada et al. (1987)
Tetracycline	200–300 mg/L, 24–48 hours	Ayu (eggs)	Tsukamoto (1985)
	200–300 mg/L, 3–24 hours	Ayu (larvae)	Tsukamoto (1985)
Oxytetracycline	500 mg/L, 1–2 hours	Pinfish, spot	Hettler (1984)
	50 mg/L, 12 hours/day for 4 days	American shad	Lorson and Mudrak (1987)
Feeding			
Strontium	10 g/kg food, 40 days	Sockeye salmon (fry)	Behrens Yamada and Mulligan (1990)
	10 g/kg food, 60 days	Sockeye salmon (fry)	Behrens Yamada et al. (1987)
	10 g/kg food, 60 days	Coho salmon (smolts)	Behrens Yamada and Mulligan (1982); Behrens Yamada et al. (1979)
	200 mg/kg food, 42–56 days	Brook trout	Guillou and de la Noüe (1987)
Oxytetracycline	0.5 g/kg fish, 14–21 days	Chum salmon	Bilton (1986)
Injection			
Tetracycline	50–100 mg/kg fish	Walleye	Babaluk and Campbell (1987)
	25 mg/kg mammal	Spinner dolphin	Myrick et al. (1984)
Oxytetracycline	25 mg/kg fish	Leopard shark	Smith (1984)

arises if the detection process will focus on a central core of the hard tissue. In this case, the chemical should be included from the first feeding, to assure that the chemical is deposited at the very center of the scales, otoliths, or vertebrae (Behrens Yamada and Mulligan 1990).

The third marking technique is injection. Injection may be necessary for large animals that can be handled readily and that cannot be marked readily by immersion or feeding. This technique is obviously useful only for highly valued individuals, such as marine mammals, spawning females, or endangered species. Tetracyclines are the most successful injected chemicals reported in the literature. Injection rates are generally high, ranging from 25 to 100 mg tetracycline/kg animal weight (Table 9.2). Myrick et al. (1984) reported that large injections of tetracycline caused tissue swelling in marine mammals; they recommended dividing the dose into three smaller amounts and injecting these doses at three different body sites.

Chemically marked fish should be released into the wild only after public regulations regarding chemical withdrawal have been satisfied.

9.5.3 Detecting a Chemical Mark

Detection processes are different for elemental analysis and fluorescent analysis. All detection, however, is based on the excitation of the chemical in the animal tissue, causing it to emit detectable and identifiable energy. For elemental analysis, emissions are generally not visible; for fluorescent analysis, the emissions are visible under ultraviolet light.

Detection is influenced by the concentration of chemicals in various tissues. For complete chemical characterization of small animals, such as eggs or larvae, the whole body may have to be used. For larger animals, specific tissues will give more accurate or conclusive chemical profiles.

For chemical marks that are calcium analogues, hard tissues are generally analyzed. Based on the rate of tissue and elemental turnover (slower is better), the best structures for elemental analysis are otoliths, followed by vertebrae and other bones, and then by scales (Tsukamoto 1985). Fluorescent chemicals, especially oxytetracycline, however, are best revealed in bones.

The standard detection technique is atomic absorption spectroscopy. Before a sample is analyzed, it generally must be leached in acid or ashed. Behrens Yamada and Mulligan (1982) leached coho salmon tissues by placing a scale sample or vertebral core in 1 or 2 mL (respectively) of 0.1 normal HCl in 10% glycerol for 48 hours at room temperature. Guillou and de la Noüe (1987) dried soft tissues at 60°C for 48 hours and then ashed them by heating to 550°C. After preparation, the sample is ignited in the presence of specific elemental gases, producing a spectrum of emissions corresponding in wavelength and intensity to the presence and concentration of the sample's component elements. Atomic absorption has been used most successfully for strontium detection and for creating profiles of common elements (Belanger et al. 1987). These techniques require the services of experienced technicians and well-equipped laboratories.

The process for detecting fluorescent chemicals is familiar to most of us from our adolescent fascination with black lights—which cause things to glow in the dark. Tetracyclines generally appear yellow or green and calcein appears green under ultraviolet light. They are most visible under an ultraviolet wavelength of 366 nm (Bilton 1986). Although the technique is simple, detection can be complicated by the natural fluorescence of tissue. This is especially troublesome with otoliths.

Marked tissues must be handled carefully to retain their utility. If exposed to visible light for extended periods, the tissue will lose its fluorescence. Therefore, tissues should be stored in the dark and handled in subdued light in preparation for and after examination. Because the marks may fade through time, the marks should be photographed. Babaluk and Campbell (1987) recommended using Tri-X 400 ASA film, exposed in ultraviolet light.

If fluorescence cannot be observed directly, chemical tests have been developed to allow detection of the chemicals analytically. Koenings et al. (1986) described grinding the tissue, extracting the fluorescent chemical, and measuring the fluorescence via spectroscopy.

Chemical marks tend to become less detectable over time as the marked tissue becomes a smaller part of the entire tissue mass. This problem can be corrected by dissecting the marked tissue from the total tissue sample. For scales marked by feeding early in the life cycle, for example, the central core of the scale can be punched out of the scale and only that core analyzed. Behrens Yamada and Mulligan (1982) punched 2.2-mm-diameter plugs from the center of coho salmon scales and vertebrae with a leather punch. This allowed the separation of marked and unmarked fish, whereas whole-scale comparisons were inconclusive. Similar measures, such as grinding vertebrae and otoliths down to a predetermined diameter, can be used to isolate the most concentrated areas of other hard tissues.

9.5.4 Analyzing Chemical Marking Data

Chemical marks, especially elemental marks, produce statistical data rather than absolute identification. If the marking involves a single chemical element, then the analysis is simple, like genetic identification based on a single polymorphic locus (Chapter 8). However, if the marking process involves a profile of many chemicals, the statistical analysis probably will require multivariate techniques, such as principal component analysis and discriminant analysis. Pielou (1984) is a most lucid reference on these techniques.

9.6 NEW TECHNIQUES

Chemical marking is difficult. Its utility for most practical fisheries work has yet to be proven, despite massive improvements in analytic chemistry. Although most fisheries researchers studying chemical marks are convinced of their value, some question both the sensitivity and field applicability of current detection techniques (Lapi and Mulligan 1981; Muncy et al. 1990).

The promise for chemical marking lies in access to improved detection technology. Such improvements may be possible as chemists and physicists continue to invent new and more subtle techniques. The array of possibilities is dazzling, including stable isotope analysis, dye applications, laser technologies (Muncy et al. 1990), electron microprobe analysis (Coutant 1990), scanning electron microscopy in conjunction with X-ray energy dispersion (Lapi and Mulligan 1981), and X-ray-excited optical luminescence (Muncy and D'Silva 1981). Any of these techniques may provide the key to chemical identification.

9.7 REFERENCES

Babaluk, J. A., and J. S. Campbell. 1987. Preliminary results of tetracycline labelling for validating annual growth increments in opercula of walleyes. North American Journal of Fisheries Management 7:138–141.

Beckman, D. W., C. A. Wilson, F. Lorica, and J. M. Dean. 1990. Variability in incorporation of calcein as a fluorescent marker in fish otoliths. American Fisheries Society Symposium 7:547–549.

Behrens Yamada, S., and T. J. Mulligan. 1982. Strontium marking of hatchery reared coho salmon, *Onchorhynchus kisutch* Walbaum, identification of adults. Journal of Fish Biology 20:5–9.

Behrens Yamada, S., and T. J. Mulligan. 1987. Marking nonfeeding salmonid fry with dissolved strontium. Canadian Journal of Fisheries and Aquatic Sciences 44:1502–1506.

Behrens Yamada, S., and T. J. Mulligan. 1990. Screening of elements for the chemical marking of hatchery salmon. American Fisheries Society Symposium 7:550–561.

Behrens Yamada, S., T. J. Mulligan, and S. J. Fairchild. 1979. Strontium marking of hatchery-reared coho salmon (*Oncorhynchus kisutch,* Walbaum). Journal of Fish Biology 14:267–275.

Behrens Yamada, S., T. J. Mulligan, and D. Fournier. 1987. Role of environment and stock on the elemental composition of sockeye salmon (*Oncorhynchus nerka*) vertebrae. Canadian Journal of Fisheries and Aquatic Sciences 44:1206–1212.

Belanger, S. E., D. S. Cherry, J. J. Ney, and D. K. Whitehurst. 1987. Differentiation of freshwater versus saltwater striped bass by elemental scale analysis. Transactions of the American Fisheries Society 116:594–600.

Bilton, H. T. 1986. Marking chum salmon fry vertebrae with oxytetracycline. North American Journal of Fisheries Management 6:126–128.

Coutant, C. C. 1990. Microchemical analysis of fish hard parts for reconstructing habitat use: practice and promise. American Fisheries Society Symposium 7:574–580.

Grahl-Nielsen, O., and K. A. Ulvund. 1990. Distinguishing populations of herring by chemometry of fatty acids. American Fisheries Society Symposium 7:566–571.

Guillou, A., and J. de la Noüe. 1987. Use of strontium as a nutritional marker for farm-reared brook trout. Progressive Fish-Culturist 49:34–39.

Hettler, W. F. 1984. Marking otoliths by immersion of marine fish larvae in tetracycline. Transactions of the American Fisheries Society 113:370–373.

Knutsen, H., E. Moksnes, and N. B. Vogt. 1985. Distinguishing between one-day-old cod (*Gadus morhua*) and haddock (*Melanogrammus aeglefinus*) eggs by gas chromatography and SIMCA pattern recognition. Canadian Journal of Fisheries and Aquatic Sciences 42:1823–1826.

Koenings, J. P., J. Lipton, and P. McKay. 1986. Quantitative determination of oxytetracycline uptake and release by juvenile sockeye salmon. Transactions of the American Fisheries Society 115:621–629.

Lapi, L. A., and T. J. Mulligan. 1981. Salmon stock identification using a microanalytic technique to measure elements present in the freshwater growth region of scales. Canadian Journal of Fisheries and Aquatic Sciences 38:744–751.

Lasswell, L. D., III. 1990. Tagging at the FBI, present and future. American Fisheries Society Symposium 7:572–573.

Lorson, R. D., and V. A. Mudrak. 1987. Use of tetracycline to mark otoliths of American shad fry. North American Journal of Fisheries Management 7:453–455.

Mulligan, T. J., R. Kieser, S. B. Yamada, and D. L. Duerver. 1983. Salmon stock identification based on elemental composition of vertebrae. Canadian Journal of Fisheries and Aquatic Sciences 40:215–229.

Muncy, R. J., and A. P. D'Silva. 1981. Marking walleye eggs and fry. Transactions of the American Fisheries Society 110:300–305.

Muncy, R. J., N. C. Parker, and H. A. Poston. 1988. Marking striped bass with rare earth elements. Proceedings of the Annual Conference Southeastern Association of Fish and Wildlife Agencies 41(1987):244–250.

Muncy, R. J., N. C. Parker, and H. A.Poston. 1990. Inorganic chemical marks induced in fish. American Fisheries Society Symposium 7:541–546.

Myrick, A. C., Jr., E. W. Shallenberger, I. Kang, and D. B. MacKay. 1984. Calibration of dental layers in seven captive Hawaiian spinner dolphins, *Stenella longirostris,* based on tetracycline labeling. U.S. National Marine Fisheries Service Fishery Bulletin 82:207–225.

Pielou, E. C. 1984. The interpretation of ecological data. Wiley-Interscience, New York.

Smith, S. E. 1984. Timing of vertebral-band deposition in tetracycline-injected leopard sharks. Transactions of the American Fisheries Society 113:308–313.

Tsukamoto, K. 1985. Mass-marking of ayu eggs and larvae by tetracycline-tagging of
    otoliths. Bulletin of the Japanese Society of Scientific Fisheries 51:903–911.
Ulvund, K. A., and O. Grahl-Nielsen. 1988. Fatty acid composition in eggs of Atlantic
    cod (*Gadus morhua*). Canadian Journal of Fisheries and Aquatic Sciences 45:898–901.
Wilson, C. A., D. W. Beckman, and J. M. Dean. 1987. Calcein as a fluorescent marker of
    otoliths of larval and juvenile fish. Transactions of the American Fisheries Society
    116:668–670.

Appendix: Guidelines for Use of Fishes in Field Research

American Society of Ichthyologists and Herpetologists (ASIH)

American Fisheries Society (AFS)

American Institute of Fishery Research Biologists (AIFRB)

Protocols for working with wild and captive fishes have been jointly drafted and approved by ASIH, AFS, and AIFRB. The protocols, published in *Fisheries* in 1988, are reproduced below, lacking only the references.[1]

INTRODUCTION

Respect for all forms and systems of life is an inherent characteristic of scientists and managers who conduct field research on fishes. Consistent with our long standing interests in conservation, education, research, and the general well-being of fishes, the ASIH, AFS, and AIFRB support the following guidelines and principles for scientists conducting field research on these animals. As professional scientists specializing in fish biology concerned with the welfare of our study animals, we recognize that guidelines for the laboratory care and use of domesticated stocks of fishes are often not applicable to wild-caught fishes, and in fact may be impossible to apply without endangering the well-being of these fishes. Laboratory guidelines may also preclude techniques or types of investigations known to have minimal adverse effects on individuals or populations, and which are necessary for the acquisition of new knowledge.

The respectful treatment of wild fishes in field research is both an ethical and a scientific necessity. Traumatized animals may exhibit abnormal physiological, behavioral, and ecological re-

sponses that defeat the purposes of the investigation. For example, animals that are captured, marked and released must be able to resume their normal activities in an essentially undisturbed habitat if the purposes of the research are to be fulfilled.

The acquisition of new knowledge and understanding constitutes a major justification for any investigation. All effects of possibly valuable new research procedures (or new applications of established procedures) cannot be anticipated. The description and geographic distribution of newly discovered species justifies studies of organisms that are poorly known. It is impossible to predict all potential observation or collection opportunities at the initiation of most fieldwork, yet the observation or acquisition of unexpected taxa may be of considerable scientific value. Field studies of wild fishes often involve many species, some of which may be unknown to science before the onset of a study. A consequence of these points is that frequently investigators must refer to taxa above the species level, as well as to individual species in their research design.

Because of the very considerable range of adaptive diversity represented by the over 20,000 species of fishes, no concise or specific compendium of approved methods for field research is practical or desirable. Rather, the guidelines presented below build on the most current information to advise the investigator, who will often be an authority on the biology of the species under study, as to techniques that are known to be

---

[1]For full documentation of these guidelines see: American Society of Ichthyologists and Herpetologists, American Fisheries Society, and American Institute of Fishery Research Biologists. 1988. Guidelines for use of fishes in field research. Fisheries (Bethesda) 13(2):16–23.

appropriate and effective in the conduct of field research. Ultimate responsibility for the ethical and scientific validity of an investigation and the methods employed must rest with the investigator. To those who adhere to the principles of careful field research these guidelines will simply be a formal statement of precautions already in place.

GENERAL CONSIDERATIONS

Research proposals may require approval of an Institutional Animal Care and Use Committee (see below). In situations requiring such approval, each investigator must provide written assurance in applications and proposals that field research with fishes will meet the following requirements.

(a) The living conditions of animals held in captivity at field sites will be appropriate for fishes and contribute to their health and well-being. The housing, feeding, and nonmedical care of the animals will be directed by a scientist (generally the investigator) trained and experienced in the proper care, handling, and use of the fishes being maintained or studied. Some experiments (e.g., competition studies) will require the housing of mixed species in the same enclosure. Mixed housing is also appropriate for holding or displaying certain species.

(b) Procedures with animals must avoid or minimize distress to fishes, consistent with sound research design.

(c) Procedures that may cause more than momentary or slight distress to the animals should be performed with appropriate sedation, analgesia, or anesthesia, except when justified for scientific reasons in writing be the investigator.

(d) Fishes that would otherwise experience severe or chronic distress that cannot be relieved will be euthanized at the end of the procedure, or, if appropriate, during the procedure.

(e) Methods of euthanasia will be consistent with the rationale behind the recommendations of the American Veterinary Medical Association (AVMA) Panel on Euthanasia, but fishes differ sufficiently that their specific techniques do not apply. The method listed by the Royal Society may be followed.

Additional general considerations that should be incorporated into any research design using wild fishes include the following.

(f) The investigator must have knowledge of all regulations pertaining to the animals under study, and must obtain all permits necessary for carrying out proposed studies. Investigators must uphold not only the letter but also the spirit of regulations. (Most applicable regulations are referenced in publications of the Association of Systematics Collections.) Researchers working outside the United States should ensure that they comply with all wildlife regulations of the country in which the research is being performed. Work with many species is regulated by the provisions of the Convention on International Trade in Endangered Species of Wild Fauna and Flora (CITES). Regulations affecting a single species may vary with country. Local regulations may also apply.

(g) Individuals of endangered or threatened taxa should neither be removed from the wild (except in collaboration with conservation efforts), nor imported or exported, except in compliance with applicable regulations.

(h) Investigators must be familiar with the fishes to be studied and their response to disturbance, sensitivity to capture and restraint and, if necessary, requirements for captive maintenance to the extent that these factors are known and applicable to a particular study.

(i) Taxa chosen should be well-suited to answer the research question(s) posed.

(j) Every effort should be made prior to removal of fishes (if any) to understand the population status (abundant, threatened, rare, etc.) of the taxa to be studied, and the numbers of animals removed from the wild must be kept to the minimum the investigator determines is necessary to accomplish the goals of the study. This statement should not be interpreted as proscribing study and/or collection of uncommon species. Indeed, collection for scientific study is crucial to understanding why a species is uncommonly observed.

(k) The number of specimens required for an investigation will vary greatly, depending upon the questions being explored. As discussed later in these guidelines, certain kinds of investigations require collection of relatively large numbers of specimens, although the actual percent of any population taken will generally be very small. Studies should use the fewest animals necessary to reliably answer the questions posed. Use of adequate numbers to assure reliability is essential, as studies based on insufficient numbers of fishes will ultimately require repetition, thus wasting any benefit derived from any animal distress necessarily incurred during the study.

ROLE OF THE INSTITUTIONAL ANIMAL CARE AND USE COMMITTEE (IACUC)

Field resources for the care and use of fishes are very different from laboratory resources, and the role of the IACUC necessarily is limited to considerations that are practical for implementation at locations where field research is to be conducted. Prevailing conditions may prevent investigators from following these guidelines to the letter at all times. Investigators must, however, make every effort to follow the spirit of these guidelines to every extent possible. The omission from these guidelines of a specific research or husbandry technique must not be interpreted as proscription of the technique.

The IACUC must be aware that while fishes typically used in laboratory research represent a small number of species with well understood husbandry requirements, the classes Agnatha, Chondrichthyes, and Osteichthyes contain at least 20,000 distinct species with very diverse and often poorly known behavioral, physiological, and ecological characteristics. Therefore, "...in most cases, it is impossible to generate specific guidelines for groups larger than a few closely related species. Indeed, the premature stipulation of specific guidelines would severely inhibit humane care as well as research." The IACUC must note the frequent use of the word "should" throughout these guidelines, and be aware that this is in deliberate recognition of the diversity of animals and situations covered by the guidelines. Investigators, on the other hand, must be aware that use of the word "should" denotes the ethical obligation to follow these guidelines when realistically possible.

Before approving applications and proposals or proposed significant changes in ongoing activities, the IACUC shall conduct a review of those sections related to the care and use of fishes and determine that the proposed activities are in accord with these guidelines, or that justification for a departure from these guidelines for scientific reasons is presented.

When field studies on wild vertebrates are to be reviewed, the IACUC must include personnel who can provide an understanding of the nature and impact of the proposed field investigation, the housing of the species to be studied, and knowledge concerning the risks associated with maintaining certain species of wild vertebrates in captivity. Each IACUC should therefore include at least one institution-appointed member who is experienced in zoological field investigations. Such personnel may be appointed to the committee on an ad hoc basis to provide necessary expertise. When sufficient personnel with the necessary expertise in this area are not available within an institution, this ad hoc representative may be a qualified member from another institution.

Field research on native fishes usually requires permits from state and/or federal wildlife agencies. These agencies review applications for their scientific merit and their potential impact on native populations, and issue permits that authorize the taking of specified numbers of individuals, the taxa and methods allowed, the period of study, and often other restrictions that are designed to minimize the likelihood that an investigation will have deleterious effects. Permission to conduct field research rests with these agencies by law, and the IACUC should seek to avoid infringement on their authority to control the use of wildlife species.

If manipulation of parameters of the natural environment (daylength, etc.) is not part of the research protocol, field housing for fishes being held for an extended period of time should approximate natural conditions as closely as possible while adhering to appropriate standards of care. Housing and maintenance should provide for the safety and well-being of the animal, while adequately allowing for the objective of the study.

An increasing body of knowledge indicates that pain perception of the many species of vertebrates is not uniform over the various homologous portions of their bodies. Therefore, broad extrapolation of pain perception across taxonomic lines must be avoided. For example, what causes pain and distress to a mammal does not cause an equivalent reaction in a fish.

FIELD ACTIVITIES WITH WILD FISHES

Collecting

Field research with fishes frequently involves capture of specimens, whether for preservation, data recording, marking, temporary confinement, or relocation. While certain of these activities are treated separately below, they form a continuum of potential field uses of fishes.

The collection of samples for museum preservation from natural populations is critical to: (1) understanding the biology of animals throughout their ranges and over time; (2) the recording of biotic diversity, over time and/or in different habitats; and (3) the establishment and maintenance of taxonomic reference material essential to understanding the evolution and phylogenetic relationships of fishes and for environmental impact studies. The number of specimens collected should be kept at the minimum the investigator determines necessary to accomplish the goal of a study. Some studies, e.g., diversity over geographic range or delineation of variation of new species, require relatively large samples.

Capture Techniques

Capture techniques should be as environmentally benevolent as possible within the constraints of the sampling design. Whenever feasible, the potential for return to the natural environment must be incorporated into the sampling design. Current literature should be reviewed to ascertain when and if capture distress has been properly documented. Those capture techniques (seines, traps, etc.) that have minimal impact on the target fishes are not discussed below. Many capture techniques must mimic those of commercial and recreational fishermen in order to obtain reliable data on population trends for the regulation of such fisheries.

Gill netting and other forms of entangling nets are an accepted practice in fish collecting. Many studies contrast recent and prior sampling and thus repetition of a prior technique is mandated for sampling reliability. Net sets should be examined at a regular and appropriate schedule, particularly in warm water, to avoid excessive net mortality.

Collecting fish using ichthyocides is often the only and by far the most efficient sampling technique. Use of ichthyocides should be accomplished with maximal consideration of physical factors such as water movement and temperature, so as to avoid extensive mortality of natural populations and nontarget species.

Electrofishing is a suitable sampling technique in water of appropriate conductivity inasmuch as fish mortalities will be minimal. Proper adjustment of current will stun fishes and complete recovery is possible. Fish can be returned with minimal adverse impact. Care must be exercised to avoid excessive electric currents that may injure or harm the operators as well as the fish.

Capture of fishes by hooks or spears is an accepted practice of recreational fishermen. Spearfishing is appropriate to cases in which capture in special environments is necessary, e.g., deep reefs, caves, kelp beds, etc., and to provide comparable data for recreational fishing statistics. Similarly, many fishes are most efficiently captured by hooks.

Museum Specimens and Other Killed Specimens

The collection of live animals and their preparation as museum specimens is necessary for research and teaching activities in systematic zoology and for many other types of studies. Such collections should further our understanding of these animals in their natural state. Descriptions of ichthyological collecting techniques and accepted practices of collection management have been compiled, as have references to field techniques. Whenever fishes are collected for museum deposition, specimens should be fixed and preserved so as to assure the maximum utility of each animal and to minimize the need for duplicate collecting. In principle, each animal collected should serve as a source of information on many levels of organization from behavior to DNA-sequencing. Whenever practical, for example, blood and other tissues should be collected for karyotypic and molecular study prior to formalin fixation of the specimen.

Formalin fixation of specimens is an acceptable practice; however, fishes that do not die rapidly following immersion in a formalin solution should be killed before preservation by means of a chemical anesthetic such as sodium pentobarbital, hydrous chlorobutanol, MS-222, urethane or similarly acting substances, unless justified in writing by the investigator. When field fixation of formalin resistant fishes without prior introduction of anesthetics is necessary, prior numbing of the specimen in ice water should be considered. Several kinds of anesthetics and their efficacy have been reviewed in the Investigations in Fish Control series [U.S. Fish and Wildlife Service]. Their use requires little additional time and effort and adds little to the bulk or weight of collecting equipment. Urethane has been shown to be carcinogenic; thus, caution should be observed with its use and field disposal.

Live Capture

Investigators should be familiar with the variety of ichthyological capture techniques and should choose a method suited to both the species and the study. Capture techniques should prevent or minimize injury to the animal. Care should be exercised to avoid accidental capture or insure field release of nontarget species. The interval between visits to traps and net sets should be as short as possible, although it may vary with species, weather, objectives of the study, and the type of trap or net.

Habitat and Population Considerations

Whether collecting for future release or for museum preparation, each investigator should observe and pass on to students a strict ethic of habitat conservation. Collecting always should be conducted so as to leave the habitat as undisturbed as possible. The collection of large series of animals from breeding aggregations should be avoided if possible. Systematists should be familiar with extant collections of suitable specimens before conducting field work. If the purpose of an experiment is to alter behavior, reproductive potential, or survivability, the interference should be no more than that determined by the investigator to accurately test the hypothesis.

Restraint and Handling

General Principles

Restraint of wild fishes ranges from confinement in an aquarium through various types of physical restrictions or drug-induced immobilization. The decision whether to use physical or chemical restraint should be based upon the design of the experiment, knowledge of behavior of the animals, and the availability of facilities. Investigators must use the least amount of restraint necessary to do the job. When not under study, aggressive species should not be confined with other animals (other than food) which they may injure or which may injure them. The well-being of the animal under study is of paramount importance, and we emphasize that improper restraint, especially of traumatized animals, can lead to major physiological disturbances that can result in any of a series of deleterious or even fatal consequences.

Animals should be handled quietly and with the minimum personnel necessary. Darkened conditions tend to alleviate stress and subdue certain species, and are recommended whenever possible and appropriate.

Hazardous Species

Sharks and other large or venomous fishes are potentially dangerous to the investigator, and thus require special methods of restraint that must involve a compromise between potential injury to the handlers and injurious restraint of the animal. The particular method chosen will vary with the species and purpose of the project. Adherence to the following general guidelines is recommended when working with hazardous fishes.

(a) Procedures chosen should minimize the amount of handling time required and reduce or eliminate contact between handler and animal.

(b) One should never work alone. A second person, knowledgeable in capture and handling techniques and emergency measures, should be present at all times.

(c) Prior consultation with workers experienced with these species, as well as a review of the relevant literature, is of particular importance since much of the information on handling dangerous species has not been published, but is simply passed from one investigator to another.

Prolonged distressful restraint should be avoided. In some cases, utilization of general anesthesia for restraint in the field may be advisable. If so, the anesthetic chosen should be a low risk compound that permits rapid return to normal physiological and behavioral status, and the animal must be kept under observation until appropriate recovery occurs. The relatively unpredictable response of some poikilotherms to immobilants or anesthetics under field conditions may contraindicate field use of these chemicals under certain conditions.

Chemical Restraint

Many chemicals used for restraint or immobilization of fishes are controlled by the Federal Bureau of Narcotics and Dangerous Drugs/Drug Enforcement Administration (DEA). A DEA permit is required for purchase or use of these chemicals. Extensive information on these substances and their use is available, and permit application procedures are available from regional DEA offices. Investigators should choose the chemical for immobilization with consideration of

beyond the native range of distribution of a fish without prior approval of the appropriate state and/or federal agencies, and approved relocations should be noted in subsequent publication of research results.

(b) If their ability to survive in nature has not been irreversibly impaired.

(c) Where it can be reasonably expected that the released animal will function normally within the population.

(d) When local and seasonal conditions are conducive to survival.

(e) When a release is not likely to spread pathogens.

Captured animals that cannot be released or are not native to the site of intended release should be properly disposed of, either by distribution to colleagues for further study, or if possible by preservation and deposition as teaching or voucher specimens in research collections.

In both the field and laboratory, the investigator must be careful to ensure that animals subjected to an euthanasia procedure are dead before disposal. In those rare instances where specimens are unacceptable for deposition as vouchers or teaching purposes, disposal of carcasses must be in accordance with acceptable practices as required by applicable regulations. Animals containing toxic substances or drugs (including euthanasia agents like T-61) must not be disposed of in areas where they may become part of the natural food web.

Index